A Structural Atlas
—— of the ——
English Dialects

This atlas grew out of a need for information about the structural realities underlying the dialect material presented in the *Survey of English Dialects*. In the published material the presentation is generally orientated towards displaying the variety of forms which exist rather than indicating how those forms function within a particular sound system.

The present study seeks for the first time to identify the *structural patterns* which exist in the sound systems of the dialects of England and seeks to regard variation not as something to be ignored or side-stepped but rather as a central and essential feature of dialect which must be accounted for in a systematic way. A more practical aim of this study is to identify some of the more prominent structural boundaries between dialect areas. Discrete boundaries do not exist: rather there are a number of areas separated by bands of dialects in which conflicting partial systems exist.

This atlas suggests some topics which may be fruitful fields for future investigation. For example, phonology is essentially concerned with perceptual differences. Are the structural distinctions which the survey material suggests supported by the speakers' own reactions? If it is appropriate to formulate an overall structure for dialects of English, is the historical structural analysis suggested here the most functional? Are the techniques of linguistic geography capable of being adapted to the problems of language variation and indeed of contemporary structural dialectology? The analysis of the distribution of lingusitic forms, whether one calls it linguistic geography, area studies or geolinguistics, occupies the middle ground between theoretical linguistics and human geography in its widest sense, and functions as a bridge between the two disciplines.

Peter Anderson studied dialectology with Stanley Ellis MA
and Professor John Widdowson at Leeds and Sheffield Universities

A Structural Atlas
— of the —
English Dialects

Peter M. Anderson

CROOM HELM
London • New York • Sydney

© 1987 Dr Peter Anderson
Croom Helm Ltd, Provident House, Burrell Row,
Beckenham, Kent BR3 1AT
Croom Helm Australia, 44-50 Waterloo Road,
North Ryde, 2113, New South Wales

British Library Cataloguing in Publication Data

Anderson, Peter
    A structural atlas of the English dialects.
    1. English language — Dialects — England
    — Maps
    I. Title
    912'.1427   PE1705
    ISBN 0-7099-5116-7

Published in the USA by
Croom Helm
in association with Methuen, Inc.
29 West 35th Street
New York, NY 10001

Library of Congress Cataloging-in-Publication Data

Anderson, Peter, 1953–
    A structural atlas of the English dialects.

    Bibliogrpahy: p.
    1. English language — Dialects — England — Maps.
I. Title.
PE1705.A53   1987   912'.1427'00942   87-8937
ISBN 0-7099-5116-7

Typeset in 10pt Times Roman by Leaper & Gard Ltd, Bristol, England
Printed and bound in Great Britain by Mackays of Chatham Ltd, Kent

Contents

Acknowledgements

Mr S.F. Sanderson, director of the Institute of Dialect and Folk-Life Studies at the University of Leeds for permission to use the SED Basis Material.
The International Phonetic Association for permission to reproduce the chart on page xii.
Mr S. Ellis MA and Prof. J.D. Widdowson for helpful comments.
Finally my wife Lynne for gallant attempts to stem the rising tide of index slips.

Peter M. Anderson

Abbreviations

e early
EEP Early English Pronunciation (See Bibliography under Ellis 1889)
eME Early Middle English
ME Middle English
NME Northern Middle English
OE Old English
p page
RP Received Pronunciation
SED Survey of English Dialects

The ME phoneme is often used to indicate the descendant of the phoneme in the modern dialect or dialects, e.g. 'ME /a:/' may mean 'the reflex of ME /a:/'

SED County Abbreviations

Beds Bedfordshire
Berks Berkshire
Bk Buckinghamshire
C Cambridgeshire
Ch Cheshire
Co Cornwall
Cu Cumberland
D Devon
Db Derbyshire
Do Dorset
Du Durham
Ess Essex
Gl Gloucestershire
Ha Hampshire
He Herefordshire
Herts Hertfordshire
Hu Huntingdonshire
K Kent
L Lincolnshire
La Lancashire
Lei Leicestershire
Man Isle of Man
Mon Monmouthshire
Mx Middlesex
Nb Northumberland
Nf Norfolk
Nt Nottinghamshire
Nth Northamptonshire
O Oxfordshire
R Rutland
Sa Shropshire
Sf Suffolk
So Somerset
Sr Surrey
St Staffordshire
Sx Sussex
W Wiltshire
Wa Warwickshire
We Westmorland
Wo Worcestershire
Y Yorkshire

List of Maps

THE INTERNATIONAL PHONETIC ALPHABET

(Revised to 1979)

CONSONANTS

	Bilabial	Labiodental	Dental, Alveolar, or Post-alveolar	Retroflex	Palato-alveolar	Palatal	Velar	Uvular	Labial-Palatal	Labial-Velar	Pharyngeal	Glottal
Nasal	m	ɱ	n	ɳ		ɲ	ŋ	ɴ				
Plosive	p b		t d	ʈ ɖ		c ɟ	k ɡ	q ɢ		k͡p ɡ͡b		ʔ
(Median) Fricative	ɸ β	f v	θ ð s z	ʂ ʐ	ʃ ʒ	ç ʝ	x ɣ	χ ʁ			ħ ʕ	h ɦ
(Median) Approximant		ʋ	ɹ	ɻ		j	ɰ		ɥ	w ʍ		
Lateral Fricative			ɬ ɮ									
Lateral (Approximant)			l	ɭ		ʎ	ʟ					
Trill			r					ʀ				
Tap or Flap			ɾ	ɽ				ʀ				
Ejective	p'		t'				k'					
Implosive	ɓ		ɗ				ɠ					
(Median) Click	⊙		ʇ	ʗ								
Lateral Click			ʖ									

S (pulmonic air-stream mechanism) / *N (non-pulmonic air-stream)*

VOWELS

	Front		Back
Close	i y	ɨ ʉ	ɯ u
Half-close	e ø	ɘ ɵ	ɤ o
Half-open	ɛ œ	ɜ ɞ	ʌ ɔ
Open	a ɶ		ɑ ɒ
	Unrounded		Rounded

DIACRITICS

- ° Voiceless n̥ d̥
- ˬ Voiced s̬ t̬
- ʰ Aspirated tʰ
- ·· Breathy-voiced b̤ a̤
- ˛ Dental t̪
- ˛ Labialized t̫
- ʲ Palatalized t̪
- ˗ Velarized or Pharyn-gealized ɫ, ɫ̵
- ˌ Syllabic n̩ l̩
- ˋ or ˬ Simultaneous ʃ and x (but see also under the heading Affricates)
- ˈ or ˎ Raised e̝, e̝, ̝w
- ˌ or ˎ Lowered e̞, ̞, e̞ ɤ
- ˖ Advanced u̟+, ̟
- ˗ or ˗ Retracted i̠, ̠-, t̠
- ·· Centralized ë
- ˜ Nasalized ã
- ˞, ˞, ɚ r-coloured a˞
- ː Long aː
- ˑ Half-long aˑ
- ˘ Non-syllabic ŭ
- ˓ More rounded ɔ̹
- ˒ Less rounded y̜

OTHER SYMBOLS

- ɕ, ʑ Alveolo-palatal fricatives
- ɫ, ʓ Palatalized ʃ, ʒ
- ɺ Alveolar fricative trill
- ɺ Alveolar lateral flap
- ɧ Simultaneous ʃ and x
- ʃˢ Variety of ʃ resembling s, etc.
- ɪ = ι
- ʊ = ω
- ɜ = Variety of ə
- ɚ = r-coloured ə

STRESS, TONE (PITCH)

- ˈ stress, placed at beginning of stressed syllable :
- ˌ secondary stress : ˉ high level pitch, high tone : ˊ high rising : ˋ low level : ˏ low rising : ˎ high falling : ˋ low falling : ˆ rise-fall : ˇ fall-rise.

AFFRICATES can be written as digraphs, as ligatures, or with slur marks; thus ts, tʃ, dʒ : t͡s t͡ʃ d͡ʒ : t̑s t̑ʃ d̑ʒ. c, ɟ may occasionally be used for tʃ, dʒ.

1

Introduction

This atlas grew out of a need for information about the structural realities underlying the dialect material presented in the *Survey of English Dialects*.[1] In the published material (Basic and Incidental) the presentation is generally orientated towards displaying the variety of forms which exist rather than indicating how those forms function within a particular sound system. This style of presentation was carried over into the *Linguistic Atlas of England*[2] (and also the *Phonological Atlas of the Northern Counties*[3] though the format is rather different).[4] The concept is broadly that each map portrays a single word and the responses are displayed on the map as fully as space allows. Such an approach is often justified by the nature of dialect evidence which rarely lends itself or appears to lend itself to systematically consistent patterning. A glance at the SED material for any item at once demonstrates the truth of Gillieron's dictum that 'every word has its own history'. An obvious drawback to this approach is that one never obtains an overall view of dialectal structure, wider trends tending to be overlooked in a mass of detail. Nor can the approach really claim to have dealt systematically with the problem of variability, since it has not initially defined any structural framework by reference to which problems of variation can be studied. The present study seeks for the first time to identify the structural patterns which exist in the sound systems of the dialects of the SED and seeks to regard variation not as something to be ignored or side-stepped but rather as a central and essential feature of dialect which must be accounted for in a systematic way.

The orientation of most dialect surveys has largely been diachronic, the discovery of the relationship between the current dialectal type and its historical ancestor. The validity of this approach has rightly been questioned and as a result linguists sought to study dialectal material without any reference to its history and with regard only to its current structural reality. This treatment was no less extreme than the approach which preceded it and there is no doubt that analyses produced by this method do not account in any way convincingly for the variability that is usually, though not invariably, present.

A primary aim of this study is to deal with this variability within a comparative framework. Given the diversity of the dialects involved, this is no easy task. The problems involved in formulating a methodology are well summarised by Petyt.[5] The attempts at formulating an 'overall system', incorporating the essential features of the individual systems have given rise to many of the difficulties encountered, since because the approach was concerned with similarities and differences in phonemic inventories rather than with the lexical incidence of particular phonemes, the resultant correlations often indicated surface similarities or differences rather than more fundamental structural relationships.

On this point Kurath and Lowman comment:

'The question has been raised whether a "diasystem" spanning the systems of a group of dialects on a purely synchronic basis can serve as a meaningful frame of reference in dialectology. I don't think so. If the concept of a phonemic system as an organisation of interdependent units — as a set of interrelated habits of articulation and perception — is accepted, an abstract scheme of units spanning diverse systems is meaningless. To call it a "diasystem" or an "overall system" does not endow it with scientific relevance.'[6]

Kurath and Lowman demonstrate by reference to two dialects of English that surface similarities are irrelevant. Further difficulties arise when many sound systems have to be compared rather than just a few. A purely synchronic approach cannot provide a solution. What is needed is an overall system, primarily defined in terms of phonemic incidence, which embodies or is able to generate the structural contrasts of the constituent dialect systems. A historically based analysis does just this by setting up a basic phonemic system which underlies all forms of English. In a study of conflicting phonological systems in the speech of certain Central American Indians, Fries and Pike remark:

'It is impossible to give a purely synchronic description of a complex mixed system, at one point in time, which shows the pertinent facts of that system; direction of change is a pertinent characteristic of the system and must also be known if one wishes to have a complete description of the language as it is structurally constituted.'[7]

The synchronic approach to linguistic description received a major impetus following its application to the native languages of North America where historical information was lacking or only available by extrapolation from modern forms. Where historical material is available, it seems shortsighted to restrict analyses to synchronic material only. In fact, the historical approach is not merely compatible with the structural approach but essential if systems are to be properly compared and the nature of structural contrasts understood. Both generative/structuralist and historical linguists have much to learn from each other's methodologies. McDavid's plea for a variety of approaches is apt:

'In fact it is doubtful ... whether one should work all the time within any single framework. The mere fact that there are differences in approach should lead to cross-fertilisation, to the discovery of phenomena that might be overlooked if one stuck to one framework.'[8]

A secondary aim of this study is to suggest that a suitable way of analysing dialectal systems and the variability in them is by reference not to a single phonemic system but to a number of partial systems often operating in conflict with one another. In an opening remark to their study of variability, Fries and Pike state:

'The speech of monolingual natives of some languages is comprised of more than one phonemic system; the simultaneously existing systems operate partly in harmony and partly in conflict. No rigidly descriptive statement of the facts about such a language accounts for all the pertinent structural data without leading to apparent contradictions. These are caused by the conflict of statements about the phonemic system with statements about another system or part of a system present in the speech of the same individual.'[9]

A particular sound system can be seen as the interaction of a number of co-existent systems, some of which are present only in fragmentary form. The task of the dialectologist is to analyse the material into these sub-systems and to seek explanation for the form which they take. The analyses which emerge will take fully into account the systemic variation present in the dialect and enable comparisons to be made between the dialect under examination and other dialects.[10] It follows from this type of analysis that neither phonological distinctions nor dialect boundaries are clear-cut but rather they should be measured by the relative predominance of different phonological systems. The discreteness suggested by isoglosses is unreal. At best they represent only approximations.

Partial phonemic systems may be expected to arise whenever two differing systems come into contact. This contact may be internal or external to the system in its method, and historical, geographical or social in type of contact. This gives six types of contact which may give rise to partial phonemic systems:

(a) *Historical internal*, i.e. contact between a current system and an earlier historical system. It reflects a purely internal change in the dialect, part of its natural 'drift'. This is a rare source of internal conflict in a dialect system since change is largely conditioned by outside pressure, i.e. the geographical spread of differing forms. Normally this type of contact will be implicated only when no other source can be ascertained, i.e. the development is unique.

(b) *Historical external*, i.e. the influence of a historical form of a language on a current vernacular. This is not of great significance for English but is more important elsewhere, e.g. modern Arabic which has been strongly influenced by the classical form of the language.

(c) *Geographical internal*, i.e. a structural change takes place in a dialect by analogy with structural features of a neighbouring dialect. Certain mid Buckinghamshire dialects show a twofold development of ME /aː/ in *bake* etc. to /eə/, /eɪ/ but develop ME /ai/ in *day* etc. to /eɪ/. Two systems operate, one of which follows neighbouring systems to the east, merging the two groups, and one which maintains a distinction.

(d) *Geographical external*, i.e. direct structural borrowing from neighbouring linguistic systems. This arises primarily because of linguistic diffusion with the result that each dialectal sound system tends to resemble its neighbour. Changes which derive from this type of contact are typically phonetic changes but very often the effects are structural. For example, the dialects of Suffolk are recorded in the Lowman's survey of the 1930s as contrasting /oː/ from ME /ɔː/ in *clothes* etc. with /ʌʊ/ from ME /ɔu/ in *snow* etc.; i.e. *nose* ≠ *knows*. [ʌʊ] for ME /ɔː/ spreading from the Home Counties has tended to replaced /oː/ by a phonetic process. The result is the phonemic merger of ME /ɔu/ and ME /ɔː/ as /ʌʊ/.[11]

(e) *Social internal*, i.e. contact of different systems in use by different social classes within the same community. This aspect of structural influence has tended to be ignored until recent years but obviously assumes greater importance in larger communities where there are well-marked class differences in speech.

(f) *Social external*, i.e. contact with a socially more prestigious form of speech — a standard or local koine. This has always been an important source of structural change in dialect systems. The major difficulty is in identifying this type of contact-induced change. Often it is only possible by inference. For example, EEP records /ɪə/ and /e:/ to represent ME /ɛ:/ in *team, eat* etc. in the South of England. SED records /ɪə/ with a very much reduced frequency, usually noting /e:/. It is possible that EEP did not fully record the presence of /e:/, but on the other hand, the mixed distribution of the two types tends to suggest that the /e:/ type had infiltrated into the rural dialects of the South and has continued to do so since the mid nineteenth century. Since the type became obsolete in Standard English in the eighteenth century the source of the forms must be elsewhere. One is inclined to suggest that some urban centres (and some regional standardised accents) of the nineteenth century had /e:/ for ME /ɛ:/ and that this is the source of the innovation.

A more practical aim of this study is to identify some of the more prominent structural boundaries between dialect areas. As has already been noted, discrete boundaries do not exist. Rather there are a number of areas separated by bands of dialects in which conflicting partial systems exist.

The regions which show systems differing widely from Standard English are generally those along the margins of the country. There is thus a general contrast between peripheral/divergent systems and central/standardised ones. In nearly all the dialects evidence can be found of partial phonemic systems corresponding to the Standard English phonemic system. This is hardly surprising in view of the dominant position of Standard English. Nonetheless, it will be apparent from the maps presented in this atlas that the relationship between dialect and standard has not been exclusively one-way. There appear to be certain structural features in the dialects of the South East (and in Standard English) that can only be attributed to contact with dialects of the central Midlands. The features involved are the following:

(a) Merger of ME /a:/ and ME /ai/ (*sale* = *sail*) (Map 44)
(b) Merger of ME /e:/ and ME /ɛ:/ (*meet* = *meat*) (Map 56)
(c) Merger of ME /ɔ:/ and ME /ɔu/ (*nose* = *knows*) (Map 97)
(d) ME /i:/ in *knife* etc. is represented by /ɑɪ ~ ɔɪ/

(e) ME /o:/ in *stool* etc. is represented by fronted types /ü:/

Of these features it is the structural mergers which entered Standard English, presumably from the dialects of the South East. All of the features, however, contrast sharply with the dialects of the surrounding South and East Anglia where there are usually contrasts in (a), (b) and (c) and where (d) is usually represented by /əɪ/, (e) is usually /u:/, in the South at least. The South East is separated from the central Midlands, with which it shares these features by a band of residual southern systems in Bedfordshire and Buckinghamshire. This suggests that the Midland features have not reached the South East by direct diffusion from the central Midlands. The evidence points to a transfer of population from the central Midlands to the South East such as is known to have occurred in the medieval period.[12] The nature of the structural similarities also suggest a continuing contact between the central Midlands and the South East. Now, it is hardly likely that the dialects involved would have been rural dialects lacking in prestige and it is therefore necessary to suppose that in the area of Northamptonshire and Leicestershire and possibly more extensively, a socially prestigious koine had come into existence in the early modern period. There are good reasons for this supposition. Central areas are innovative and dialect features originating there tend to spread to outlying dialects. Central dialects also tend to have features in common with the whole dialect continuum whilst avoiding the extremes of the peripheral dialects. For this reason they are more comprehensible and each is more likely to be used as a lingua franca. Higden's comments that the dialects of the Midlands were the best understood of all English dialects is well known. Finally the region in which this Midland koine arose was that in which distinct dialect areas came into contact — the southern and the eastern, in the neighbourhood of Watling Street, long a significant boundary. Sternberg, writing in 1851 about the dialects of Northamptonshire, distinguishes three dialects; the southern, the eastern and a third, central, type of speech.

'In the central districts of Northamptonshire where the two dialects come into contact and the Anglian speech of Mercia blends with the Saxon idiom of the West, a third and intermediate variety is current, partaking in some measure of the peculiarities of both, which from its utter want of tone and freedom from dialectal inflexion, has become proverbial among the neighbouring counties for its superior purity and resemblance to our present Standard English.'[13]

After some comments on the similarity between the

3

Authorised Version of the Bible and Northampton-shire speech, he continues:

> 'It is to this *Lingua Franca* which at the present day presents precisely the same analogy to the National speech that the Northamptonshire dialects of the seventeenth century did to the language of the Church historian — and which is current in slightly different forms along the whole line of the March counties — that we must, in all probability look for the origin of our present literary language.'

There is thus evidence for a corridor of 'neutral' speech, neither eastern nor southern which could form the basis for a prestige koine which influenced the dialects of a substantial area of the South East. Because of the closeness of the sound systems of the koine areas and Standard English, the diffusion of standardised types could take place in the opposite direction at a later date without much opposition. Arguably, the central Midlands continue to influence Standard English, e.g. the substitution of /a/ for /æ/, the development of diphthongs with more open or retracted first elements ([εɩ~ɛɩ] for ME /a:/, [äɩ] for ME /i:/).

Dialect boundaries[14]

Much of the value of linguistic geography as a discipline stems from its use not merely to display linguistic patterns but also to suggest links with other patterns, whether geographical, political or cultural. In this way it can sometimes support hypotheses developed in quite different fields just as the findings of a brooch or a bag of coins may help to illuminate and clarify problems of linguistic diffusion. Primarily dialect boundaries are determined by geographical factors and only secondarily by political or demographic considerations and often these ultimately mirror geographical boundaries.

Geographical features

Rivers — Non-navigable rivers create good boundaries where they cut across advancing innovations. The rivers Wharf and Ouse mark the boundary between the northern and the north Midland dialects and have done so since the medieval period. On the other hand navigable rivers flowing along the line of an innovation tend to aid the spread of the dialect feature. Shropshire dialects have reverted /r/ and a southern type of front vowel system which is most likely due to settlement of the county from the South along the river Severn.

Hills — Dialect relic areas frequently coincide with higher ground, such as the Pennines, the Cotswolds and the Chilterns. In all of these regions more conservative dialectal systems are maintained. Hills also tend to limit the spread of dialectal features and a good example of this is the chain of limestone hills from the Cotswolds to south Leicestershire. It coincides with the northern limit of lengthening of ME /a/ and ME /o/ in *grass, off* etc. and also the northern limit of unrounding of ME /u/ in *butter, sun* etc. except in the West where southern types have moved further north along the Severn. On the other hand, passes through chains of hills tend to channel innovations. For instance the Calder valley and the Aire valley are the major routes across the south Pennines and it is noticeable that the dialects of the Upper Calder valley show distinct Lancashire traits such as /wɷm/ *home* in contrast to west Yorkshire /ɷəm/, long forms /a:/ and /ɔ:/ in *laugh, trough* and the presence of final post-vocalic /r/.[15] Likewise north Midland forms have moved up the Aire valley. SED records /ɔɩ/ forms in *coal* etc. which have spread from further east.

Marshes — Linguistic boundaries which seem to bear little relation to current geographical features often follow the edges of earlier marshes or forests. Perhaps the most important boundary of this type is the Fens which, until the seventeenth century, was an impassible morass with a few scattered island communities. The dialects of these areas contrast sharply with Lincolnshire to the north and Norfolk to the east, the systems used being of a type very close to Standard English. Other areas of marsh existed which must have had the effect of halting linguistic advances, for example the meres of north Shropshire and the marshland around the Ouse in Yorkshire.

Political features

Political borders are very often, perhaps usually, a reflection of appropriate geographical boundaries. As Moore, Meech and Whitehall note:

> 'A glance at a political map of England will show how often the boundaries of the Midland Counties were established along the marshy banks of unnavigable streams situated about one day's journey from the county towns, and the sometimes quite disproportionate influence upon dialect limits of unnavigable rivers and smaller streams may be thus partially explained.'[16]

In this way political boundaries serve to reinforce geographical boundaries. The northern-most limits of the Mercian Kingdom of Offa coincide with the North/north Midland dialect boundary. The homogenous dialect area of north and mid Lincolnshire coincides with the boundaries of the kingdom of Lindsey even though this was absorbed into Mercia by AD 700.[17] On the other hand political boundaries without the support of geographical features are much less strong. The Scots/English linguistic frontier is determined by the Tweed rather than the political border. The speech of Berwick-on-Tweed, politically in England, is Scots rather than English in many of its features. The best example of a political boundary without any correlation with geographical features is Watling Street and the importance of this boundary as a dialectal 'watershed' cannot be understated. It formed the boundary between Danish and English Mercia and between Norse-influenced speech and native West Saxon speech, allowing the latter to spread north west but restricting its eastward advance. The dialects to the west of Watling Street are southern dialects although, because the southern features are recessive, there exists a transitional area covering much of southern England.[18] Map (A) shows some of the significant features. The features shown are:

(1) ME /ɛ:/ > /eɪ~e:/
(2) Retention of ME /or/ as short vowel + /r/
(3) Non-southern development of ME /i:/ to /aɪ~ɔɪ/
(4) Non-southern development of ME /o:/ to /ü:/
(5) Development of ME /ɔ:/ to /o:/
(6) Voicing of initial /f/ to /v/

Patterns of settlement are frequently reflected in political boundaries (e.g. Sussex is the territory of the South Saxons). Sometimes political boundaries cut across settlement areas. Some fourteen features mark Devon apart from surrounding dialects (see Map (B). The features mapped are:

(1) Raising of ME /ɔ:/ to /u:/
(2) Merger of ME /ɛ:/ and ME /ai/ *wheat = wait*
(3) Development of ME /ɔu/ to /ɔ:/
(4) Absence of /h/
(5) Development of ME /u:/ to /œY/
(6) Merger of ME /o:/, /iu/ and /ɛu/ as /Y:/
(7) Absence of lengthening of ME /o/ before /k,g/
(8) Absence of merger of ME /or/ and ME /ar/ *farm ≠ form*
(9) Development of ME /i:/ to /æ:/ in contrast to Southern /əɪ/
(10) Absence of shortening in *dead, head* etc.
(11) Voicing of initial /θ/ to /ð/
(12) Voicing of initial /s/ to /z/
(13) Voicing of initial /f/ to /v/
(14) Development of ME /u/ to /ɪ/ in certain fricative contexts, e.g. *sun, brother*

What is most noticeable about the distribution of these features is that none of the isoglosses coincide

with the political border between Devon and Cornwall. The linguistic border is well into Cornwall corresponding probably to the limit of the West Saxon advance by conquest culminating with the battle of Hingston Down in AD 838.[19] Other links between political units and dialectal areas are much more speculative. What are we to make of the Cotswolds area which shows a number of common features (see Map (C))? These are:

(1) Development of ME /a/ (OE *ĕ*?) to /æ/
(2) Development of ME /o/ to /a/
(3) Development of ME /ɛ:/ to /jɒ~jʌ/
(4) Development of ME /ɔ:/ to /wɒ~wʌ/
(5) Retention of stress-shifted forms in *dew, few,* i.e. [djaɒ] [fjaɒ]

The last of these features must date from the Old English times indicating that this region had dialectal features that set it apart even then. Is it therefore merely coincidental that the isoglosses mark out an area which corresponds remarkably well to the territory occupied by the tribe of the Hwicce in the seventh century? (An area later absorbed into the Kingdom of Wessex, though continuing to be reflected in the boundaries of the Anglo Saxon diocese of Worcester.) Though the features may not be the same, the dialect boundaries surely continue more ancient political divisions.

Cultural features

Cultural boundaries are the product of processes often analogous to those which have produced linguistic boundaries and also they are often related to geographical, political and demographic patterns. Research is only just beginning in this field and is likely to show major links between cultural and linguistic boundaries. Dr David North demonstrates the existence of a series of important linguistic and cultural boundaries which mark off the South East of England as a distinctive area.[20] Undoubtedly there are similar cultural/linguistic boundaries elsewhere. For instance it has already been noted that north north Shropshire and adjoining Cheshire are quite different linguistically, as a result of the coincidence of a geographical boundary (marshland) and a demographic boundary (the limit of settlement along the Severn from the south). Not surprisingly there are a number of cultural differences. Because of the orientation of SED these appear to be differences of farming practices. The name for the strawyard used for fattening cattle especially during winter is not found in most of south Cheshire but it is common in Shropshire (SED I. 1. 9). The curb-stone in the old fashioned cow-shed is generally called a heel-tree in south Cheshire but is unnamed in Shropshire (SED I. 3. 9). In carrying hay or corn, the body of the cart is extended by a horizontal frame in Cheshire

DIALECT LIMITS IN SOUTHERN ENGLAND

Map (A)

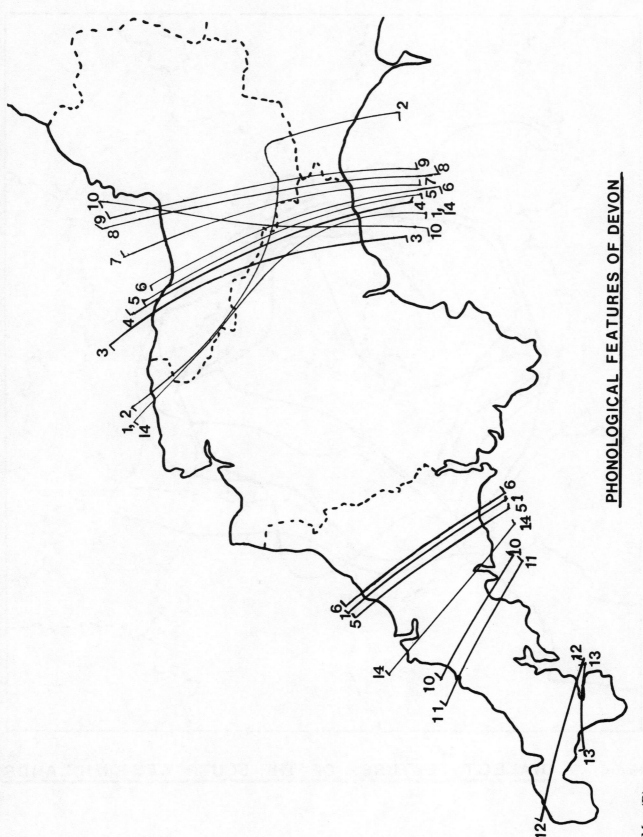

PHONOLOGICAL FEATURES OF DEVON

Map (B)

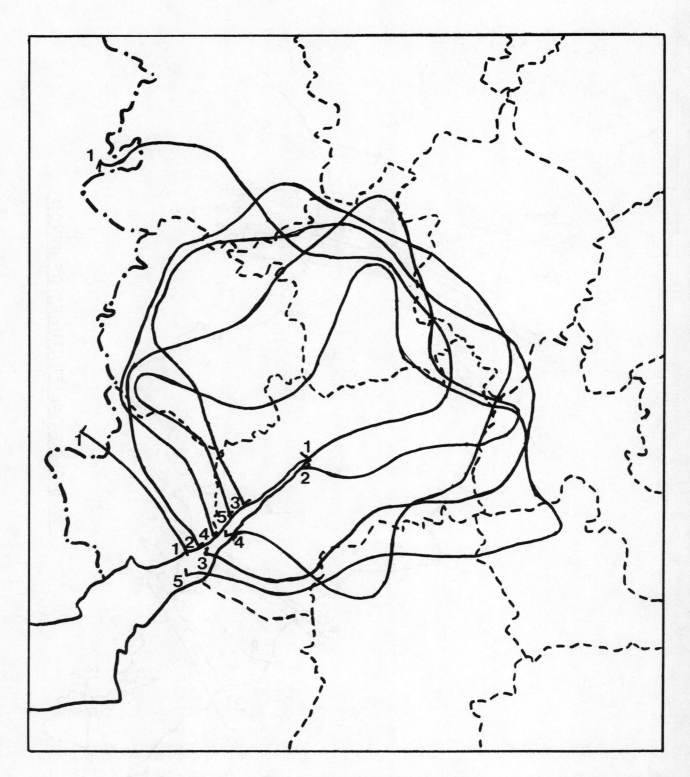

Map (C)   **DIALECT FEATURES OF THE SOUTH WEST MIDLANDS**

(*thrippers*) but the concept is absent in north Shropshire (SED I. 10. 6). On the other hand cart-ladders placed at the front and back of the cart are, according to the SED evidence, never used in Cheshire but are found in Shropshire (SED I. 10. 5). The design of the plough, it seems, also differed between the two counties. The evener for equalising the pull of the horses is invariably a large swingle-tree regulating the subsidiary swingle-trees in Cheshire. In Shropshire, on the other hand, says SED, it is a permanent attachment to the plough beam end as it seems to be throughout the border counties (SED I. i. 4). These correlations help to set linguistic differences within the more general framework of cultural distribution patterns, a field which merits further attention but which is beyond the scope of the present study.

This atlas suggests some topics which may be fruitful fields for future investigation. For example, phonology is essentially concerned with perceptual differences; it would be interesting (and perhaps humbling for dialectologists) to discover whether the structural distinctions which the SED material suggests are supported by the speakers' own reactions. If it is appropriate to formulate an overall structure for dialects of English, is the historical structural analysis suggested here the most functional? One ought to perhaps, at the outset, ask whether such a structure is necessary or even desirable. Finally, are the techniques of linguistic geography capable of being adapted to the problems of language variation and indeed of contemporary structural dialectology? This study may not answer or even begin to answer the first two questions but the reply to the final question is an unambiguous yes. The analysis of the distribution of linguistic forms, whether one calls it linguistic geography, area studies or geolinguistics, occupies the middle ground between theoretical linguistics and human geography in its widest sense and functions as a bridge between the two disciplines.

Cartographic techniques and the sed

SED

No analysis of the SED material has yet been prepared on the basis suggested in this introduction. The maps presented here give a broad indication of its potential but closer study of the individual dialects would certainly reveal a more complex and variable picture.

The SED material represented here covers some 106,000 items excerpted from the Basic and Incidental Material over a period of four years and organised to provide a phonemic analysis of the sound-system of each locality. Lack of space pre-vents publication of the structural analyses but the essential features appear in the atlas.

Analytical and cartographic techniques

Here follows a brief description of the cartographic techniques which have been employed in preparing this atlas.

All atlases of English dialects published to date display the reflexes of an individual word rather than a particular phoneme. In this the map-maker's method reflects the historical reaction against the Neo-Grammarian view of sound change. Perhaps the more balanced view is to see a particular change as essentially regular but liable to deflection for all sorts of reasons — social, historical or structural. This view is taken by Kurath in a study of the dialectal structure of southern England:

'By choosing three or more words containing the same ME parent phoneme, one can usually determine its normal development in the several regions of present-day England with some assurance. This is not surprising. Past experience in diachronic linguistics has shown that phonological change takes place with considerable regularity.'[21]

From an early stage it was decided that the atlas should be structural in orientation and truly interpretive of the SED material. The map-making technique is described below but it will be useful at this stage to set out the essential characteristics of the atlas itself.

1. Each map is drawn on the basis of a number of responses having a common ME phoneme. (Frequently all relevant responses in the Basic and Incidental Material.) The maps are therefore *diachronic*.

2. Whilst they are diachronic, the maps are also *structural* insofar as the intention is to compare system with system, firstly historically and secondly synchronically. Both comparisons are needed because synchronic distinctions can often only be understood in the light of historical differences and developments.

3. Because structural maps are provided, phonetic maps can be used to show up trends in dialect developments, e.g. all ingliding diphthongs can be mapped for a particular ME phoneme. Not all important differences are 'distinctive'. In deciding what phonetic types are to be mapped it is necessary to select judiciously from the material. In this respect this atlas is *interpretive*.

The Linguistic Atlas of England claims to be interpretive through being 'isoglossic'. The editors state in the introduction:

9

'In presenting interpretive maps one sometimes has to make arbitrary decisions about where to draw isoglosses. It was Harold Orton's usual practice, though not his invariable one, to emphasize the older forms or those forms which showed the greatest deviation from Standard English.'

I have tried to avoid this sort of presentation but clearly any interpretive analysis is subjective and reflects a particular point of view. None of the decisions have been arbitrarily or lightly taken and frequently a single map represents a considerable number of drafts and reworkings.

A. Descriptive maps

Material was selected for each Middle English sound group, usually at least ten words for each group. The relative frequencies of the phonetic types were then scored up or down to a base of 100 and the resultant percentages were mapped using symbols of differing sizes.

B. Structural maps

The structural maps could not be prepared until the analysis of the material on a phonetic basis had been completed (A above). The method used was to compare the phonetic scores for two ME phonemes locality by locality, for example:

2 Cu 3 *Brigham*

	[ɪə~ẹa]	[e:~e:ə]
ME/a:/	50%	50%
ME/ai/	—	100%
Difference	+50	−50

The 'differences' were then converted to a percentage measure of distinctiveness, in this case 50%. ($\frac{50+50}{200}$). ME /a:/ is thus 50% distinct from ME /ai/. Alternatively, in 50% of environments the contrast between ME /a:/ words and ME /ai/ words is neutralised. This method can be used to indicate maximally contrasting forms, e.g.:

6 Y 7 *Askrigg*

	[ɪə]	[ɛ̌ə]	[ɛə]	[e:]	
ME/ :/	73	27	7	20	= 127
ME/ i/	9	18	18	73	= 118
	+64	+9	−11	−53	= 137

$\frac{137}{245}$ = 56% distinction

The major contrast is between [ɪə] and [e:]. (Postulated contrast /iə/ v /e:/.) [ɛə] and [eə] are of doubtful status but clearly help to maintain the contrast between the two main types. [eə] is associated with [ɪə] and [ɛə] with [e:] and they have been treated as 'belonging' to the postulated phonemes /ɪə/ and /e:/. This general principle has been consistently applied throughout the analysis work.

The type of development known as 'split and merger' is not amenable to precisely the same sort of treatment and the word groups have been split on the basis of the Standard English distribution. The maps will therefore represent the degree of divergence from the Standard English structural contrast and it is acknowledged that this may *potentially* obscure systems where a contrast exists but which is not precisely the same as Standard English. On the other hand this atlas is not intended to be exhaustive but merely to show some of the structural differences present in the dialects of the SED. Complete uniformity in technique is impossible to achieve and the presentation (but not the underlying analyses) has been varied in the interests of comprehensibility.

Conclusion

It is fashionable to criticise the SED for its failure to gather adequate phonemic material and for ignoring the majority of English speakers. These maps presented here suggest that quite adequate structural conclusions can be drawn from the SED material even though the SED itself is essentially phonetic in presentation. The phonemic realities are rarely in doubt and where the position is not clear, the ambiguity is very often in the phonemic system itself. As regards the non-coverage by the SED of substantial numbers of speakers, the orientation of the survey was towards the oldest type of dialectal English spoken. The success of the project was in obtaining a genuine cross-section of that type of English and in completing a national survey with limited financial support. Let the structuralists produce their comprehensive survey of English speech before they criticise the SED. The remarkable feature of the survey is not its inadequacy but its richness, a comparative body of material to which linguists of all persuasions can turn to test their hypotheses. The same cannot be said of all surveys. At least the bulk of the SED material is published and has already proved indispensable to the publications of some of its critics.

The SED provides this study with virtually all its material, but for comparative purposes, material from *Early English Pronunciation* (EEP)[22] part V, by A.J. Ellis has also been used. A.J. Ellis collected phonological material from a variety of sources covering the dialects of England, Wales and

Scotland. These sources were often informants who were lifelong residents of the place in which they lived and the material was recorded phonetically by trained fieldworkers. His coverage was unfortunately patchy and he often had to rely on written information from educated informants which he endeavoured to check by direct and indirect enquiry. The result was a study of dialectal phonology which set new standards of accuracy and began a fresh approach to dialect study. Ellis's material lends itself to a structural approach and maps based on it have been provided in this atlas where there has been a need for a nineteenth century perspective. This is the first time that his material has been used in this way and the results suggest that further structural analysis would repay the work involved in extracting the information.

ME sound system

Short vowels /a/ /e/ /i/ /o/ /u/
Long vowels /a:/ /ɛ:/ /e:/ /i:/ /ɔ:/ /o:/ /u:/
Diphthongs /iu/ (/eu/) /ɛu/ (/ou/) /ɔu/ /au/ /ai/ /ɔi/ /ui/

The forms /ɛ:/$_1$ and /ɛ:/$_2$ are used to represent the ME sounds which arose from OE *ǣ, ēa* and eME /e/ respectively. Likewise the forms /ɔ:/$_1$ and /ɔ:/$_2$ are used to represent the ME sounds which arose from OE *ā* and eME /o/ respectively.

Notes on the SED basic material

Inevitably, certain inconsistencies come to light on examining the Basic Material, partly due to the number of fieldworkers involved in the survey. The editors admit as much in the introduction to Volume IV — *The Southern Counties*:

'The more closely we studied the field recordings, the more convinced we became of the need for collating them with the tapes.'[23]

In the phonetic notes the fieldworkers' records are compared with the tape recordings made of selected informants. LAE chose to follow the printed responses but I have felt no compulsion to do so and have used the material in the phonetic notes to supersede the fieldworkers' notations in certain instances. (ME /u:/, /i:/, /ɔ:/ in the Southern Counties and ME /u/ and /a/ in Monmouthshire.) I have taken the balance of the material at its face value although I suspect that it would be illuminating to compare the Basic Material with the tape recordings for other areas also. It is to be hoped that this will be done in the not too distant future. Maps 89 and 96 are somewhat uncertain as far as parts of the South are concerned but I have assumed that even if the fieldworkers misheard the sounds, they misheard them consistently, their interpretation being essentially phonemic. If this assumption is wrong, then the material is of little value phonologically if not worthless.

NOTES

1. Orton and Dieth, 1962.
2. Orton et al. 1978.
3. Kolb, 1966.
4. *The Linguistic Atlas of England* is also to a certain extent interpretive, often idiosyncratically so.
5. Petyt, 1980, p. 117 et seq.
6. Kurath and Lowman, 1970, p. 44.
7. Fries and Pike, 1949, pp. 29-50.
8. McDavid, 1979, p. 15.
9. Fries and Pike, op. cit.
10. For a partial system analysis see Anderson, 1977.
11. Trudgill, 1974, p. 69.
12. Samuels, 1969, pp. 408-18.
13. Sternberg, 1851, p. xii.
14. A summary of the relationship between linguistic areas and geographical features in relation to ME dialects is to be found in Moore, Meech and Whitehall, 1935.
15. Patchett, 1981, p. 35.
16. Moore, Meech and Whitehall, 1935, p. 29.
17. Stenton, 1971, p. 49.
18. Sternberg, 1851, p. xii.
19. Stenton, 1971, p. 235.
20. North, 1979, p. 8 et seq.
21. Kurath and Lowman, 1970, p. 2.
22. Ellis, 1889.
23. Orton and Dieth, 1961, p. 10.

2

Middle English Short Vowels

2.1 ME /a/ (ă)

ME /a/ is represented by a number of different phonemes in Standard English, each having its origin in conditioned phonetic changes which affected the realisations of the parent phoneme. Within Standard English, the major changes in phonetic structure have come about as a result of raising, lengthening or retraction (see Table 2.1). Similar changes have affected the dialects but the structural effects have not necessarily been the same. These developments will now be considered.

Table 2.1: A broad outline of the descendants of ME /a/ in Standard English

/a/ + /s,f,θ,r/	>	/ɑː/
/a/ + /l/	>	/ɔː~ɒ/
/w/ + /a/	>	/ɒ/
/w/ + /ar/	>	/ɔː/
/a/ in other positions	>	/æ/

2.2 Raising of ME /a/

(a) Raising before a consonant (excluding /s,f,θ,r,l/) (Map 1)

ME /a/ is raised in East Anglia and the South East as well as parts of Somerset and the south west Midlands (Hereford, Worcester and Gloucester). It is also raised in west Cornwall and the Isle of Man, both of which the English language has reached at a comparatively recent date. In parts of Essex, Kent, Surrey and Sussex, ME /a/ appears as [ɛ] representing a merger with ME /e/ which is known from the OE period onwards.[1]

ME /a/ is raised sporadically in parts of the West Riding of Yorkshire and also before a following /k,g/ in north west Derbyshire and parts of south east Lancashire, partially merging with ME /e/.

(b) Raising before /f,s,θ/ (Map 2)

Raising of ME /a/ was less general in this position, being found usually in the same areas as raising in other positions but also in a more extensive area of South West England. It is interesting to note that raising in this position was relatively less frequent in East Anglia than isolative raising but that the position is reversed in the South West. There, [a] occurs in isolative position and [æː] before voiceless fricatives. Kurath and Lowman remark:

'It is a curious fact that in the East and in the West [æ] makes its appearance in mutually exclusive positions.'[2]

(c) Raising before /r/ (Not mapped)

Raising before /r/ is relatively uncommon, many apparent instances being probably due to by-forms with ME /aːr/. Regular raising occurs in north Oxfordshire (25 0 1/2), north Cambridgeshire (20 C 1), west Lancashire (5 La 3/4, 6/7, 10, 13/14) and the Isle of Man. It also occurs in south Durham (3 Du 4/5) where it merges with ME /aːr/.[3]

2.3 Lengthening of ME /a/

ME /a/ remained only in closed syllables following lengthening in eME in open syllables everywhere. It was later lengthened in other positions in certain dialects.

(a) Lengthening before /f,s,θ/ (Maps 3–4)

Lengthening before voiceless fricatives occurs throughout southern England, southern central England and East Anglia. Lengthening also occurs in south Lancashire (5 La 12) and to a minor extent in north Derbyshire and contiguous areas and also on the Isle of Man. The Lancashire development appears to be an independent innovation. (See also Map 11 for a similar development after ME /o/.)

(b) Lengthening before /r/

ME /a/ has been lengthened everywhere with subsequent loss of /r/ in some areas. /r/ is retained south of a line approximately coinciding with Watling Street and also in Lancashire, south Westmorland, the northern Dales of Yorkshire and also

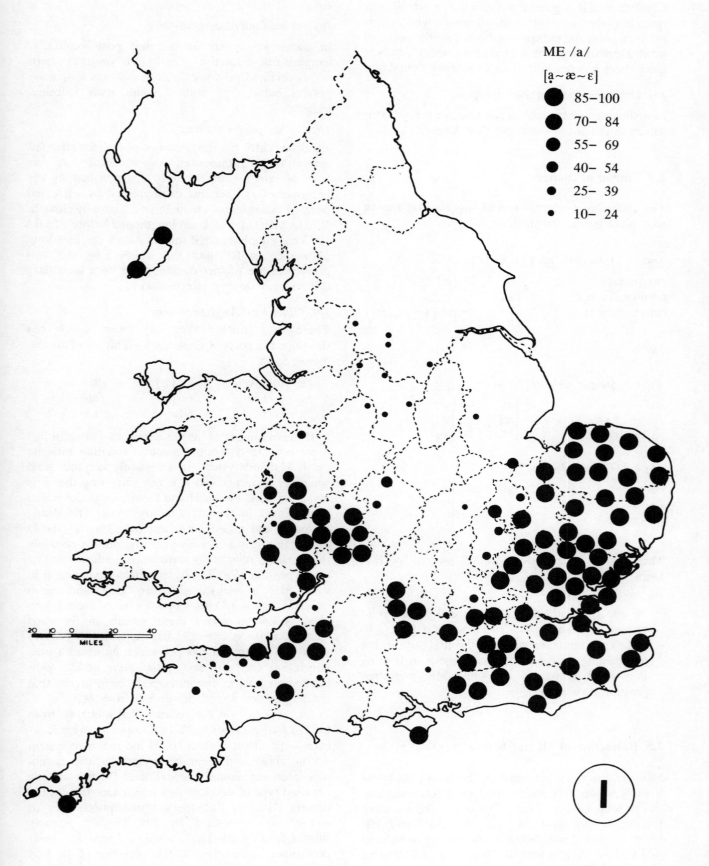

ME /a/

[a̠ ~ æ ~ ɛ]

● 85–100
● 70– 84
● 55– 69
● 40– 54
● 25– 39
● 10– 24

MILES
20 10 0 20 40

Ⅰ

Northumberland, north Durham and north Cumberland. It is generally realised as a retroflex or retracted alveolar sound in all areas where it is retained, with the exception of Northumberland and north Durham where it is uvular and north Cumberland where it is retained as an alveolar or dental tap.

(c) Other lengthening (Not mapped)

Lengthening occurs sporadically before a final consonant in the South West and East Anglia.

2.4 Timing of changes

The following examples would suggest that raising took place before lengthening.

Type 1 Ashwellthorpe (21 Nf 10)

/a/ (in all		> [æ]
positions except	> [æ]	
before /r/)(4)		> [æ:] (+ /s,f,θ/)
/a/ + /r/		> [a:]

Type 2 Steeple Ashton (32 W 5)

/a/	> [a]	> [a]
/a/ + /f,s,θ/	> [æ]	> [æ:]
/a/ + /r/		> [a:r]

Type 3 Tiptree (29 Ess 9)

/a/	> [æ]	> [æ/
/a/ + /r/		> [a:]
/a/ + /f,s,θ/		> [a:]

This view would appear to be shared by E.J. Dobson.

> 'In the case of ME *ǎ*, the normal direction of change is from its ME pronunciation [a] ... to [æ]. The retraction which is the first step in the lengthening process therefore consists in holding the vowel at palatal [a] while ME *ǎ* in free position goes to [æ].'[4]

2.5 Retraction of ME /a/ before /r/ (Map 5)

ME /a/ has been retracted in the South East and Norfolk when it is conditioned by a following /r/ and to some extent /f,s,θ/. This is also the Standard English development. ME /a/ + /f,s,θ/ and ME /a/ + /r/ are clearly being levelled under one sound [ɑ:] in East Anglia and the South East. (Compare Map 5 and Map 2.)

2.6 Structural significance of developments (Map 6A)

(a) /r/ retained post-vocalically

In areas where /r/ is retained post-vocalically, length is not distinctive. (See Map 6 for areas where /r/ is retained post-vocalically.) /a/ has long allophones before /r/ and in some areas voiceless fricatives.

(b) /r/ lost post-vocalically

Elsewhere ME /a/ split into two phonemes after /r/ ceased to be pronounced post-vocalically. A pair such as *cart — cat*, formerly distinguished by the presence of /r/ became distinguished by what had been a secondary characteristic, namely length. Where ME /a/ had been lengthened before /f,s,θ/ the long allophones fell together with the new long phoneme. In RP and the South East the two phonemes are further distinguished by a secondary difference in quality. (Retraction to /ɑ:/.)

(c) Older East Anglian system

There is a further type of system which has developed in parts of East Anglia. This takes the following form:

/a/ isolatively	> [æ]	/æ/
/a/ + /f,s,θ/	> [æ:]	/æ/ (?)
/a/ + /r/	> [a:~a:]	/a:~a:/

If the treatment of [æ:] as a long allophone of [æ] is correct, the system has much in common with the north Midland system. It is certainly very marginal wherever it occurs and it is not surprising that it is being replaced by the Home Counties system which is dominant in the surrounding areas. The distribution of the raised long [æ:] (see Map 2) shows clearly that it is a recessive feature; almost certainly the separate relic areas were once continuous. The two types therefore imply two dialect types, one in which ME /a/ was raised before /f,s,θ/ and one in which it was not. This seems to be in accord with what is known about these sounds in Standard English. Dobson cites the late seventeenth century work of Christopher Cooper which indicates a pronunciation [æ:] in *last, past, path* and a pronunciation [a:r] in *barge, carp*. Dobson argues that the lengthened sound developed from ME /a/ + /s,f,θ/ was [a:] on the grounds that a change from [æ:] to [ɑ:] is rather unlikely. Cooper's system however is the direct antecedent of the recessive system set out above and it can be argued that this system was later supplanted in Standard English by the unraised type of development which accounts for the current RP type.[6] Cooper's transcriptions may of course be influenced by his origins: possibly Buntingford, north Hertfordshire. There are however other testimonies to the presence of [æ:] in Standard English in the early eighteenth century.[7]

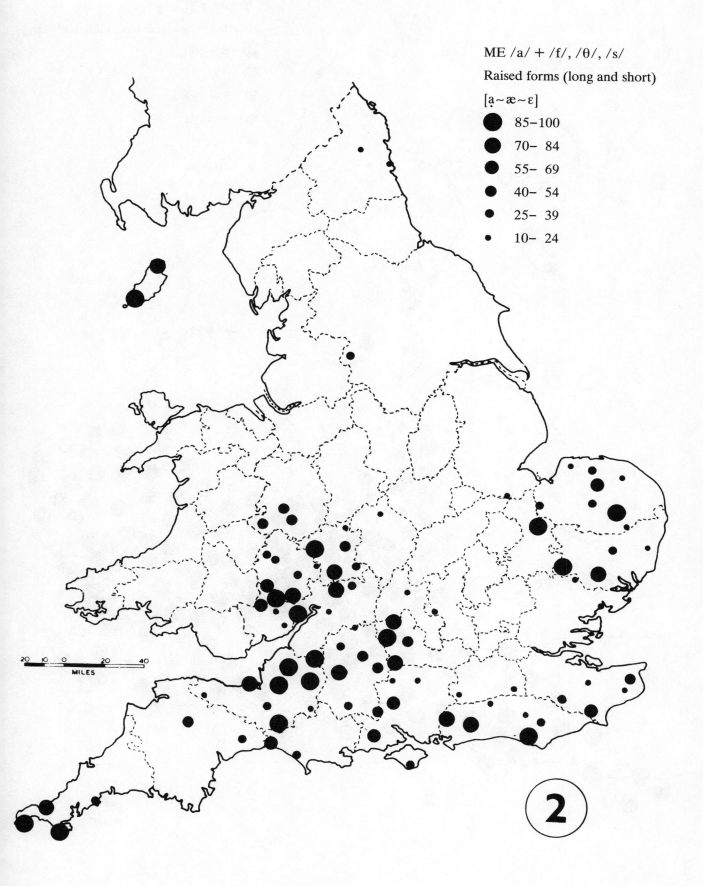

ME /a/ + /f/, /θ/, /s/

Raised forms (long and short)

[a̞~æ~ɛ]

● 85–100

● 70– 84

● 55– 69

● 40– 54

• 25– 39

· 10– 24

②

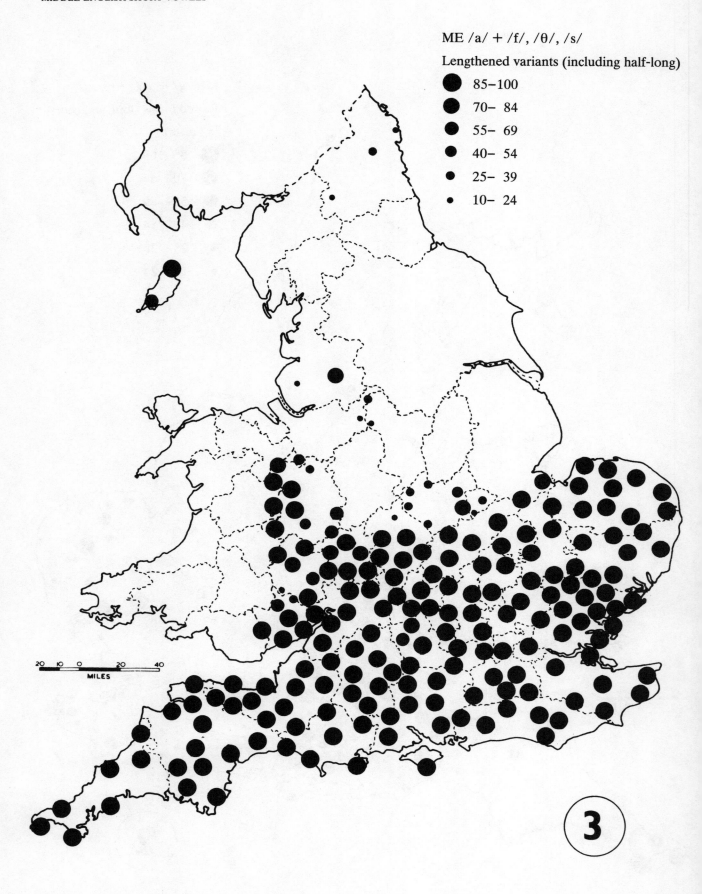

ME /a/ + /f/, /θ/, /s/

Lengthened variants (including half-long)

- 85–100
- 70– 84
- 55– 69
- 40– 54
- 25– 39
- 10– 24

3

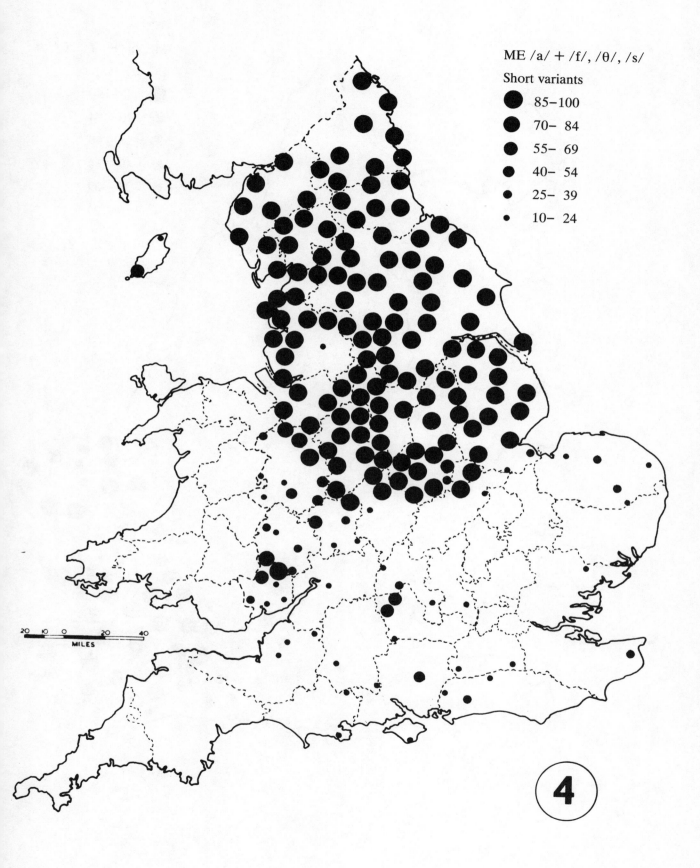

ME /a/ + /f/, /θ/, /s/

Short variants

● 85–100

● 70– 84

● 55– 69

● 40– 54

• 25– 39

• 10– 24

MILES

④

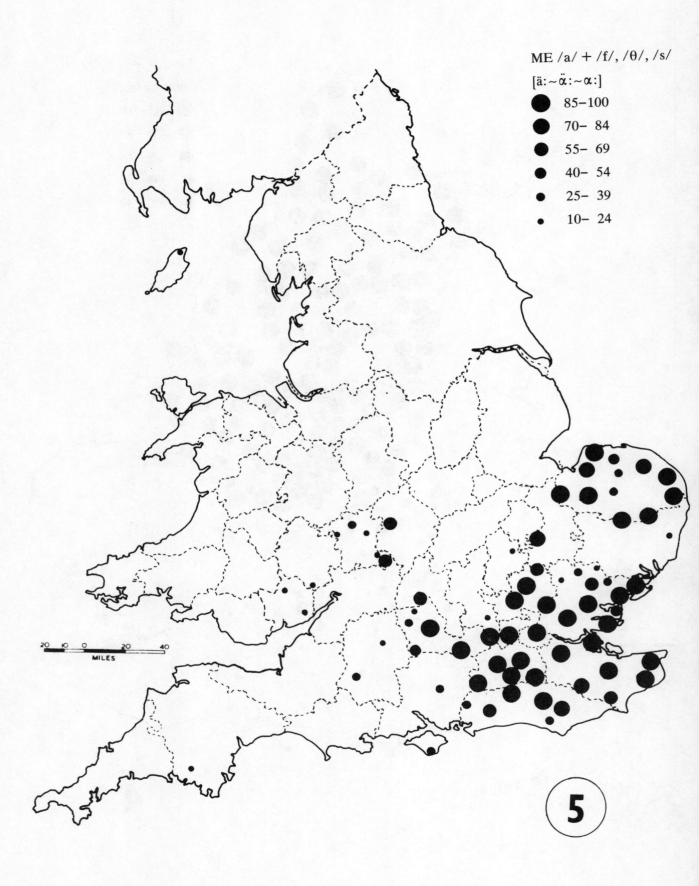

ME /a/ + /f/, /θ/, /s/

[ä:~ä̈:~α:]

- ● 85–100
- ● 70– 84
- ● 55– 69
- ● 40– 54
- ● 25– 39
- ● 10– 24

MILES

⑤

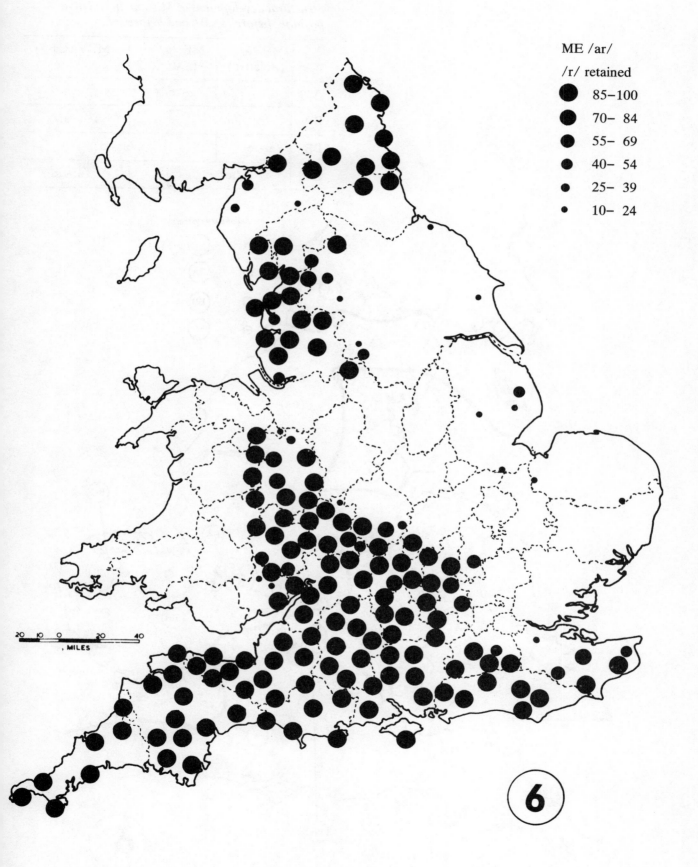

ME /ar/
/r/ retained

● 85–100
● 70– 84
● 55– 69
● 40– 54
● 25– 39
● 10– 24

MILES

6

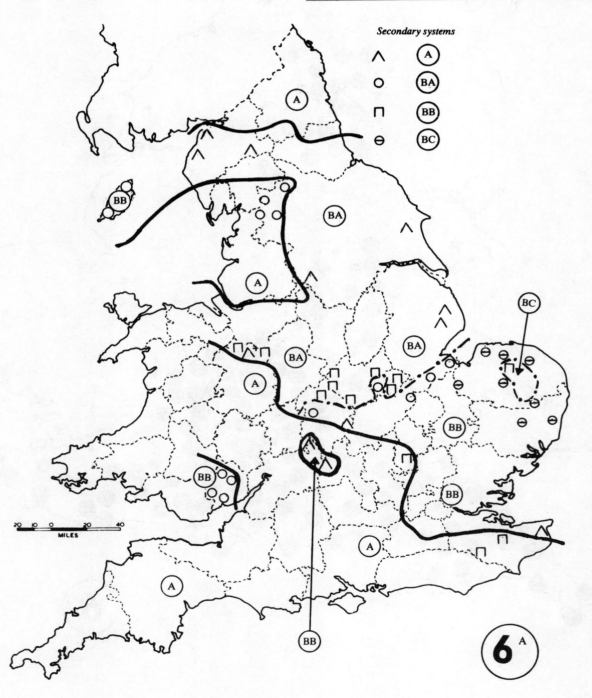

Key to Map 6A

Structural development of ME /a/ in isolative position, before /f,s,θ/ and before /r/.

	ME /a/ (isolative)	ME /a/ + /f,s,θ/	ME /a/ + /r/
A	/a~æ/		
BA	/a/		/a:/
BB	/a~æ/	/a:~ɑ:/	
BC	/æ/		/a:~ɑ:/

Secondary systems

∧ Ⓐ

○ ⒷⒶ

⊓ ⒷⒷ

⊖ ⒷⒸ

6 ᴬ

2.7 ME /o/ (ǒ)

The development of ME /o/ may be usefully compared with ME /a/ in that there are similarities in the processes which have affected the two sounds. It is also useful to consider the development of ME /au/ which is partially merged with ME /o/ in many parts of England. Standard English shows a typical 'split and merger' pattern, the lengthened allophones of ME /o/ falling in with ME /au/. Only the major developments of ME /o/ are considered here.

Table 2.2: A broad outline of the descendants of ME /o/ in Standard English

/o/	>	/ɒ/
/o/ + /r/	>	/ɔ:/
/o/ + /f,s,θ/	>	/ɒ~ɔ:/
/au/	>	/ɔ:/

2.8 Lowering of ME /o/

ME /o/ has generally been lowered in the dialects to a low back position [ɒ~ɑ].[8]

2.9 Unrounding of ME /o/ (Map 7)

The degree of rounding retained varies from area to area. In three areas, Norfolk, south Northamptonshire and north Buckinghamshire, and the south west Midlands including the Cotswolds, ME /o/ has been completely unrounded to [ɑ], and over much of south western England rounding is rather weaker than in Standard English.

2.10 Fronting of ME /o/

ME /o/ has been fronted sporadically in many dialects of southern and western England, a change which has found its way into Standard English on occasion (e.g. the alternation in *strap — strop*). The effect of this fronting is to merge ME /o/ in part with ME /a/ with subsequent sharing of the developments of ME /a/. The development appears to be of fairly long standing.[9] Also, such forms as [æ:f] at 40 Sx 6 (*OFF* SED IX.2.13) tend to support this view. ME /or/ appears to have been very frequently fronted in central southern England so that such pairs as *form* and *farm* are homophones. The relic forms in Norfolk and Sussex suggest a wider distribution in the past (Map 15). A second trend towards fronting can be distinguished. ME /o/ frequently appears as [ɞ] in the field recordings of the Southern Counties. A completely separate fronting has taken place in Northumberland giving a half-

open rounded front vowel, usually long — [œ:~œ] (Map 8).

2.11 Lengthening of ME /o/

(a) Lengthening before /f,s,θ/ (Maps 9–10)

Lengthening occurs in approximately the same areas as lengthening of ME /a/ in the same position, but the South Pennine enclave is rather larger, extending into Yorkshire. A long sound is heard in Northumberland but this is a change affecting ME /o/ in all positions except before /r/. It is clear from Map 12 that the lengthened forms are to some extent being replaced in all areas with the exception of East Anglia and the South West.

(b) Lengthening before /k,g/ (Map 11)

Lengthening occurs before /k/ and /g/ in East Anglia, Somerset, Dorset and the West Midlands. This distribution seems to suggest that the lengthening in this position never reached the extreme South West and also that the lengthened forms are being supplanted by shortened forms from the central and east Midlands.

(c) Lengthening before /r/ (Not mapped)

Lengthening occurs before /r/ in most dialects with subsequent loss of /r/ in the Midlands and East Anglia. (See Map 12.) A short vowel is retained in north Cumberland and partially in north and east Yorkshire.

(d) Lengthening before other final consonants

ME /o/ is sporadically lengthened before other final consonants in the South West and occasionally elsewhere.

2.12 ME /au/ (au)

The development of ME /au/ to some extent parallels ME /o/. Over most of England /au/ becomes [ɔ:], a long back sound varying in quality from area to area. Over most of southern England south of the Thames and in west England, ME /au/ is a more open sound than in Standard English and frequently only weakly rounded (Map 13). The most extreme development of this type is found in the Cotswolds where [ɑ:], a low back unrounded vowel occurs. In distinction, the east Midlands and South East including parts of Kent, East Anglia and the central Midlands show a much closer fully rounded sound [ɔ:]. The ME diphthong is lost over the whole of England with the exception of a small area of north Staffordshire which shows /oʊ/ representing a a merger with ME /ɔu/.[11]

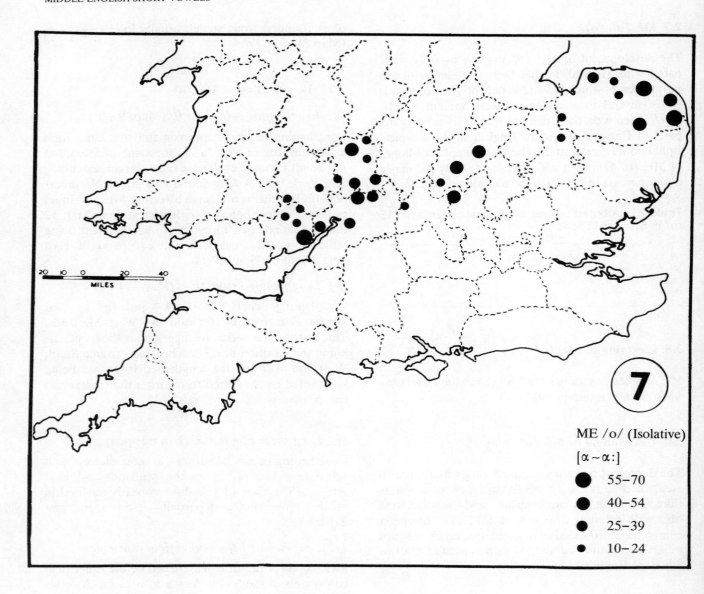

ME /o/ (Isolative)

[α ~ α:]

- ● 55–70
- ● 40–54
- ● 25–39
- ● 10–24

⑦

2.13 Fronting of ME /au/ (Map 14)

ME /au/ is not always retained as a back sound but is fairly frequently fronted to /a:/ in north Lancashire, the northern Dales of Yorkshire, Northumberland and Durham. A further area of fronting in final position occurs in Oxfordshire and Wiltshire.

2.14 Effects of lengthening and unrounding on ME /o/ and ME /au/

The phonetic effects of lengthening and unrounding differ from area to area. In the south west Midlands both ME /o/ and ME /au/ have unrounded descendants, for example:

ME /o/	>	[α]
ME /o/ + /f,s,θ/	>	[α:]
ME /au/	>	[α:]

In Norfolk and East Anglia, on the other hand, unrounding is restricted to ME /o/ in unconditioned position, for example:

ME /o/	>	[α]
ME /o/ + /f,s,θ/	>	[ɔ:]
ME /au/	>	[ɔ:]

2.15 Structural significance of the developments of ME /o/ and ME /au/ (Map 15A)

Because of the overlapping developments ME /au/ and ME /o/, the structural position is rather complex. However, a basic distinction can be drawn between those dialects in which /r/ is retained post-vocalically and those in which it is lost.

(a) Dialects in which /r/ is lost post-vocalically

These dialects show a wide variety of systems based

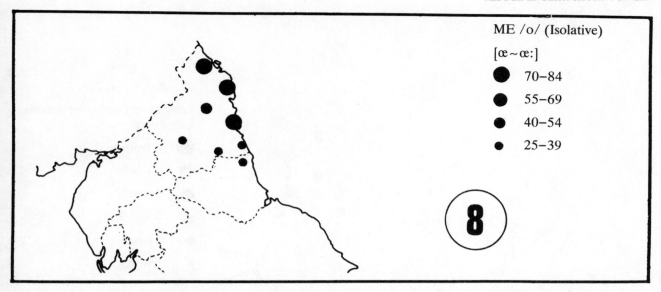

ME /o/ (Isolative)

[œ ~ œ:]

- ● 70–84
- ● 55–69
- ● 40–54
- • 25–39

8

on two phonemes contrasted by length. The way in which these phonemes are distributed varies considerably (see Map 15A). A three-way contrast appears in south Durham (/ɒ/~/ɔ:/~/a:/). The developments suppose the evolution of long allophones in certain positions varying from area to area. The difference became phonemic with the loss of /r/ in post-vocalic position, long allophones merging with the reflex of ME /au/.

(b) Dialects in which /r/ is retained post-vocalically

Two areas may be distinguished — the North and the South (see Map 12).

(i) Northern area ME /o/ is represented by /ɒ/ in all positions contrasting with /ɔ:~a:/ from ME /au/, with some neutralisation of the opposition before /r/ in most of the area and before /f,s,θ/ in south Lancashire.

(ii) Southern area There is a strong tendency to merge ME /o/ and ME /au/ in a single phoneme of variable length. ME /o/ may have allophones [ɔ:~ɑ:] ocurring before /f,s,θ,k,g,r/ and sporadically before other consonants, and allophones [ɒ~ɑ] in other positions. ME /au/ has allophones [ɔ:~ɑ:]. Since ME /o/ never occurs finally, potential contrasts will only arise in medial or initial position but will often be neutralised in this position (before /f,s,θ/ regularly, before /g,k/ frequently and before other consonants intermittently).[12] In positions where contrast is possible, certain dialects have intrusive /r/, e.g. Shropshire [dɔʳ:təʳ], in which /ɔ:/ is reinterpreted as /or/.

2.16 ME /u/ (ŭ)

ME /u/ was lowered in Standard English but

remained in certain positions, mainly labial. (The development is not uniform — compare *put* /pʊt/ and *putt* /pʌt/.) On the whole such differences remained allophonic until ME /o:/ was shortened and distinctions such as *buck — book* were reinterpreted as /bʌk/ — /bʊk/.

2.17 Lowering and unrounding of ME /u/

ME /u/ has been lowered and unrounded over most of southern England and East Anglia and also in the Welsh border counties from Shropshire southwards (Map 17). Unrounding is also characteristic of north Northumberland which follows the development of the neighbouring Scots dialects in this respect. Rounded vowels are generally retained in the neighbourhood of labials but not always in the same words as Standard English.

Unrounding to [ɤ] without lowering is common in Norfolk and to a minor extent in east Northumberland. Elsewhere, ME /u/ remains as a rounded close vowel in all positions (Map 16).

ME /u/ retained in proximity to labials in southern England tends to remain as [ʊ] but has been fronted to [ʏ] in Devonshire and adjoining parts of Cornwall and Somerset.

The unrounded vowel found on the Welsh border is to some extent separated from the main [ʌ] area. The distribution suggests either independent development or else the reintroduction of rounded forms from the central Midlands into the intervening area. Ellis records [ʌ] relatively frequently from north Gloucester but remarks that this is a 'mixed area', i.e. that [ʊ] and [ʌ] occur in free variation.[13] In the SED records, there is not much trace of this in Gloucestershire although Oxfordshire is more mixed.

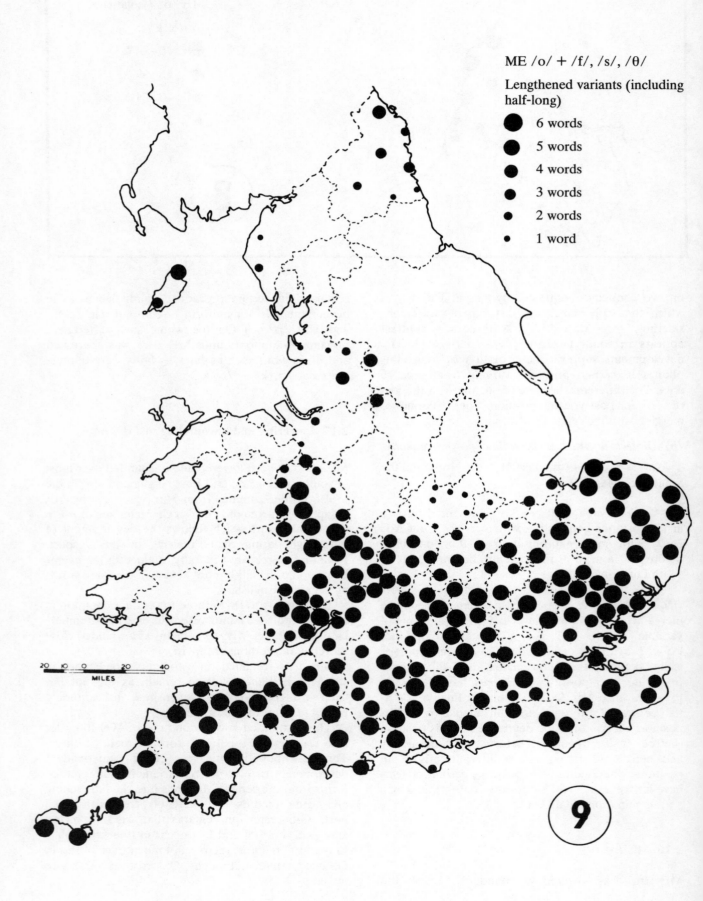

ME /o/ + /f/, /s/, /θ/

Lengthened variants (including half-long)

● 6 words
● 5 words
● 4 words
● 3 words
● 2 words
• 1 word

MILES
20 10 0 20 40

9

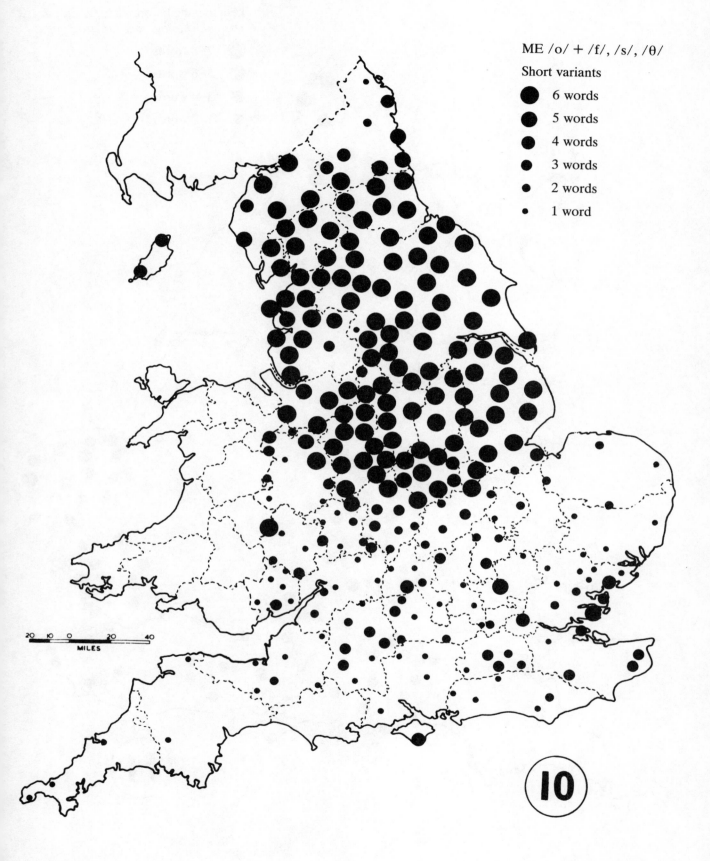

ME /o/ + /f/, /s/, /θ/

Short variants

● 6 words

● 5 words

● 4 words

● 3 words

• 2 words

· 1 word

10

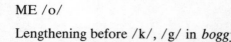

ME /o/

Lengthening before /k/, /g/ in *boggy, cock, dock, dog, fog, fox, frog, hog.*

● 7–8 words

● 5–6 words

● 3–4 words

● 1–2 words

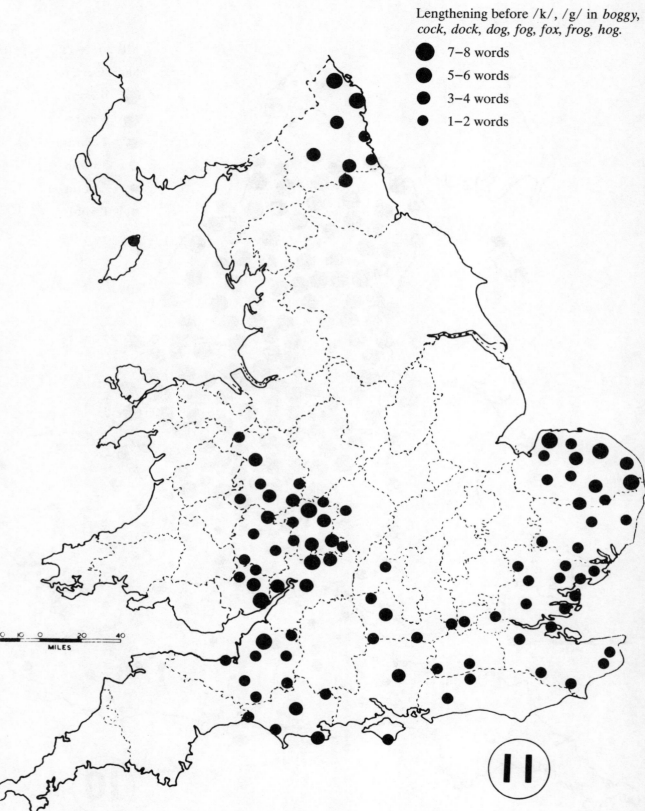

ME /or/ (final and pre-consonantal)
/r/ retained.

●   7 words

●   5–6 words

●   3–4 words

●   1–2 words

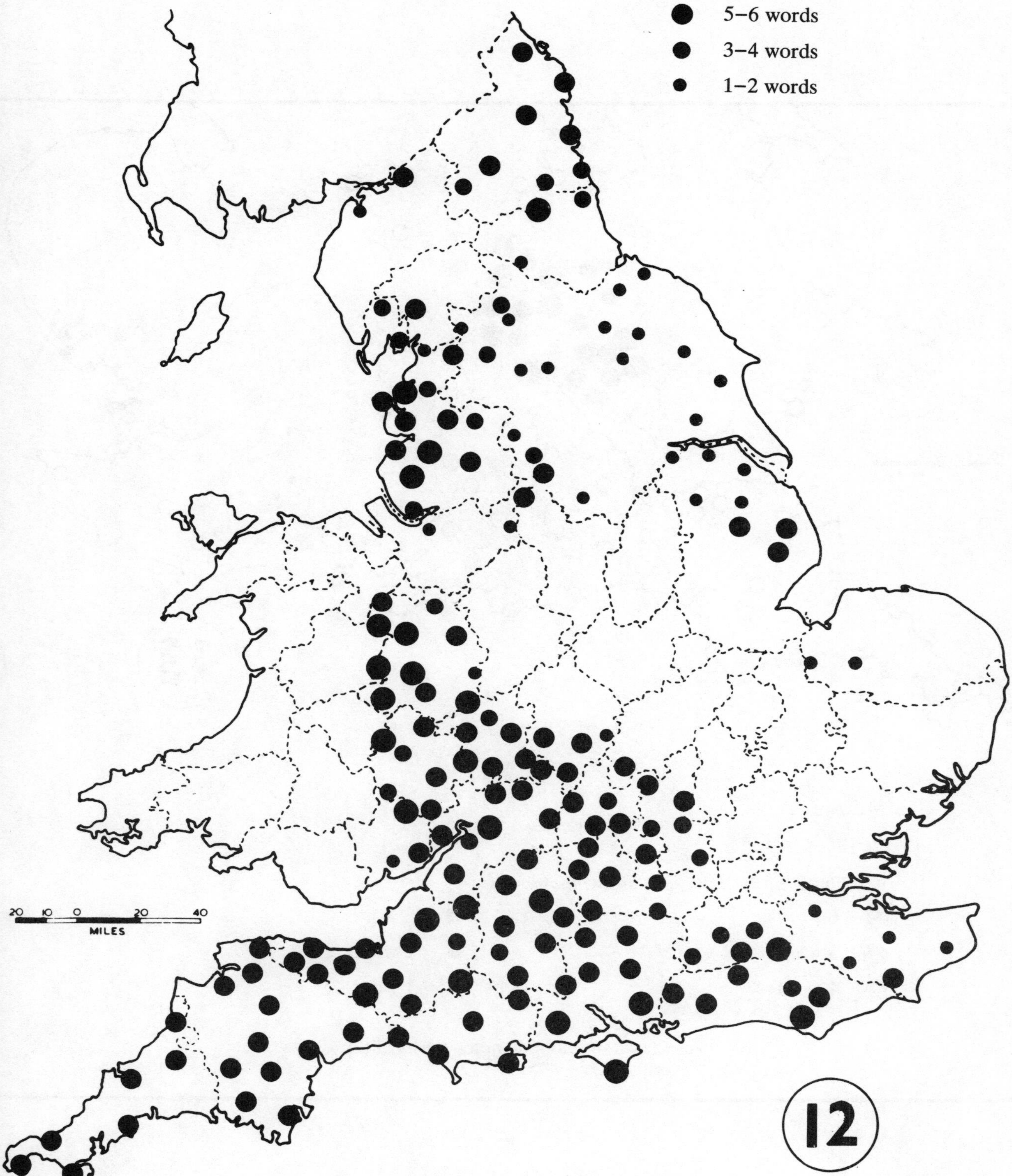

20 10 0   20   40

MILES

(12)

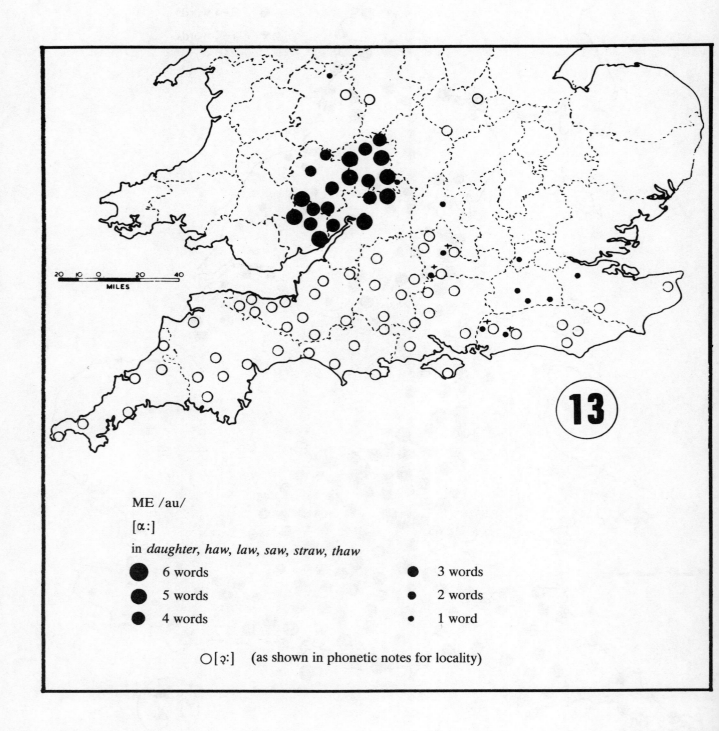

ME /au/

[ɑ:]

in *daughter, haw, law, saw, straw, thaw*

⬤   6 words   ●   3 words

⬤   5 words   •   2 words

●   4 words   ·   1 word

○ [ɔ:]   (as shown in phonetic notes for locality)

ME /au/

[a:~æ]

in *daughter, haw, law, saw, straw, thaw.*

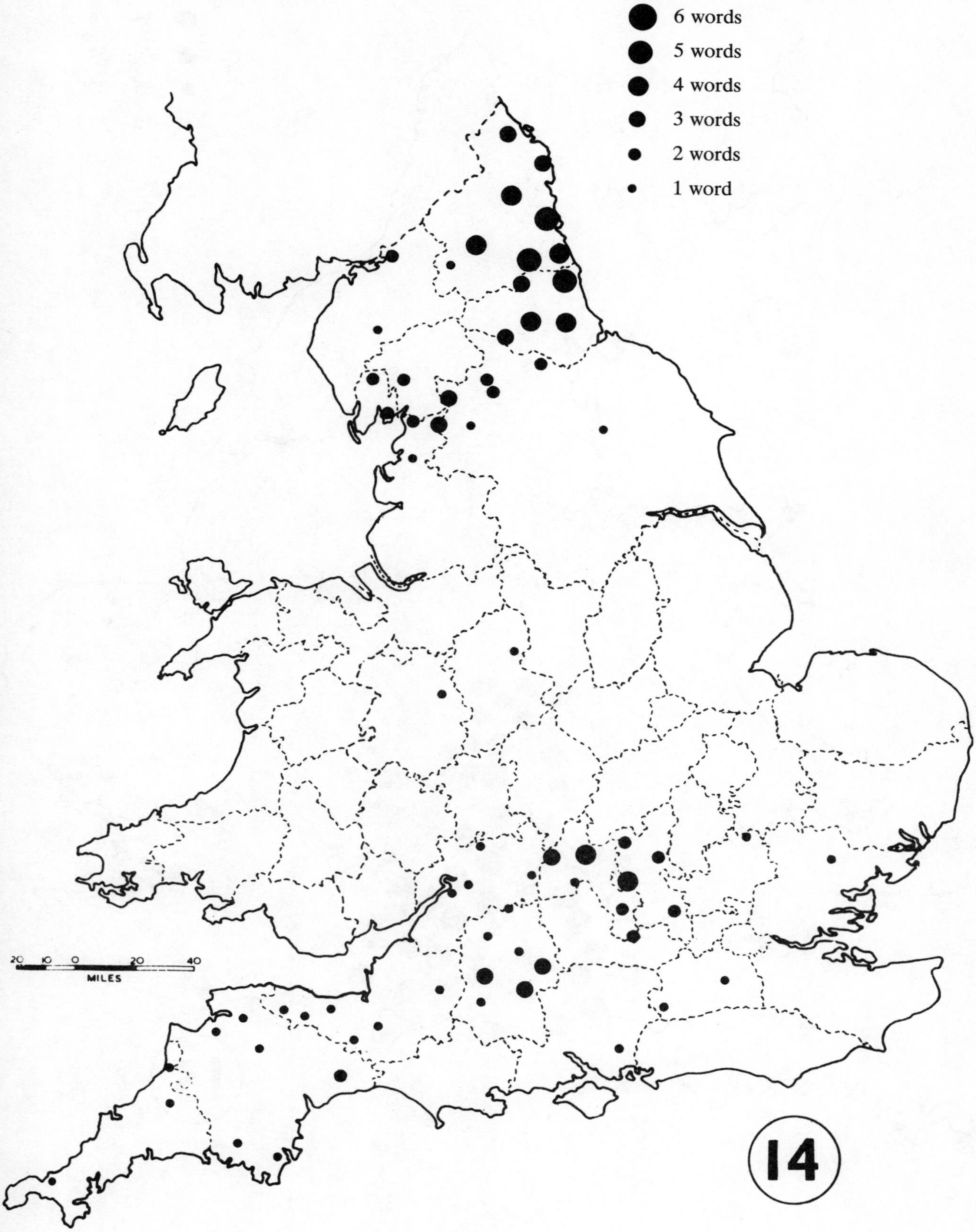

- ● 6 words
- ● 5 words
- ● 4 words
- ● 3 words
- • 2 words
- · 1 word

MILES

20 10 0 20 40

⑭

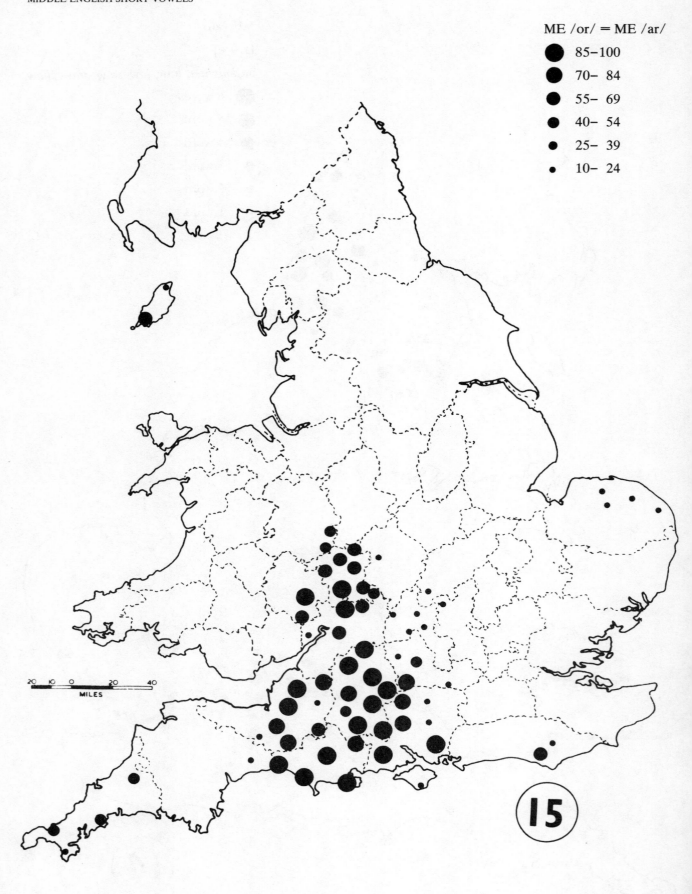

ME /or/ = ME /ar/

- 85–100
- 70– 84
- 55– 69
- 40– 54
- 25– 39
- 10– 24

MILES

15

2.18 Structural significance of the developments of ME /u/

To understand the structural position of ME /u/, the shortening of ME /o:/ must be considered. The position here is rather complex as the shortening has been gradual, that is different phonetic environments have been affected at different times and in varying geographical areas. Maps 18, 62, 63, 64 show the different developments. The earliest shortening (in for example *mother, brother, month*) appears to have taken place everywhere. A later shortening in words like *foot, soot* extended as far north as the Humber (Map 63). ME /o:k/ has been shortened (in *cook, look, book*) but not in the north Midlands or the North (Map 62). The trend towards shortening has affected a further ill-defined groups of words such as *broom, goose, roof* (Map 18). This change has reached only the south Midlands, East Anglia and the west Midlands and has not been adopted in Standard English. Map 64 summarises the different shortenings.

ME /o:/ has been most shortened in East Anglia and the south Midlands and in the former area the /ʊ/ phoneme is all the more frequent because it is also often the reflex of ME /ɔ:/. The shortening of the long vowel is in part related to the lowering of ME /u/ which left a gap which the newly shortened forms could fill. None the less, the two processes do not completely overlap. In the South West, ME /u/ > /ʌ/ but shortening of ME /o:/ is relatively limited. There are areas of the south west Midlands in which ME /u/ remains as /ʊ/ whilst ME /o:/ has been shortened just as much as in the more southerly dialects. Whilst this may indicate the reintroduction of [ʊ] forms to these dialects, it may also do no more than demonstrate that pressures other than the most obvious are affecting these dialects.

In general, the later shortening processes took place after the lowering of ME /u/, but /ʌ/ forms which occur in *roof, soot* etc. in Norfolk, Bedfordshire, Hertfordshire and Shropshire indicate that in some areas, shortening occurred before lowering.

Map 19, based on ME /u/ words shows the areas in which a contrast between /ʊ/ and /ʌ/ may be presumed to exist. The boundary is reasonably sharp in the West and in the Fens but the isoglosses are far more spread in the south Midlands. The emergence of two separate phonemes is clearly in progress in parts of Buckinghamshire and Cambridgeshire, (e.g. 20 C 1 where [ɞ] corresponds to RP /ʌ/ and [ʊ] to RP /ʊ/ < ME /u/). Whether such small distinctions are phonemic is doubtful.

Although Northern England does not have the /ʊ/~/ʌ/ contrast, a distinction can still be made in consequence of the failure of shortening of ME /o:/ in these dialects, for example:

Northern	/lu:k/ ~ /lʊk/	*look ~ luck*
Southern	/lʊk/ ~ /lʌk/	—— '' ——

It is only in those Northern and Midland dialects in which shortening of /o:/ has taken place together with retention of ME /u/ that the contrast between the two groups is lost in a merged form /lʊk/.

2.19 ME /ir/, /ur/ (ir, ur)

Map 20 displays the areas in which /r/ is retained in a range of words having ME /ir/ or /ur/ and represented by /ə:/ in Standard English. If this map is compared with Map 6 and Map 12 (ME /ar/ and ME /or/), it is quite clear that /r/ has survived more widely after /ə:/. The corridor of /r/ usage which runs from the Wash to the South West is notable, as is the absence of /r/ in the north east Midlands. Possibly this points to a connection between this area and the South East.

The developments which have taken place in the dialects have been very varied and are further complicated by having different etymons in different areas. The dialects of Northumberland and north Durham have merged ME /ur/ and /ir/ with ME /or/. The dialects of the South of England have tended to develop /ə:~ər:/ in the areas where /r/ is retained. Developments elsewhere are very mixed but there was apparently a tendency to develop ME /ur/ in this group and to subsequently shorten it. This was in part a positional development (in Cheshire in the combinations /urs/, /urθ/) and in part general (east Yorks, Lincolnshire /ɒ/, south Suffolk, north Essex /ʌ/).

NOTES

1. Wright, 1925, para. 54, note 1.
2. Kurath and Lowman, 1970, p. 19.
3. Orton 1933, p. 14 and para. 47.
4. Dobson, 1968, para. 54.
5. Excluding /w/ and /l/ environments not considered here.
6. Dobson, 1968, paras. 42, 50, 54, note 3.
7. Dobson, 1968, para. 54, note 3.
8. The fieldworkers record [ɔ] and [ɒ]. The former is frequently a feature of the transcriptional style of some of the fieldworkers. In fact some of the recording books direct that [ɔ] should be read as [ɒ].
9. Dobson, 1968, para 87.
10. ME /au/ is not considered in so far as it appears in *aunt, branch* etc. The developments are rather complex but in East Anglia, southern England and the South East, developments very similar to ME /a/ in *grass, chaff* are found. Possibly /nt, ntʃ/ formed another lengthening group which affected native and French words alike. See SED IV.8.12 *ANT* (< OE *æmete*). Lengthened forms occur as far north as south Derbyshire and these may in part derive from unrounded /ɒ:/ < /au/. Dobson 1968

Key to Maps 15A and 15B			
ME /o/	/o/ + /f,s,θ/	/o/ + /r/	/au/
A1 /ɒ/	/ɒ/	/ɔ:/	/ɔ:/
A2 /ɒ/	/ɒ/	/ɒ/	/ɔ:/
A3 /ɒ/	/ɒ/	/ɒ/	/a:/
A4 /ɒ/	/ɒ/	/ɔ:/	/a:/
A5 /ɒ~α/	/ɔ:/	/ɔ:/	/ɔ:/
A6 /ɒ/	/ɔ:/	/ɒ/	/ɔ:/
B	/ɒ~α~ɔ:~α:/		

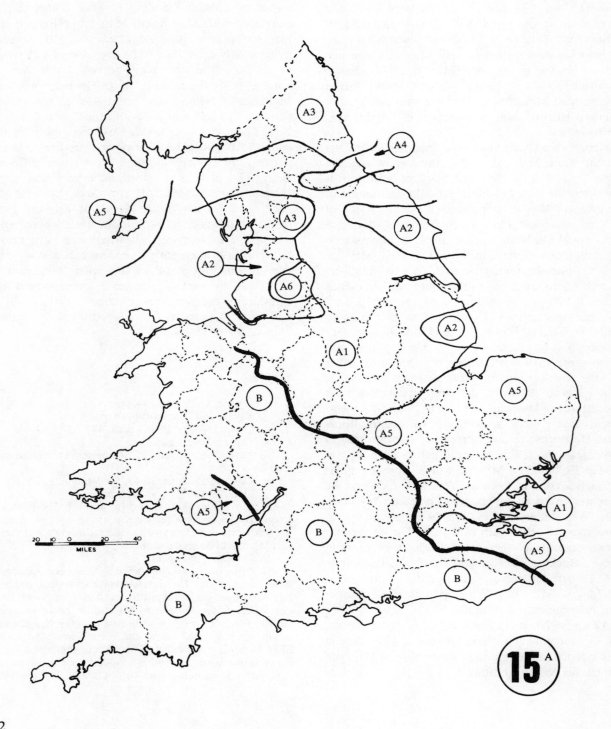

20 10 0 20 40
MILES

15ᴬ

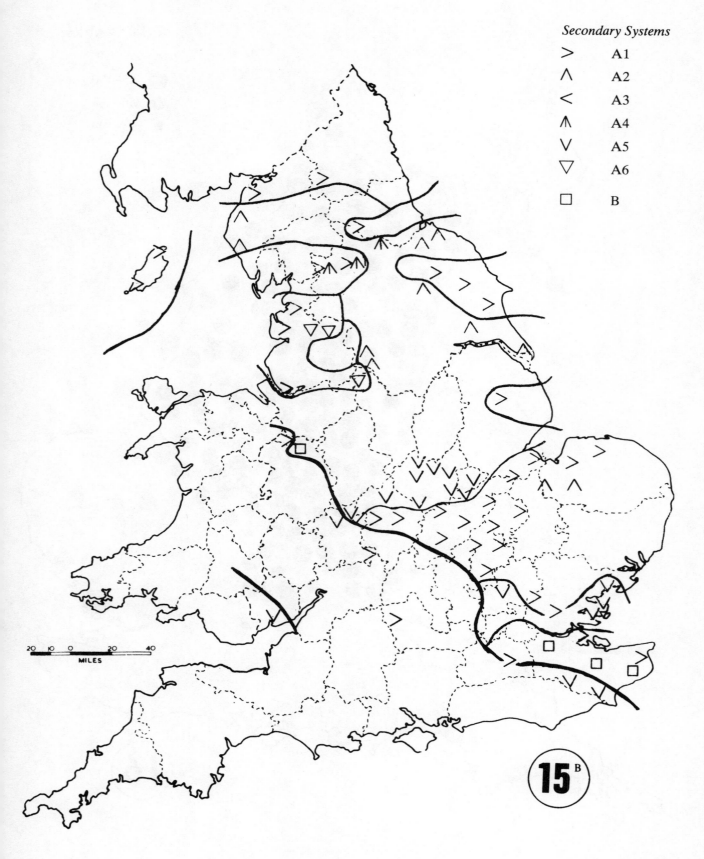

Secondary Systems

>   A1
∧   A2
<   A3
⋏   A4
∨   A5
▽   A6
□   B

MILES

15ᴮ

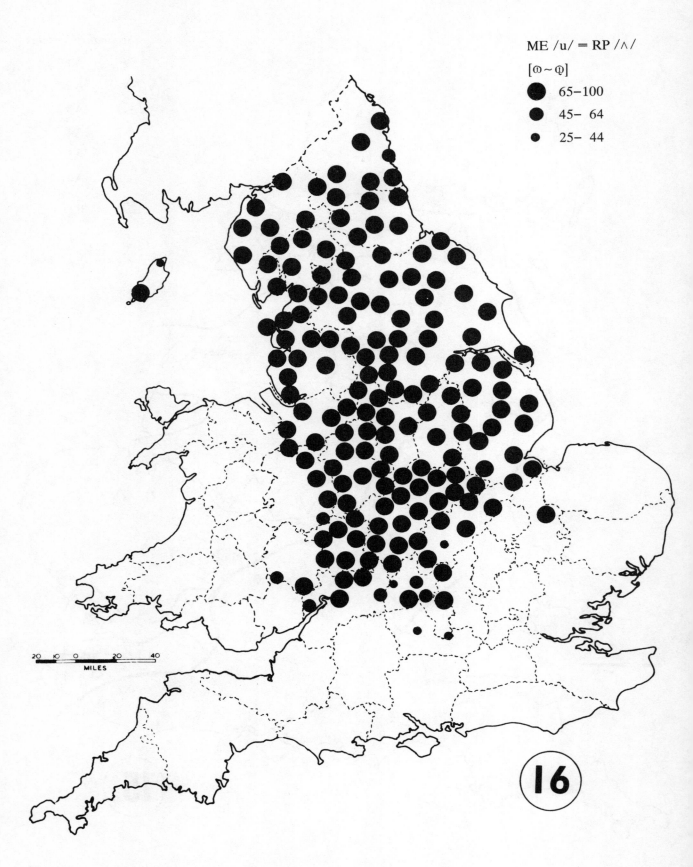

ME /u/ = RP /ʌ/

[ʊ ~ ɤ]

● 65–100

● 45– 64

· 25– 44

⑯

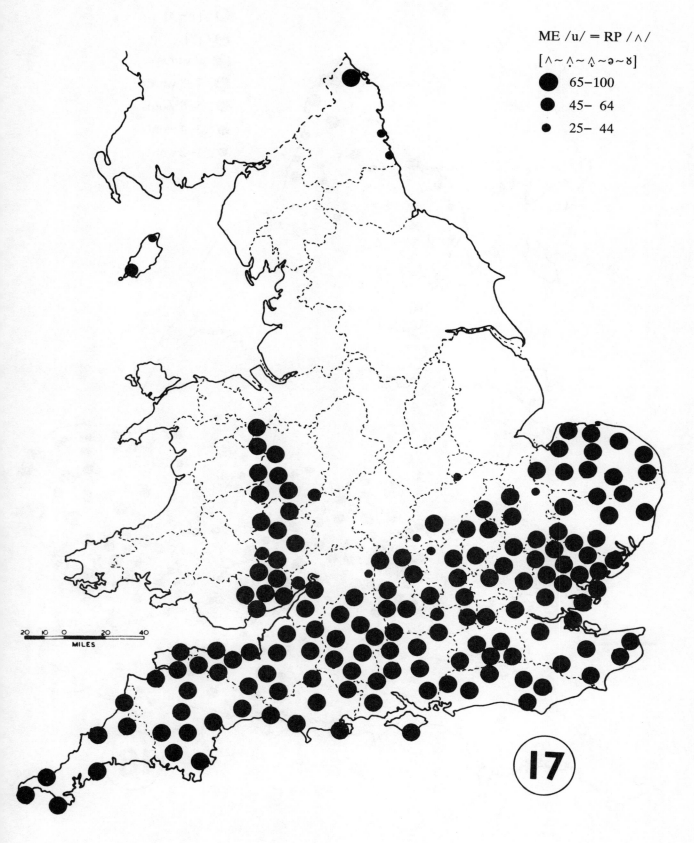

ME /u/ = RP /ʌ/

[ʌ ~ ʌ̞ ~ ɐ ~ ə ~ ɤ]

● 65–100

● 45– 64

● 25– 44

⑰

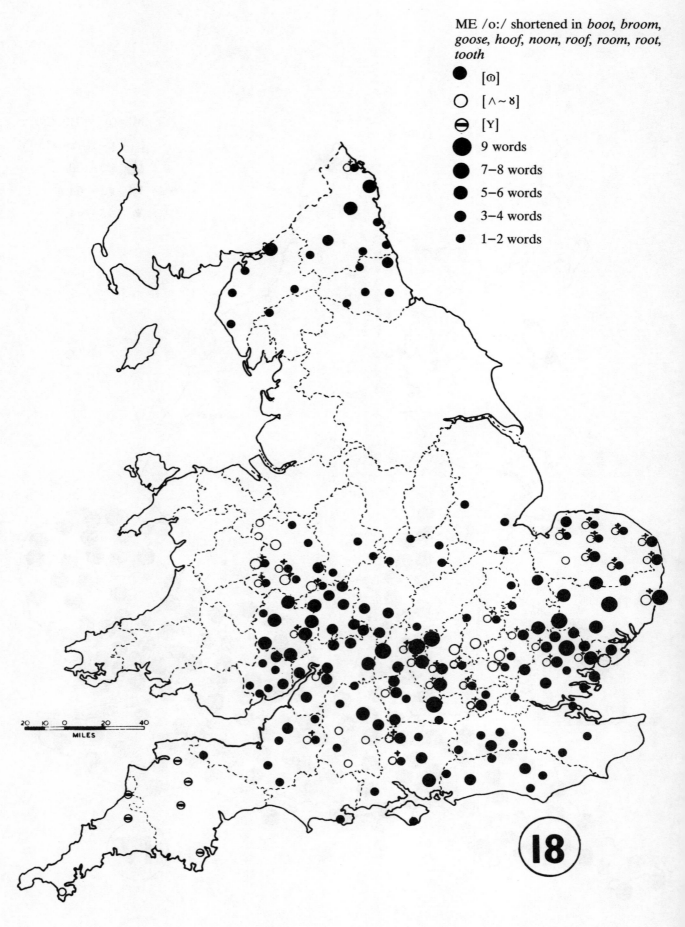

ME /o:/ shortened in *boot, broom, goose, hoof, noon, roof, room, root, tooth*

- ● [ɷ]
- ○ [ʌ ~ ɤ]
- ⊖ [ʏ]
- ● 9 words
- ● 7–8 words
- ● 5–6 words
- ● 3–4 words
- ● 1–2 words

⑱

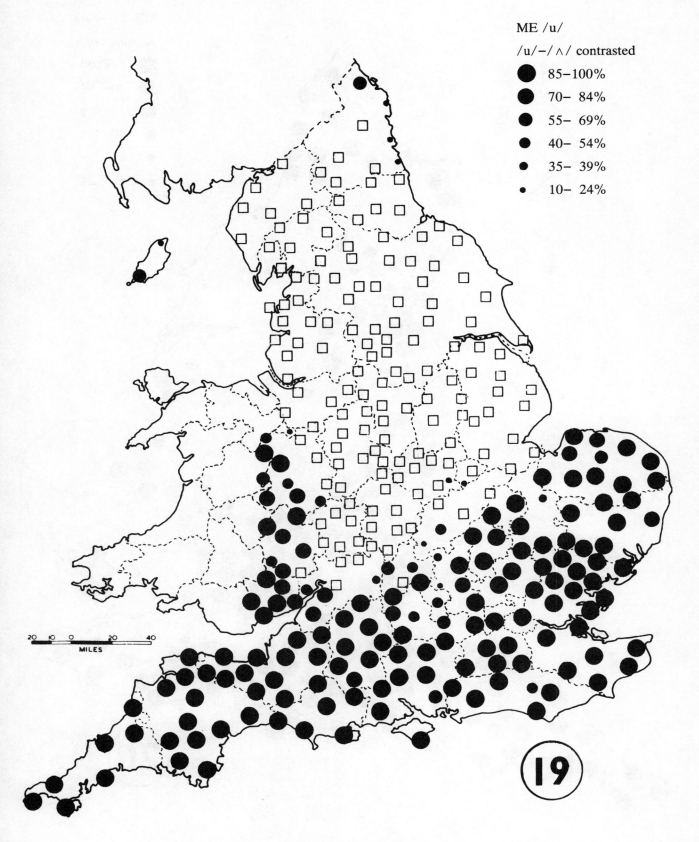

ME /u/

/u/−/ ∧/ contrasted

- ● 85−100%
- ● 70− 84%
- ● 55− 69%
- ● 40− 54%
- • 35− 39%
- · 10− 24%

19

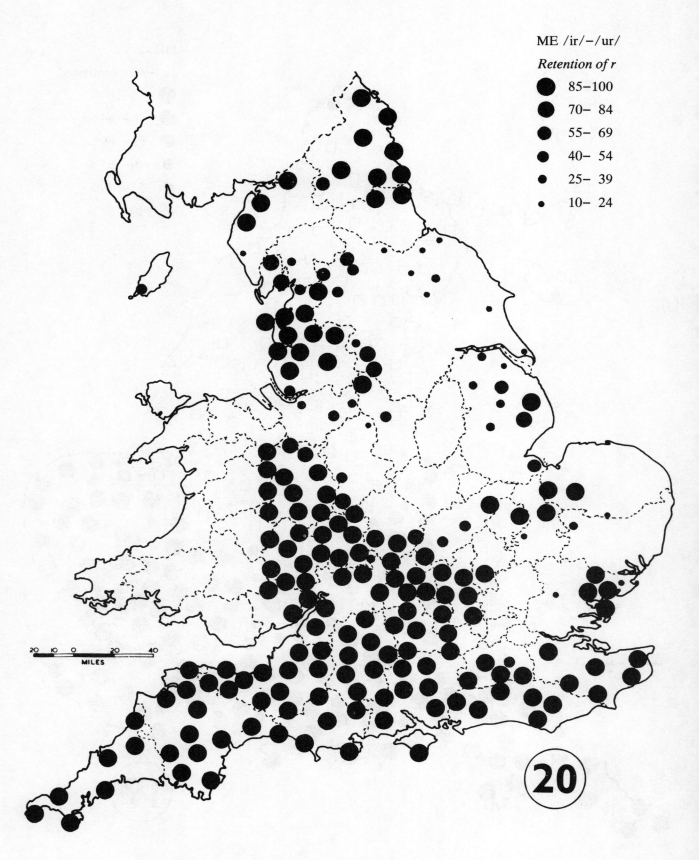

ME /ir/–/ur/

Retention of r

● 85–100

● 70– 84

● 55– 69

● 40– 54

● 25– 39

· 10– 24

MILES

20

favours unrounding of a long back vowel to /a:/ to account for present day long vowels. In part this is based on the analogous earlier ME unrounding (/a:/ < /au/ in *safe* etc.) and in part on the evidence of Cooper among other writers (para. 238 and vol. I, p. 286). Dobson admits that Cooper's evidence may also indicate [æ:], but he chooses [a:] as it appears to fit his theory of the development of ME /a/ + /f,s,θ/ better (see above para. 2.6 (b)). I would prefer to interpret Cooper and for that matter Lodwick as showing a pronunciation [æ:] which would accord with the probable isolative development of ME /a/ to [æ]. Late ME /au/ < ME /al/ in *half, calf* poses further problems. Dobson is willing to accept a change from /au/ to /a/ in *laugh* but not in *half, calf* on the grounds of the scarcity of reported contemporary pronunciations with a short vowel (Dobson, 1968, para. 28, note 3). Wyld 1927, p. 192 suggests that the origin of the present [a:~ɑ:] forms is ME /a/:

'Again as regards the suggested history of present day [kɑ̃f], it is not proved that diphthongisation before *l* was universal. What if there were ME dialects in which *l* was lost quite early before *f*? This might result in *haf caf*?'

Dobson also relies on the presence of [ɑ:~a:] in Northern dialects to discount the likelihood of lengthening of short /a/ before /f/. The dialectal situation is clearly set out in Orton *et al.*, 1978 (Maps Ph9 *CALF* and Ph10 *HALF*). [ɔ:] is common in northern England and is the direct descendant of ME /au/. A further group of pronunciations [ɛι~e:~i:] show early monophthongisation to ME /a:/ in the case of *half*. The third type of pronunciation is the [a:~ɑ:~æ:] type. In parts of the far north of England these represent the local development of ME /au/ in all positions. In the south however, they show a similar patterning to ME /a/ before /f,s,θ/. The northern boundary of [a:] forms is further north than for ME /a/ + /f,s,θ/ but probably this is due to dialect spread (i.e. forms regularly developed from ME /a/ + /f,s,θ/ have been borrowed in dialects which already had [a:] < ME /ar/. Its spread is helped by the fact that the alternative forms are more obviously dialectal than the short vowel type in *grass* etc.). The *HALF* map shows a number of areas in which a short vowel is retained, including Sussex. This may be related to the context of the response ('*half past seven*') where the stress is reduced. In my own speech I have a short vowel in this position although I normally use a vowel of the RP type. Quite clearly, there may have arisen a short vowel firstly as a prosodic variant which was later lengthened and substituted for the alternative stressed pronunciations.

11. It may be coincidental that this merger occurs in the area most favoured as the location in which *Sir Gawain and the Green Knight* was written (see McIntosh, 1963, p. 5). The text is characterised by frequent merger of ME /ɔu/ and ME /au/.

12. Contrasts are reported for the dialect of Naunton (Gloucesterhire). /ɑ:k/~/ɑk/ *hawk~hock* (Barth, 1968, para. 47, p. 11).

13. Ellis, 1889, p. 111.

3

Middle English Long Vowels

3.1 ME /i:/ (ī)

The present dialectal forms show that ME /i:/ has become a diphthong in all dialects, and that this diphthong has subsequently become a long monophthong in some areas. Maps 21–28 are arranged in pairs representing types of development before voiced and unvoiced consonants. This positional variation has been reported outside Great Britain (USA and Canada).[1] Orton 1933 reports this variation from *Byers Green* (Durham) but it also occurs elsewhere. The clearest examples are as follows:

Area	Voiceless	Voiced
Northumberland, north Durham and north Cumberland	[ɛɪ]	[ɛɪ~aɪ]
South Durham	[aɪ]	[ɑɪ][2]
east Yorks	[ɛɪ]	[aɪ~a:]
mid Lincs, north Notts	[aɪ]	[aɪ]
Huntingdonshire	[ʌʏ]	[ɑɪ]

A different type of positional development is seen in Cheshire where ME /wi:/ becomes /wɛɪ/ whilst ME /i:/ in other positions generally becomes /ɑɪ/. In this case, there is an actual split of the phoneme and merger with another phoneme.[3]

In some parts of England, ME /i:/ has moved no further than [əɪ~ʌɪ] (Maps 25–26). Pronunciations of this type are concentrated in the south west Midlands and South West with the notable exception of west Somerset, Devon and Cornwall. There are further enclaves along the South coast and in Norfolk and coastal Suffolk. These forms are clearly recessive. It would appear that ME /i:/ tended to develop a central onset in southern England in order to avoid ME /ai/ which has generally remained in the south. In the north however, ME /ai/ was reduced to a monophthong at an early date and the evolution of ME /i:/ has been via fronted onsets. Thus, [ɛɪ] appears in Northumberland and north Cumberland (sometimes centralised [ë̞ɪ]) and in east Yorkshire. It is also found to a small extent in the west Midlands and in parts of Wiltshire, Somerset and Hampshire where it may be a further develop-

ment of [əɪ] (Maps 27–28). The development would appear to be recessive.

Maps 23–24 show the contrasting development in which ME /i:/ becomes an upgliding diphthong with a retracted first element. This type would appear to be spreading in the Midlands and southern England. Curiously, this pronunciation appears in south Devon and north Cornwall, an area which shows other innovative features in common with more central parts of England.

The type of development which occurs in Standard English (to [aɪ]) is surprisingly rare in southern England (Maps 21–23). Its presence in a small area of the South East may perhaps be attributed to Standard English influence. In Devon, it occurs alongside [æ:~a:]. It is clearly a relic form as far north as a line from Cheshire to the Wash. In the North of England, on the other hand, it is the commonest development and in some respects an innovative form which is tending to displace older [ɛɪ]. It is also worth noting that since SED it has also tended to supplant [ɑɪ~ɑ:] in Sheffield (Yorks) and Cheshire. In both cases the change seems to be due to pressure from the regional koine backed by the underlying Standard English usage.[4]

Monophthongal variants occur in several areas. In parts of north Yorkshire and positionally in east Yorkshire [a:] occurs. [ɑ:] is found in the Pennine area of Yorkshire and sporadically throughout the central Midlands. As already mentioned, [a:~æ:] occurs in Devonshire. There is a moderately strong trend in many of the Midland dialects to reduce the second element of the diphthong or to lengthen the first element.

3.2 Structural positions of ME /i:/

ME /i:/ always remains distinct from ME /a:/ and ME /ai/. The following are examples of the types of contrasts prevailing:

Locality	ME /a:/	ME /i:/	ME /ai/
1 Nb 7	/ɪə/	/ɛɪ~aɪ/	/e:/
5 La 12	/e:/	/a:~aɪ/	/e:/

21 Nf 3	/ɛ:1~ɛ:/	/ʌ1/	/æ1/
26 Bk 1	/e·ə/	/ɔ1/	/ɛ1/
31 So 8	/e:/	/æ1/	/e1/
35 K 7	/ɛ1/	/ə1/	/ɛ1/
37 D 4	/e:/	/æ1~æ:/	/ɛ1/
39 Ha 5	/e:/	/ɑ1/	/a1/

3.3 ME /u:/ (ü)

The developments of ME /u:/ and ME /i:/ are broadly analogous with the difference that ME /u:/ is retained in the North of England and in parts of the South West. In part this may be attributed to the absence of pressure from ME /o:/ which had become a centralised (fronted?) sound in northern Middle English. The correspondence is not complete however. ME /o:/ and ME /u:/ are merged as /u:/ in north Lincolnshire and there is a tendency towards the same merger in east Yorkshire. In the South West, the distinction is fairly tenuous — /u:/ contrasting with /ɷu/ in south Gloucestershire.[5] Likewise, there are areas of the Yorkshire Dales and north Lancashire where ME /u:/ has become a diphthong although ME /o:/ was fronted during the ME period. It is hard to account for this intrusion into an area which is generally highly conservative and one can only assume that the change has been introduced from the Lancashire side or possibly from more southerly parts of the West Riding. Map 29 shows the distribution of forms of the [u:~əu~ʌu] type. These are clearly recessive, being found in the North, the South West and parts of north east Norfolk.[6]

In contrast, Map 30 shows the extent of the commonest reflex of ME /u:/ — the [ɛɷ~æɷ~ɛʏ] type. In part, this is probably a further development of [aɷ] but also it is being substituted for [əɷ] via a transitional type [ëɷ] in some areas of the South. The development is found as far north as Shropshire and south Lincolnshire and it is also found in the far South West with the exception of part of Devonshire. A further area is found in east Cheshire, north west Derbyshire and Heptonstall (West Yorkshire) where it appears to be a relic form. On either side of the Pennines, [ɛɷ] has given way to ingliding diphthongs and long monophthongs of the [ɛə ~ɛ:] type. In this case, the peripheral dialects represent the innovative points whilst the central area is the most conservative. Alternatively, the outer dialects can be seen as innovative centres in their own right and the central core as being marginal to those centres. The present day advanced development of ME /u:/ is not surprising in view of Gil's comments on the seventeenth century pronunciation of ME /i:/ and ME /u:/ in Lincolnshire.[7]

The Standard English development (to [aɷ~ɑɷ]) is relatively uncommon in the dialects (Map 31). It is found bordering on the [u:] area in northern England (north west Lancashire, the Yorkshire Dales and mid Lincolnshire).[8] There is a further zone in west Cheshire and west Shropshire. The distribution appears to be recessive but the evidence from the central West Midlands tends to suggest that this is not entirely true. It is rather surprising that Standard English has selected this type. Probably it indicates the conservative nature of the standard language and its relative isolation from the sound systems of neighbouring dialects. The standard type is tending to become more retracted whilst the dialect type is becoming more fronted.

3.4 Monophthongal forms (Maps 34–35)

ME /u:/ has become a long monophthong of the [a:] type in west Yorkshire and west Lancashire and also to a lesser extent in Leicestershire and adjoining parts of south Staffordshire. It is also a feature of popular London speech. [ɛ:] occurs in south Lancashire and south Derbyshire and in the latter area it is associated with an advanced [ɛɷ] pronunciation for ME /o:/. A series of diphthongs appears in the Pennine areas of west Yorkshire and east Lancashire. ([ɛə ~ɛa~æ ~æə]). All these raised types seem to derive from earlier [ɛɷ~æɷ] which still occurs in the dialects of *Heptonstall* (6 Y 21), *Charlesworth* (8 Db 1) and *Burbage* (8 Db 3). The tendency to develop monophthongs in the dialects of west Yorkshire and south Lancashire to represent ME /i:/ and ME /u:/ is perhaps related to the large number of rising diphthongs which have arisen in these dialects.[9]

3.5 Other developments

[a1] ocurs in Cheshire and north Staffordshire though it is under pressure from [ɛɷ~æɷ] in the South and East of the county (Map 33). Probably this rather unlikely development has arisen from earlier [aɷ] which is retained allophonically in certain positions (before /l/, /r/ and /k/). The contrast with ME /i:/ is maintained as /ai/ — /ɑi/.[10] A similar type of development has taken place in North Buckinghamshire (to [ɛï]).

A round fronted [ʏ] is quite frequent as the second element of the diphthong in the South West. Devonshire and west Somerset show [œu~œʏ], a further instance of a more general fronting of back vowels in these dialects. (cf. ME /u/ > [ʏ] and ME /o:/ > [ʏ:]).

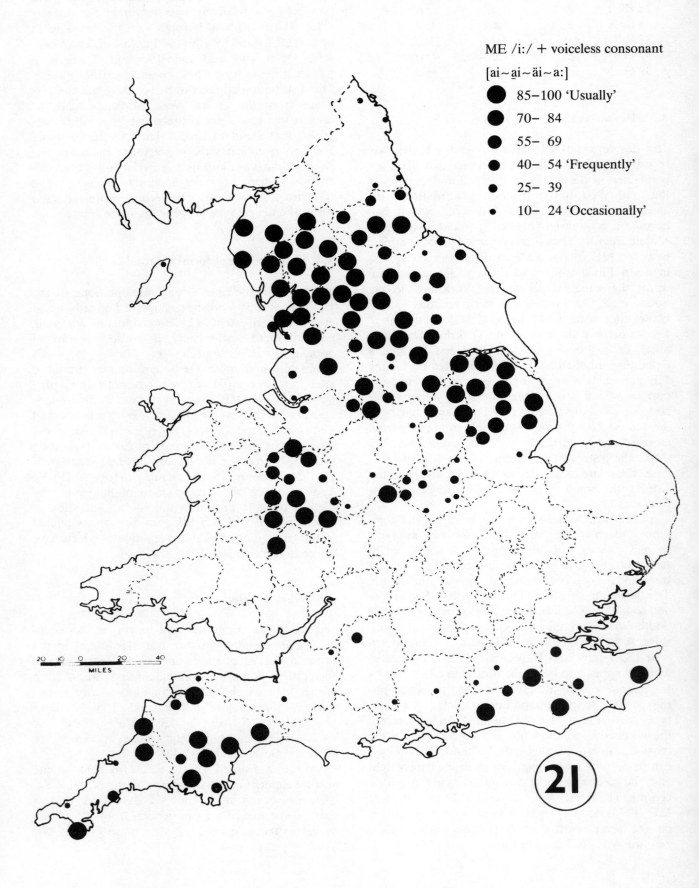

ME /i:/ + voiceless consonant

[ai~a̠i~äi~a:]

● 85–100 'Usually'

● 70– 84

● 55– 69

● 40– 54 'Frequently'

• 25– 39

· 10– 24 'Occasionally'

㉑

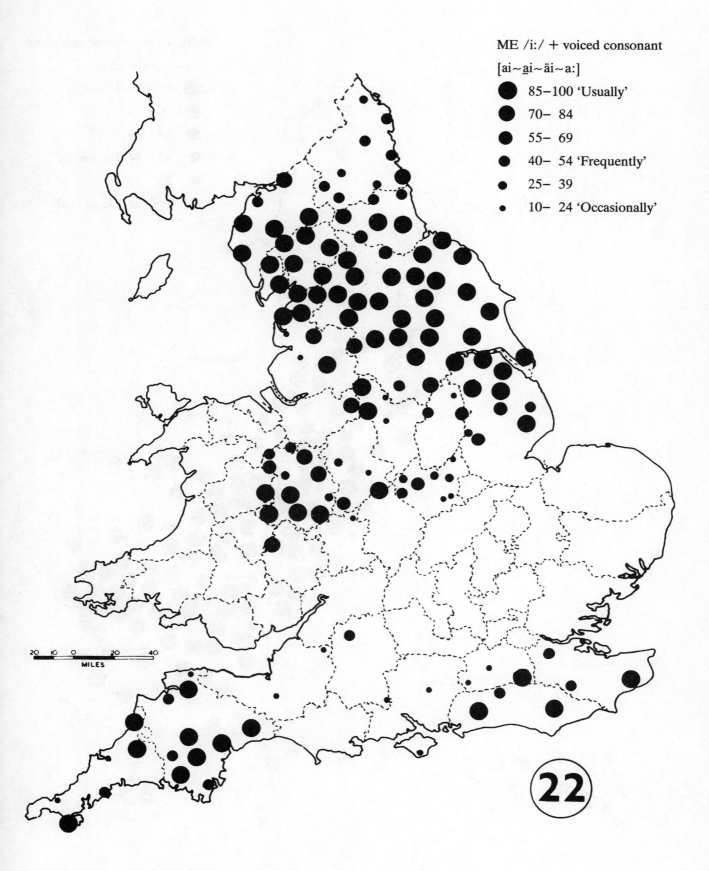

ME /i:/ + voiced consonant

[ai~ai~äi~a:]

● 85–100 'Usually'

● 70– 84

● 55– 69

● 40– 54 'Frequently'

● 25– 39

· 10– 24 'Occasionally'

MILES

22

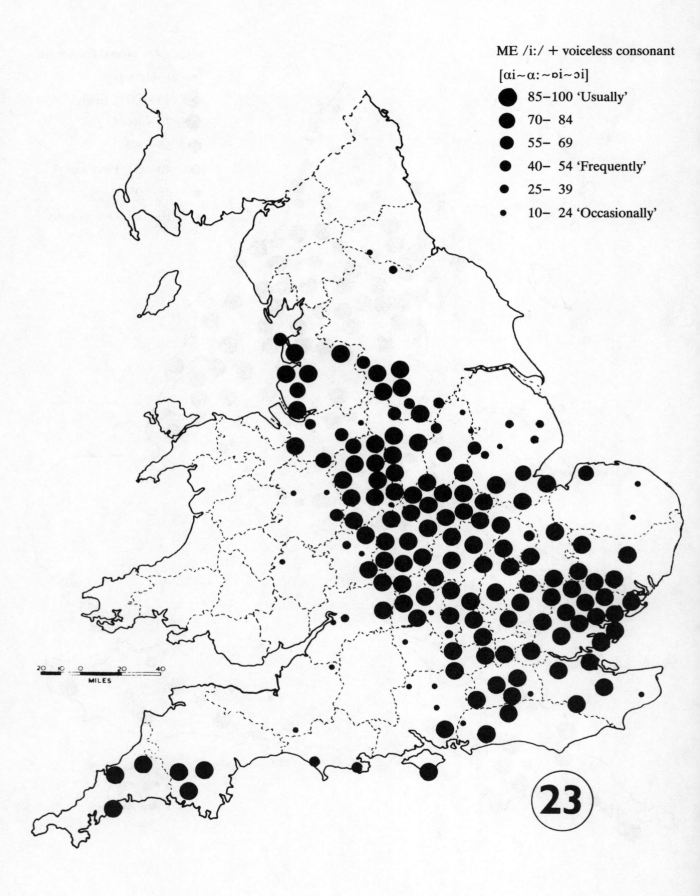

ME /iː/ + voiceless consonant

[ɑi~ɑː~ɒi~ɔi]

85–100 'Usually'

70– 84

55– 69

40– 54 'Frequently'

25– 39

10– 24 'Occasionally'

MILES

23

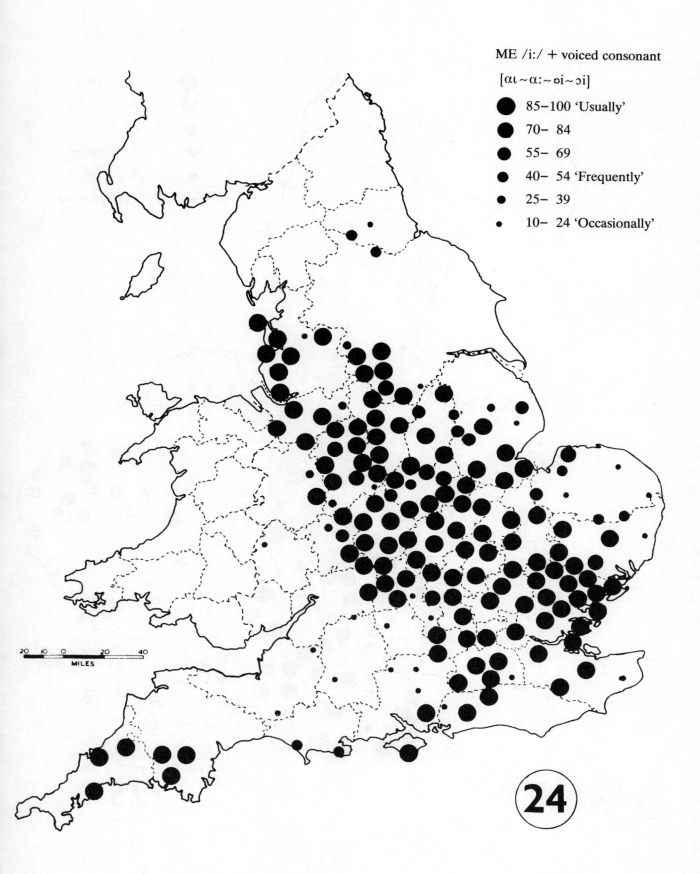

ME /i:/ + voiced consonant

[ɑɪ~ɑ:~ɒi~ɔi]

● 85–100 'Usually'
● 70– 84
● 55– 69
● 40– 54 'Frequently'
● 25– 39
· 10– 24 'Occasionally'

24

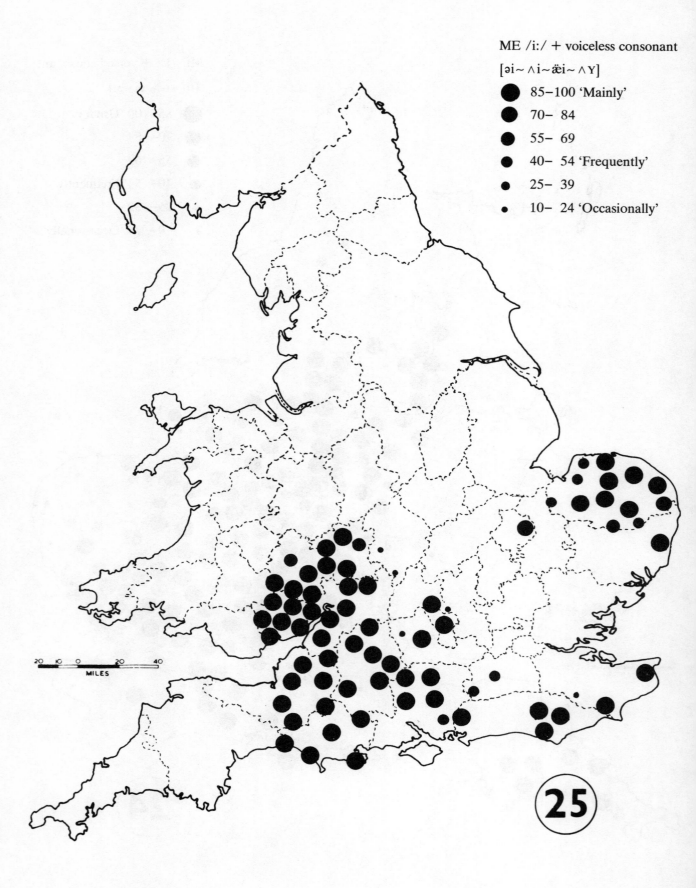

ME /iː/ + voiceless consonant

[əi~ʌi~æi~ʌɣ]

● 85–100 'Mainly'

● 70– 84

● 55– 69

● 40– 54 'Frequently'

• 25– 39

• 10– 24 'Occasionally'

25

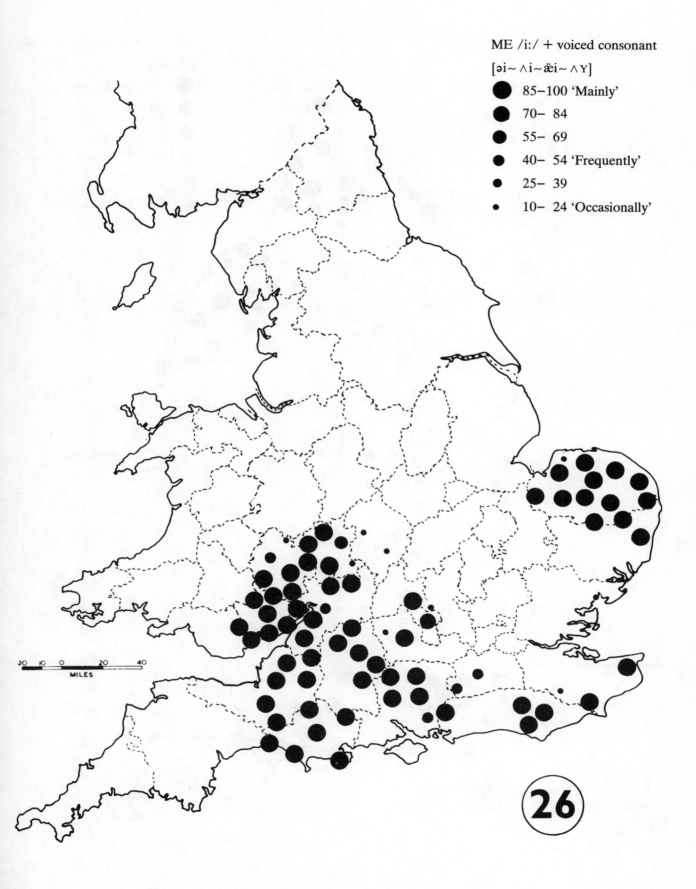

ME /i:/ + voiced consonant

[əi~ ʌi~ æi~ ʌʏ]

● 85–100 'Mainly'

● 70– 84

● 55– 69

● 40– 54 'Frequently'

● 25– 39

● 10– 24 'Occasionally'

MILES

㉖

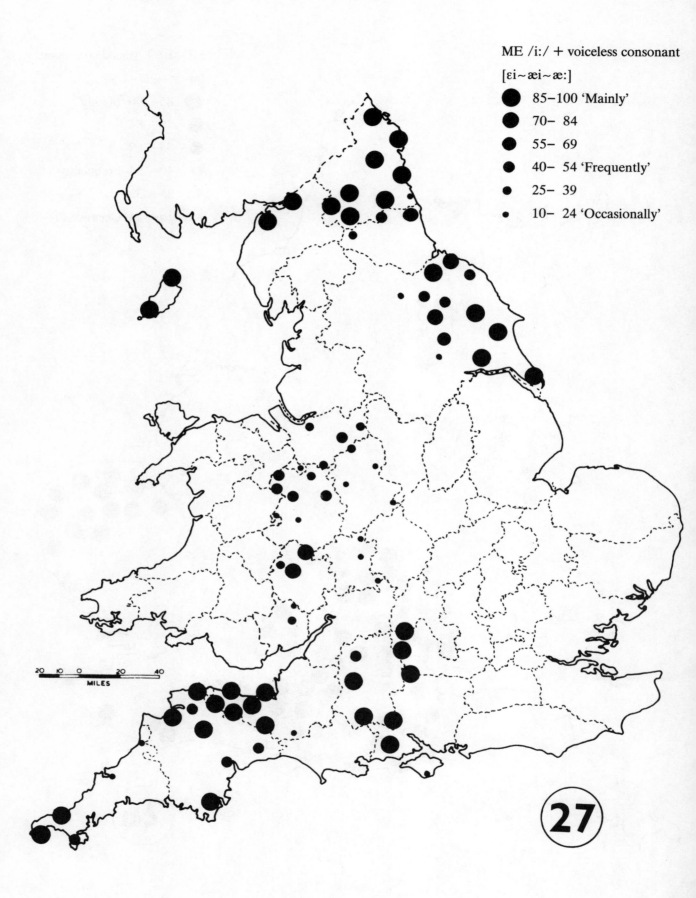

ME /i:/ + voiceless consonant
[ɛi~æi~æː]

● 85–100 'Mainly'
● 70– 84
● 55– 69
● 40– 54 'Frequently'
• 25– 39
· 10– 24 'Occasionally'

MILES
20 10 0 20 40

27

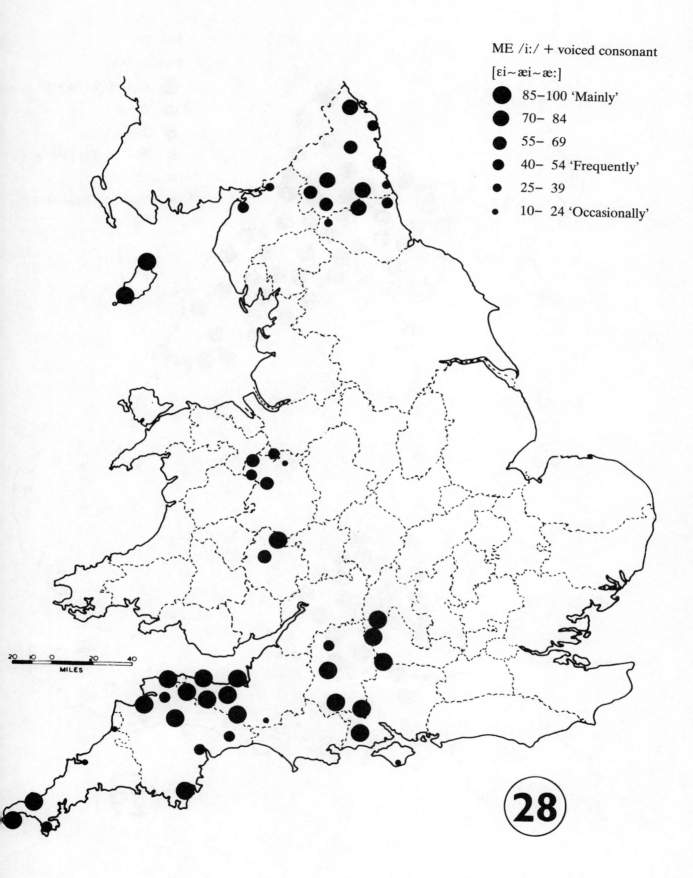

ME /iː/ + voiced consonant

[ɛi ~ æi ~ æː]

● 85–100 'Mainly'

● 70– 84

● 55– 69

● 40– 54 'Frequently'

• 25– 39

• 10– 24 'Occasionally'

MILES

28

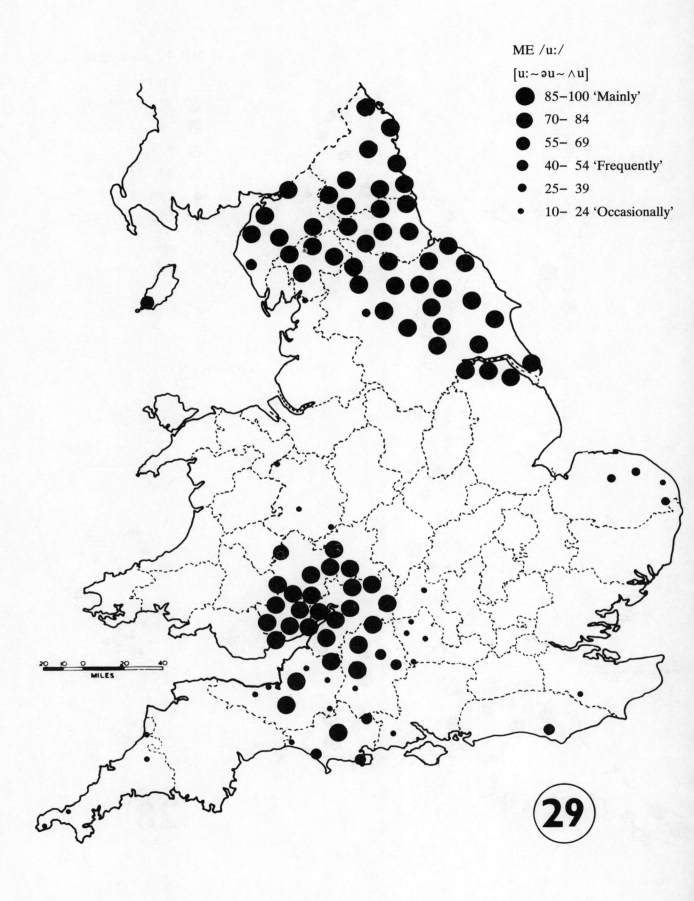

ME /u:/

[u: ~ əu ~ ʌu]

● 85–100 'Mainly'

● 70– 84

● 55– 69

● 40– 54 'Frequently'

● 25– 39

● 10– 24 'Occasionally'

MILES

20 10 0   20   40

29

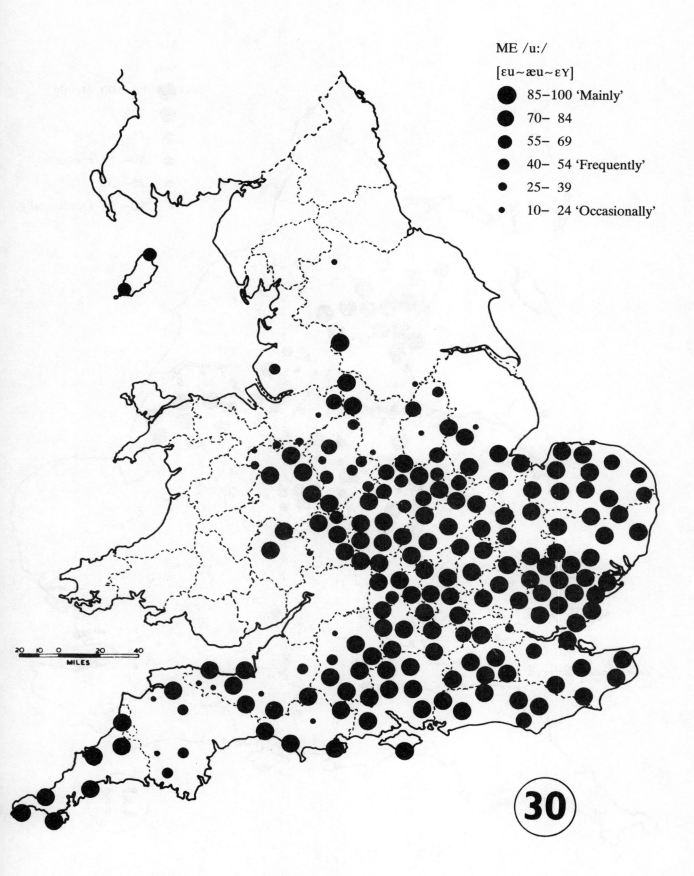

ME /uː/

[ɛu ~ æu ~ ɛʏ]

● 85–100 'Mainly'

● 70– 84

● 55– 69

● 40– 54 'Frequently'

● 25– 39

· 10– 24 'Occasionally'

30

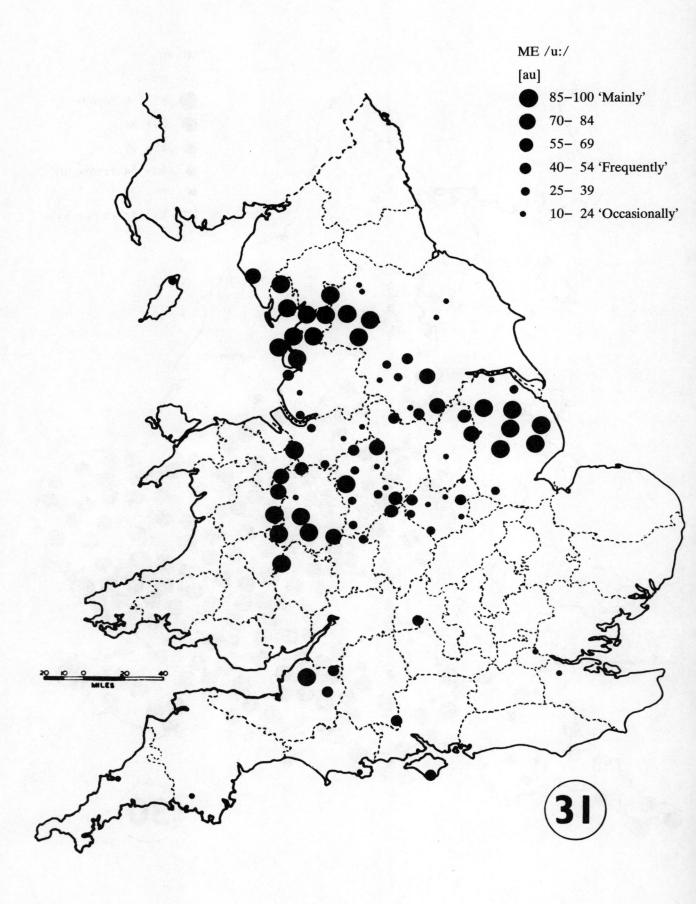

ME /u:/

[au]

●	85–100 'Mainly'
●	70– 84
●	55– 69
●	40– 54 'Frequently'
●	25– 39
·	10– 24 'Occasionally'

31

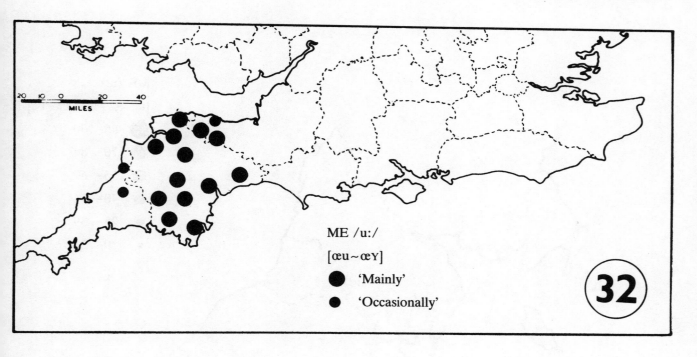

ME /u:/

[œu~œʏ]

● 'Mainly'

● 'Occasionally'

32

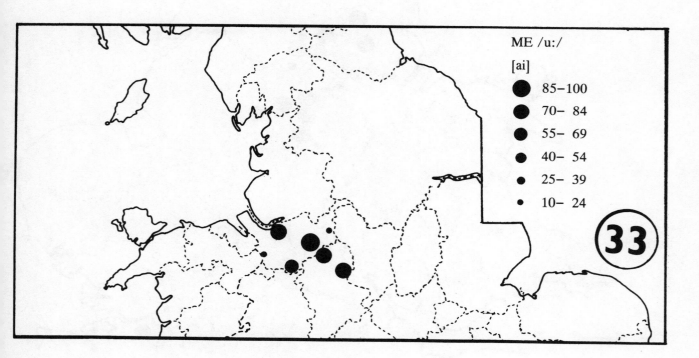

ME /u:/

[ai]

● 85–100

● 70– 84

● 55– 69

● 40– 54

● 25– 39

● 10– 24

33

3.6 Structural position of ME /u:/

ME /u:/ generally retains its separate phonemic identity but is merged with ME /o:/ in north Lincolnshire. A merger with ME /ar/ is found in south Yorkshire and the development of [ɛ:] etc. in west Yorkshire and Derbyshire entails merger with ME /a:r/.

3.7 ME /a:/ (ā)

ME /a:/ was the lowest of the long front vowels, derived from ME /a/ lengthened in open syllables. In the dialects it has generally been raised but the exact developments and mergers are complex. It is convenient to distinguish the following types of development (page 56).

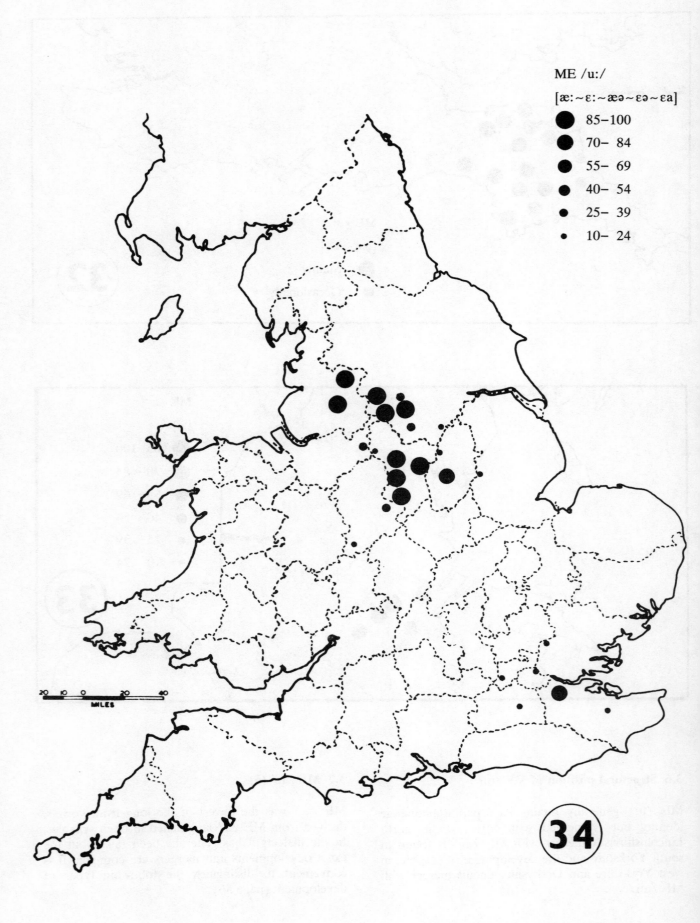

ME /u:/

[æː~ɛː~æə~ɛə~ɛa]

● 85–100
● 70– 84
● 55– 69
● 40– 54
• 25– 39
• 10– 24

34

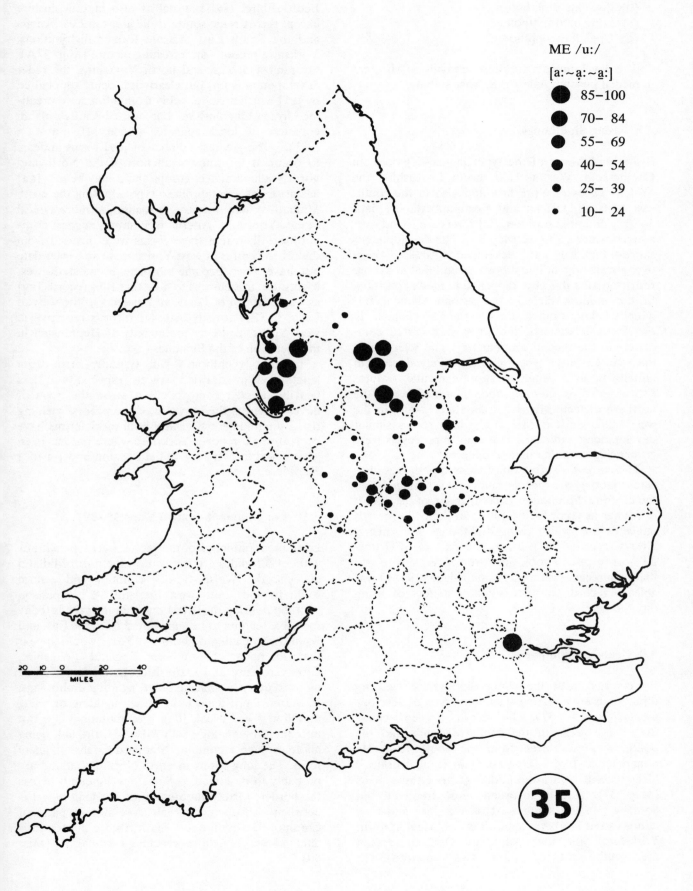

ME /u:/

[a:~a̱:~a̱:]

● 85–100

● 70– 84

● 55– 69

● 40– 54

• 25– 39

· 10– 24

(a) Rising diphthongs
(b) Ingliding diphthongs
(c) Long monophthongs
(d) Upgliding diphthongs

The developments are those applying to ME /a:/ in medial position unless otherwise stated.

3.8 Rising diphthongs

Rising diphthongs of the type [ia~ea~iɛ] occur in Cumberland, Westmorland, north Lancashire, the western Dales of Yorkshire and also in the southeast parts of Durham and Northumberland (Maps 36–37). In initial position, [ja] forms are found over a much wider area (see Map 82). The developments suggest that ME /a:/ developed a stressed onset over a wide area in initial position and that in a more restricted area this also happened in medial position. In the modern dialects the second element frequently bears as much stress as the first element. In the Tyneside dialects, the stress has shifted completely to the second element [jɛ]. The selection of the stressed onset type was most likely dependent initially upon a range of suprasegmental features ('stress, rhythm, tempo and quantity').[11] In the northern dialects ME /a:/ was affected and in the west Midlands it is ME /ɛ:/ which shows similar developments indicating that similar processes were influencing a whole range of dialects.[12]

The current distribution of rising diphthongs indicates that they are recessive and under pressure from the centring diphthongs. A comparison of the dialect of Muker as recorded by Ellis and the SED records indicates that whilst rising diphthongs were nearly always recorded by Ellis, by the time of SED only 33% of responses took this form. It remains to add that on a recent visit to the same village (1976) I was able to record only occasional instances of rising diphthongs.[13]

3.9 Centring diphthongs

By contrast with the rising diphthongs, centring diphthongs are a relatively common type of development (Maps 36–37). Ellis records [iə~eə] widely from large areas of the south Midlands and the South West and even from the South East. He remarks that [eə] is commoner in rural districts.[14] SED records centring diphthongs from three areas (Map 37). [iə] is recorded most frequently in Somerset, in the south west of Wiltshire and to a minor extent in Oxfordshire. It is also usual in north Yorkshire, Northumberland and Durham (except the south east of these two counties). In

Northamptonshire, Buckinghamshire and south Bedfordshire, [ɛə] is usual as also in Lincolnshire except the extreme south. Relic areas in East Anglia and the South East indicate former distributions. Yorkshire presents an intresting picture (Map 37A). Over most of east and north Yorkshire, the older development is [iə] but clearly it is being supplanted by [ɛə] which arises possibly from influences spreading from Lincolnshire but also because of an equation of local cognates (since ME /ai/ > [ɛə]).[15] The greatest number of [ɛə] forms appears to occur at the known junction of the North and north Midland dialect groups and it may be that [ɛə] has arisen as a compromise type adopting the north Midland system but using a realisation more typical of east Yorkshire. Alternatively it may suggest nothing more than that these forms were diffused from the urban centres of west Yorkshire at an earlier date but have since become obsolete in most of west Yorkshire. It is curious to note that Ellis records [ɛə] as being typical of Leeds and dialects to the west of Leeds.[16] SED reveals that this form is recessive in west Yorkshire being found only at Heptonstall in the seclusion of the Pennines.

Ingliding diphthongs will typically arise from lengthened or drawled vowels especially in less heavily stressed contexts. In a sense this type of development is the opposite of the process yielding rising diphthongs but clearly both mechanisms have been at work in north Yorkshire where [ja] has been generalised in ME /a:/ initial position and [iə~ɛ] elsewhere.[17]

3.10 Long monophthongs (Maps 38–39)

Long monophthongs of the [ɛ:~e:~ẹ:] type with or without off-glides are frequent in the north Midland dialects, the Welsh Border counties and central southern and south west England. A comparison with the position in EEP shows that the type is today recessive tending to be supplanted from the East and South by upgliding diphthongs. Yet it would appear that in parts of southern England (Wiltshire, Gloucestershire and Oxfordshire), [e:] has become more frequent displacing older ingliding diphthongs. In the northern dialects in which ingliding or rising diphthongs are usual, long monophthongs are not infrequent by analogy with ME /ai/, the link being made through a common Standard English cognate form. The long forms in north Northumberland are probably to be linked to Scots developments across the border. Mostly the quality of the long vowel is between half-open and half-close but in parts of Cheshire, Derbyshire and Staffordshire the sound is much closer, sometimes reaching cardinal [i:] (Map 40).

3.11 Upgliding diphthongs

Maps 41 and 42 display the distribution of upgliding diphthongs. These range from long monophthongs plus off-glide to forms of the [æɪ~aɪ] type. The former are more frequent at the points where this type is in contact with other types whilst the latter are characteristic of the South East. A comparison with the position as recorded by Ellis indicates how upgliding diphthongs have spread rapidly to represent ME /a:/ (Map 41). They were the dominant forms in the London area stretching as far as south Hertfordshire and Essex and in a small area of Cambridgeshire and Huntingdonshire. In the other areas in which they occurred they were clearly in competition with an older type. Their occurrence in the Birmingham area but not in the surrounding countryside further supports the view that upgliding diphthongs are an innovation and recent origin. (For further discussion see paragraph 3.14 below.) SED shows upgliding diphthongs as far west as Herefordshire and as far north as mid Derbyshire and also in an isolated area of Somerset (Map 42).

3.12 Structural relationship of ME /a:/ and ME /ai/

The developments of ME /ai/ are considered at paragraph 4.1 and in Maps 92–95.

Three broad areas of contrast can be distinguished: northern, midland and southern (Maps 43–44).

(a) Northern (Type 1)

The contrast is usually between ingliding/rising diphthongs and long monophthongs. The following examples may be noted:

1 Nb 5	Wark	/ɪə/	v	/e:~e:ə/
2 Cu 4	Threlkeld	/ɪa~ea/	v	/ɛ:~ɛ:/
3 Du 3	Wearhead	/ɪə~eə/	v	/eə/
6 Y 7	Askrigg	/ɪə/	v	/e:/
6 Y 15	Pateley Bridge	/ɪə/	v	/ɛə/
6 Y 18	Spofforth	/ɛə/	v	/e:/

Clearly in this group of dialects ME /ai/ became a long monophthong after ME /a:/ had developed an off-glide. In view of the early monophthongisation of ME /ai/ not long after 1200[18] the development of an off-glide cannot be any later. Within the northern area, merger is beginning to take place in most localities usually by generalisation of the ME /ai/ type, (as for example at York [ɛ:]). In Durham however, it is the [ɪə~eə] type which is becoming general.

(b) Midland (Type 2)

In east Cheshire, mid and south Derbyshire, north Staffordshire and east Leicestershire there are contrasts of the following types:

7 Ch 3	Swettenham	/e:~e̜:/	v	/i:/
8 Db 4	Youlgreave	/e:/	v	/i:/
8 Db 7	Sutton	/e·ɪ/	v	/i:/
12 St 2	Mow Cop	/ɛɪ/	v	/i:/
13 Lei 7	Sheepy Magna	/ɛɪ/	v	/i:/

All these types clearly derive from one ancestral type in which ME /ai/ was monophthongised and raised to /i:/. In all of these dialects ME /ai/ merges to some extent with ME /ɛ:/ (< OE æ, ēa) and remains distinct from ME /e:/ (> [ɛɪ]) and from ME /ɛ:/ (< eME /e/ lengthened in open syllables) which becomes [ɛɪ] in parts of Derbyshire and east Cheshire. It would follow that the ME /ɛ:~ai/ phoneme had an early development to [e:] as it was clearly able to avoid ME /ɛ:/ (< eME /e/) and ME /a:/.[19] The Great Vowel Shift appears to have started in the dialects of the north west Midlands earlier than elsewhere and to have had more far-reaching consequences. The area of type 2 contrast has shrunk somewhat since the late nineteenth century and south Staffordshire, north east Warwickshire and most of west Leicestershire have given up the distinction.

(c) Southern (Type 3)

The southern area is characterised by the preservation of ME /ai/ as an upgliding diphthong of the [ɛ~~æɪ~aɪ] type (see Map 95). The maximal distinction is ingliding versus upgliding (/ɪə/ v /æɪ/) but as upgliding diphthongs come to represent ME /a:/ the contrast is being reinterpreted as high versus low (/ɛɪ/ v /aɪ/). The village of Heptonstall in the Pennines quite surprisingly maintains a type 3 contrast as does most of surrounding Upper Calderdale. Probably ME /ai/ retained its diphthongal quality longer here than elsewhere and it was subsequently merged with ME /ɛ:/ < eME /e/ lengthened in open syllables.[20] Examples of type 3 contrasts are as follows:

6 Y 21	Heptonstall	/e:~ɛə/	v	/ɛɪ~æɪ/
15 He 3	Cradley	/e:~e:ɪ/	v	/ɛɪ~æɪ/
18 Nth 3	Little Harrowden	/ɛə/	v	/ɛɪ~æɪ/
21 Nf 3	Blickling	/ɛ:ɪ~ɛ:/	v	/æɪ/
21 Nf 7	Outwell	/eɪ/	v	/ɛɪ/
22 Sf 5	Kersey	/ɛɪ/	v	/æɪ/
26 Bk 2	Stewkley	/e·ə/	v	/ɛɪ/
29 Ess 6	West Bergholt	/ɛɪ/	v	/æɪ~aɪ/
31 So 4	Coleford	/ɪə/	v	/aɪ/
31 So 6	Stogursey	/eɪ/	v	/aɪ~æɪ/
32 W 9	Whiteparish	/e:/	v	/aɪ/
36 Co 2	Altarnum	/e:/	v	/ɛɪ/
37 D 6	South Zeal	/e:~ɛ:/	v	/ɛɪ/

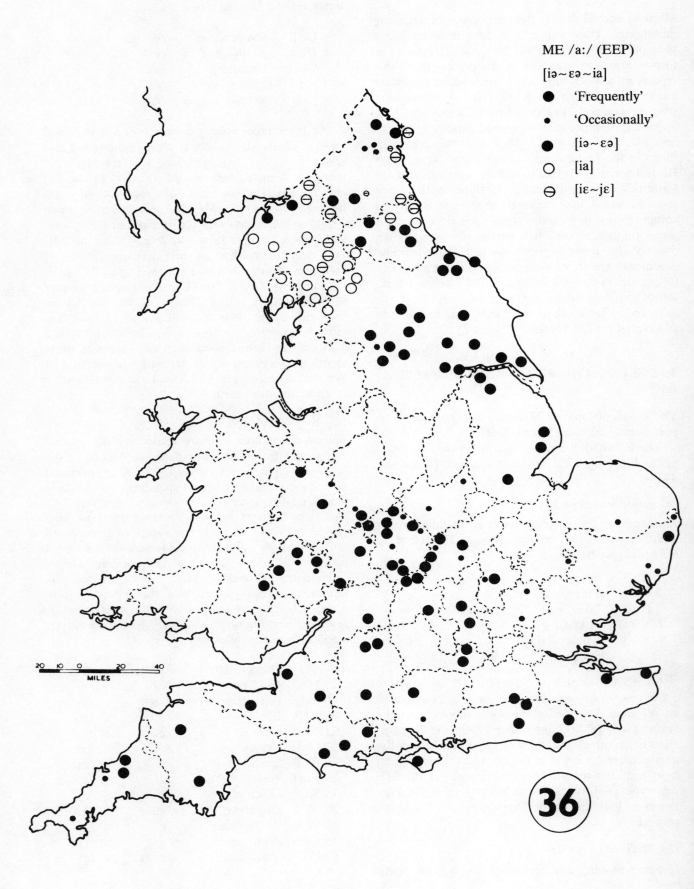

ME /a:/ (EEP)

[iə ~ εə ~ ia]

●   'Frequently'

•   'Occasionally'

●   [iə ~ εə]

○   [ia]

⊖   [iε ~ jε]

MILES

36

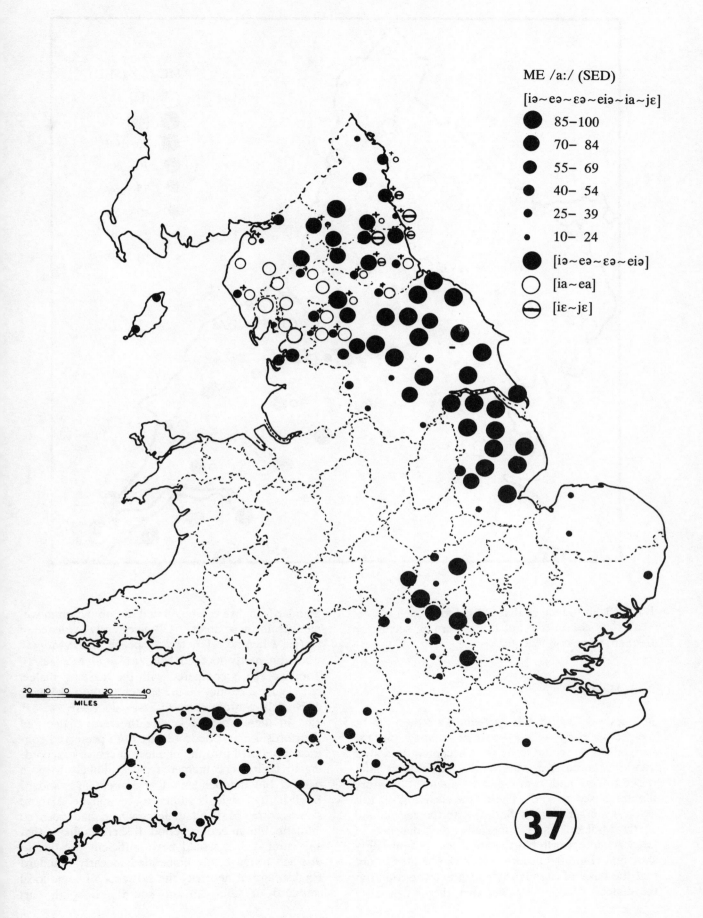

ME /a:/ (SED)

[iə~eə~ɛə~eiə~ia~jɛ]

● 85–100
● 70– 84
● 55– 69
● 40– 54
• 25– 39
· 10– 24
● [iə~eə~ɛə~eiə]
○ [ia~ea]
⊖ [iɛ~jɛ]

37

MILES

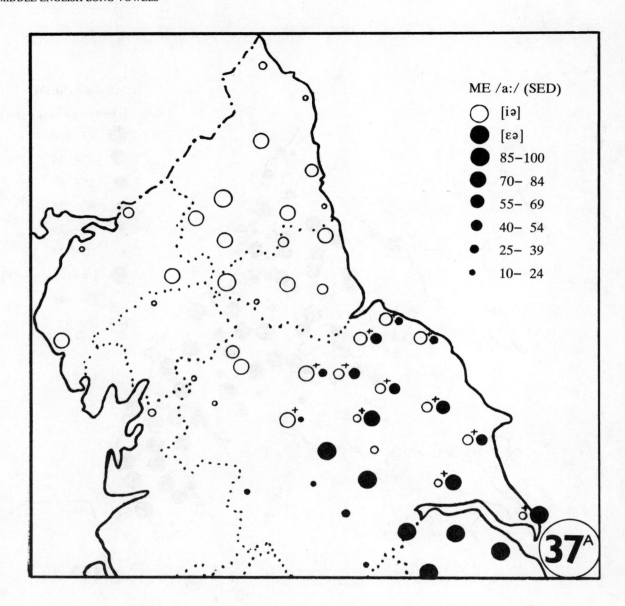

ME /a:/ (SED)

○   [iə]

●   [εə]

●   85–100

●   70– 84

●   55– 69

●   40– 54

●   25– 39

•   10– 24

37ᴬ

3.13 Mergers

It is difficult to believe that a distinction such as /εɪ/ ~ /æɪ/ is contrastive but the patterning seems too frequent to be coincidental.

In Standard English ME /a:/ and /ai/ began to be merged as early as the sixteenth century but the merger did not come to be truly accepted until after 1650.[21] The merger was to /ε:/ which was later raised to /e:/ and from the early nineteenth century diphthongised to /eɪ/. There is a clear link in this atypical merger (for the South) with the central and north Midlands and especially the dialects of Leicestershire, north Northamptonshire, Cambridgeshire and Huntingdonshire. There can be little doubt that the basis of Standard English is to be found in the dialects of this area and that changes in early

Standard English can be related to population movement from these areas.[22] Gil gives early evidence of merger when he refers to the speech of the Mopsae who apparently merged ME /a:/ and ME /ai/.[23] Their speech is compared with the 'eastern' dialect but clearly it cannot be the speech of the rural parts of Norfolk, Suffolk or north Essex since ME /a:/ ≠ /ai/ in these areas. Likewise the rural dialects of Hertfordshire and Bedfordshire both preserved contrasts until well into the nineteenth century (according to EEP). The merged type is unlikely to be a parallel but independent development in Standard English. Its origin is rather to be sought in those same central Midland dialects which had been so influential in an earlier period. It seems unlikely that any rural dialect would have sufficient prestige to displace forms firmly embedded in early Standard English and of necessity the existence of some local standard or koine in the south and south east

Midlands must be postulated. There is a common type of system which overlays older dialect systems in large parts of the south Midlands. It takes the following form:

ME /a:/
ME /ai/   >   /e:/
ME /ɛ:/

ME /e:/   >   /i:/
ME /o:/   >   /u:/
ME /ɔ:/   >   /o:/

In EEP it occurs in north east Northamptonshire (p. 254), Rutland (p. 255), mid Cambridgeshire (p. 249), mid Oxfordshire (pp. 125 ff.) and elsewhere. It is suggested that this local koine had a direct influence on Standard English and that subsequently Standard English disseminated the merged type into the dialects of south Hertfordshire and south Essex. It also helped to consolidate the position of the koine in the rural dialects surrounding the towns of Oxford and Cambridge which one might expect to follow the lead of Standard English.[24]

The most important merger types are the following:

Lincolnshire (except south)	/ɛə/
Oxfordshire	/e:~e:ə/
Cheshire	/ẹ:~i:/
Lancashire, south and west Yorkshire, Nottinghamshire and Shropshire	/e:/
South Staffordshire, Leicestershire, South East England	/ɛɪ/

The merger in the north Midlands seems to be of long standing.[25]

3.14 Further consideration of the merger of the [ɛɪ] type

The [ɛɪ] type is clearly an innovation in Standard English beside older [eɪ]. It also appears to be an innovation in London English. Ellis remarks, 'I was myself born in North London in 1814 and cannot recall it.'[26] It is strange that such a prominent feature of current London English is not reflected in popular literature before 1880.[27]

Ellis regarded [ɛɪ~æɪ] as a North and East London pronunciation[28] and this may give some clue as to the origin of the open type. During the nineteenth century the population of London increased dramatically and the period saw the extension of the city northwards and eastwards into Essex. In Essex ME /ai/ and ME /a:/ remained distinct but under the influence of a merged type in more prestigious

dialects, the development of ME /ai/ (to some diphthong of the [ɛɪ~æɪ] type) came to represent ME /a:/. The same type of formation by analogy is found in Hampshire (see Map 45A). EEP shows that [ɛɪ] (< ME /a:/) was well established in the rural dialects of Huntingdonshire and adjoining Northamptonshire and was so widespread in the east of the central Midlands that analogous formations must have taken place there as well. Quite likely such a development was a feature of the local regional standard. ([ɛɪ] is frequent for ME /ai/ in north Buckinghamshire and nearby Northamptonshire.) It very likely made its initial appearance in Standard English from this source but was supported by the spread of the Essex merger into popular London speech. In the latter respect, the substitution of the [ɛɪ] type can be seen as a change from beneath deriving especially from more casual and relaxed forms of speech.[29]

The likelihood is also that [eɪ], the conservative type in Standard English is of similar origin. It first appears in the early nineteenth century and is recorded by Ellis as the Standard English type.[30] Map 45A shows that [eɪ] is a reflex of ME /a:/ in the south east Midlands in a number of relic areas some of which may have been continuous in the past. This type is clearly not the oldest type (centring diphthongs of the [ɪə~ɛə] type underlie the dialects of this area as elsewhere in southern England) but in some of the areas in which it occurs ME /ai/ becomes [eɪ] and the same assumptions about analogical formations seem to apply here as with the development of [ɛɪ] and [æɪ].

3.15 ME /e:/ (ẹ)

ME /e:/ derives from a number of Old English sources including OE ēo (via eME /œ:/). The divergent developments of the different OE dialects present some cartographical problems as far as the descendants of Primitive Germanic ǣ and the i-mutation of Primitive Germanic ai (as in seed and deal respectively). In West Saxon both groups developed ME /ɛ:/. In Kentish both groups had ME /e:/. In other areas eOE appears to have had ē in the first group and ǣ in the second group. By the late OE, ǣ had spread into the central and east Midlands as a West Saxon innovation.[31] In most dialects Primitive Germanic ǣ has had the same development as ME /e:/ indicating that ME /e:/ is the probable ancestor. In parts of west Hampshire, Dorset and Wiltshire in the heart of the West Saxon area /e:/ appears for PG ǣ and also occurs fairly frequently for ME /e:/ of all origins. Probably there has been some sort of levelling in favour of ME /ɛ:/ in these areas whereas over the rest of the South and East, the tendency has been to select ME /e:/ types.

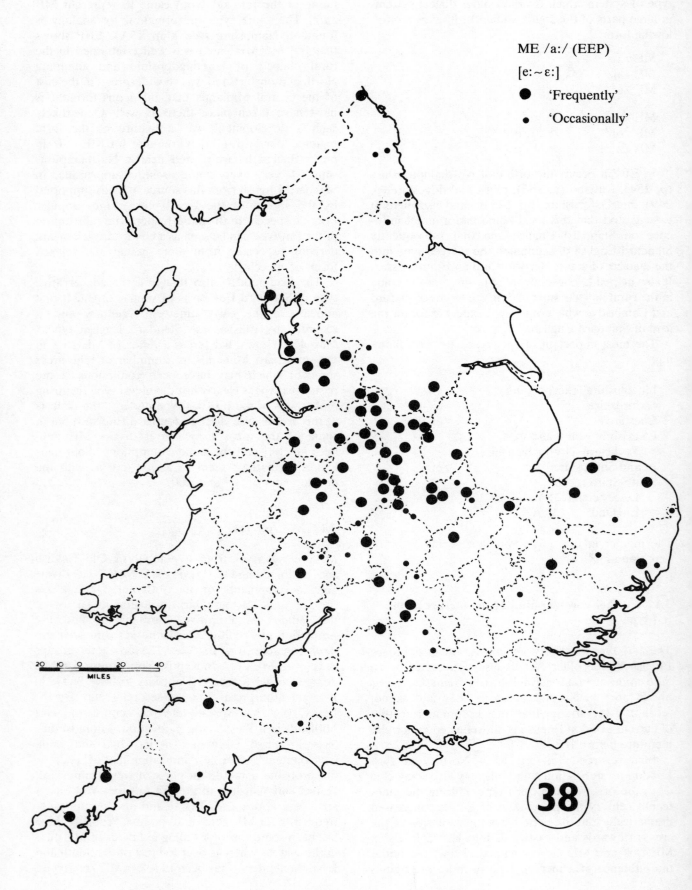

ME /a:/ (EEP)

[e:~ɛ:]

● 'Frequently'

• 'Occasionally'

MILES

38

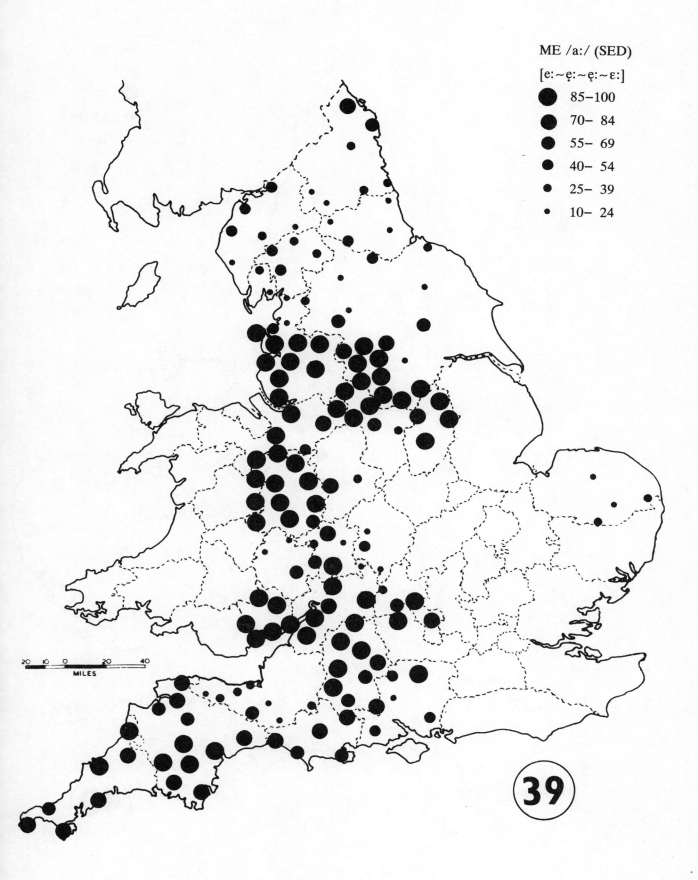

ME /aː/ (SED)

[eː~ẹː~ę̣ː~ɛː]

● 85–100
● 70– 84
● 55– 69
● 40– 54
• 25– 39
· 10– 24

39

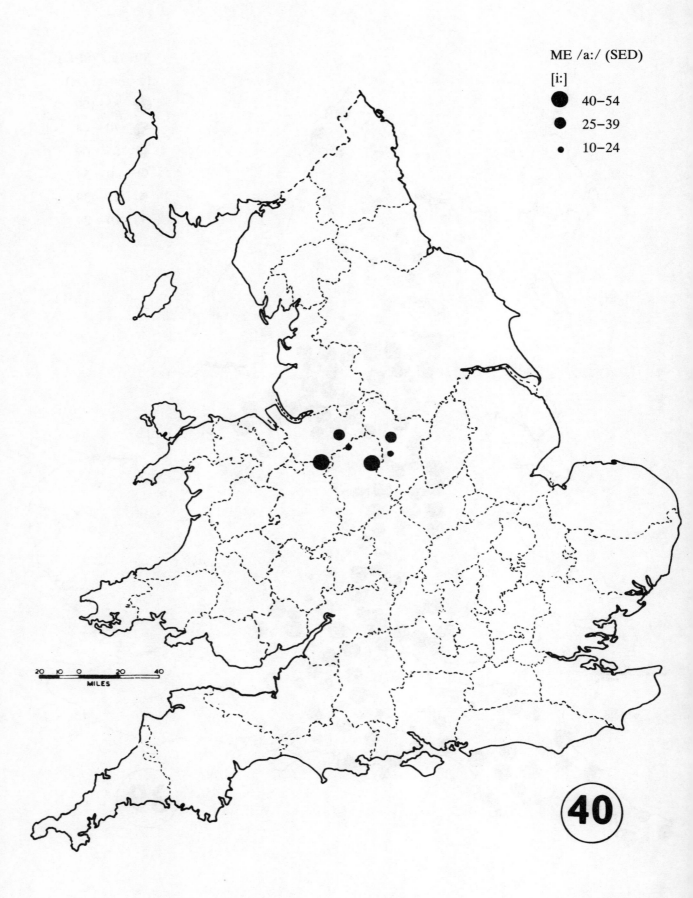

ME /a:/ (SED)

[i:]

● 40–54

● 25–39

• 10–24

MILES

40

3.16 Raising of ME /e:/ (ē)

ME /e:/ was raised in late ME to /i:/ in all dialects with the qualification for certain southern dialects where ME /ɛ:/ types have been generalised (3.17). Many of the dialects have moved further to become upgliding diphthongs usually of the [ɪi] type (Map 46). In north west Yorkshire and south Durham [ëi~əɪ] appear and in the north-west Midlands, [ɛi~ëi] is reached (Map 47).[32] In each of these areas, the diphthong appears to have arisen independently indicating how readily long close vowels become diphthongs.

3.17 Shortening of ME /e:/ (Map 48)

ME /e:/ has been shortened quite frequently in the dialects of the West and in the south Midlands and East Anglia. Shortening is not found in the north Midlands, nor does it occur in the London area or the Thames valley. The shortening of ME /e:/ may be compared with the shortening of ME /o:/, the two developments having taken place in similar contexts (Map 18). Clearly, this is also an incomplete change — *sheep* and *week* are shortened over much more extensive areas.[33] The structural position of ME /e:/ is discussed at 3.26.

3.18 ME /ɛ:/ (ę)

ME /ɛ:/ has two major sources, later OE *ǣ* (under which earlier OE *ǣ* and *ēa* were levelled by the eleventh century except in Kent and parts of the South West[34]) and eME /e/ lengthened in open syllables. The history of this group presents problems, in part due to the fact that different dialects developed the ancestral types in different ways so that there was variation between ME /ɛ:/ and ME /e:/. Usually ME /ɛ:/ has tended to merge with one or other of the front vowels in many dialects. The development of ME /ɛ:/ < eME /e/ lengthened in open syllables is considered separately (3.24).

3.19 Development of ME /ɛ:/

Map 49 shows that /i:/ is a very frequent reflex of ME /ɛ:/ in the South and Midlands. It is unlikely that these derive from ME /ɛ:/ directly but rather from variants with ME /e:/ as has been suggested by Dobson for Standard English.[35] The development in the far North cannot easily be explained in the same way. Probably ME /ɛ:/ was caught between ME /a:/ which was raised very early in the northern dialects and ME /e:/. ME /i:/ has not advanced beyond /ɛi~ai/ indicating a slower development for ME /e:/. The development to /i:/ in Derbyshire, north Staffordshire and Cheshire is rather special and contrasts with ME /e:/ (see 3.26). /i:/ tends not to occur in the South West.

3.20 Ingliding Diphthongs (Map 50)

These include forms of the /iə~ɛiə~eə/ type as well as /ju~jʌ/ forms which derive from an older type /iə/ via */ɪʊ/.[36] These forms occur in a wide belt across northern England as far south as west Cheshire and north Shropshire (/ɛiə/)[37] and Lincolnshire. They also occur sporadically in the South and South West but also with some regularity in Buckinghamshire. Earlier evidence suggests that this type was formerly very frequent in areas in which it is today a relic form[38] and like /iə/ for ME /a:/ has been ousted by other types. It is reasonable to regard this type as representing the oldest vernacular type to have developed from ME /ɛ:/ and one which evolved fairly generally in the dialects though possibly it was a conditioned development in certain areas.[39] Ingliding diphthongs do not appear to have evolved in the central Midlands, the east Midlands, Northumberland, Durham, Cumberland, Devonshire[40] or the South East. The absence in the last-named area presumably accounts for its absence in Standard English. In those areas which show only residual traces of ingliding diphthongs, the probable reason is that they have been supplanted by later types which originate either directly from earlier types of Standard English (or other local standards) or as a result of the adaptation of the internal structure of the dialect to the structure of early Standard English. This is discussed at 3.27 in greater depth.

3.21 Long monophthongs and upgliding diphthongs

Map 51 shows the distribution of /e:/ and /ɛi/ types. Both types are found with some frequency in Devon and Cornwall, south Wiltshire and Hampshire. A broad band of forms runs from the Cotswolds up to Cheshire and Derbyshire. A further enclave exists in Norfolk and north Suffolk which no doubt was once connected with the main distribution area. Over most of the western area, these forms appear beside /iə/ types (except in Devon and Cornwall) and it is likely that they represent relics of earlier regional standards or direct early Standard English influence (see paragraph 3.27).

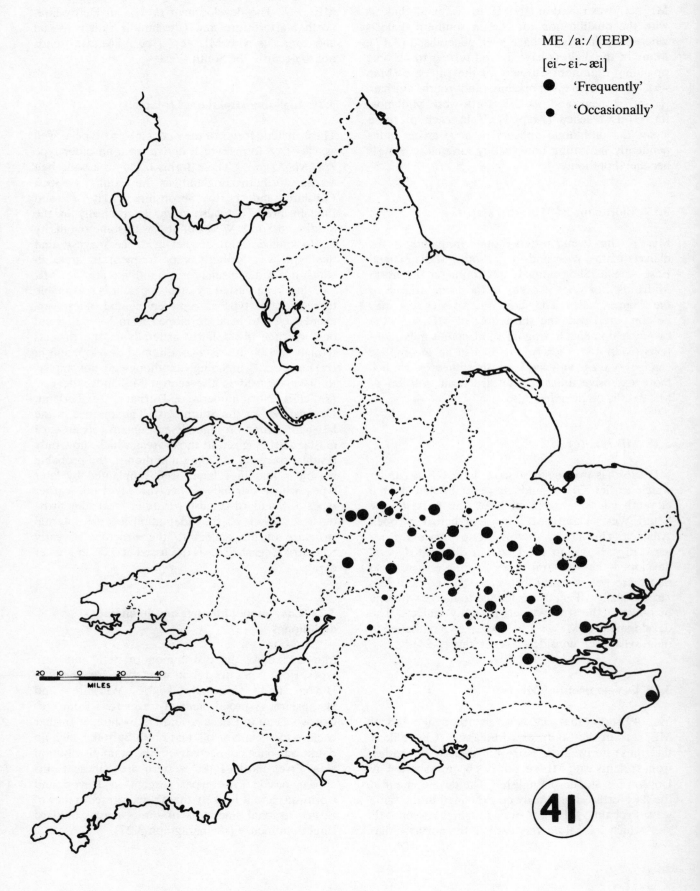

ME /aː/ (EEP)

[ei ~ εi ~ æi]

● 'Frequently'

• 'Occasionally'

MILES

41

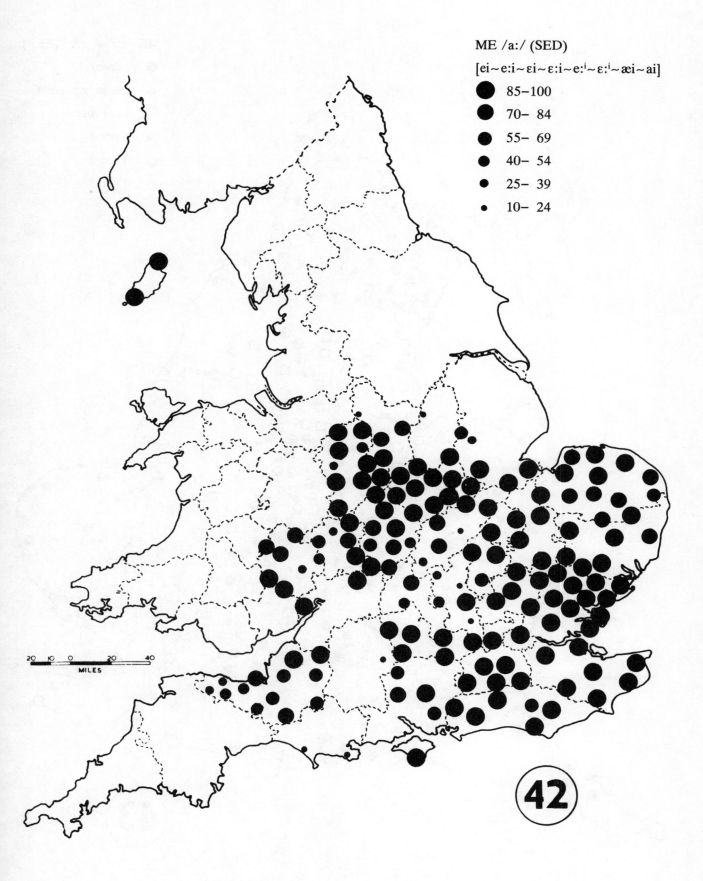

ME /a:/ (SED)

[ei~eːi~ɛi~ɛːi~eːⁱ~ɛːⁱ~æi~ai]

● 85−100
● 70− 84
● 55− 69
● 40− 54
● 25− 39
• 10− 24

20 10 0 20 40
MILES

42

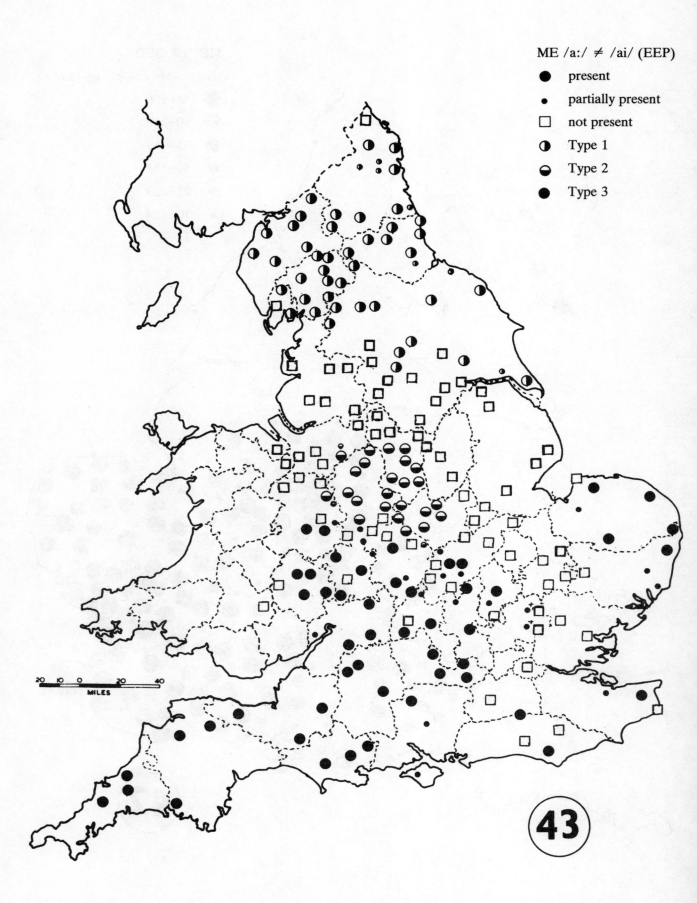

ME /a:/ ≠ /ai/ (EEP)

● present

• partially present

□ not present

◑ Type 1

⊖ Type 2

● Type 3

43

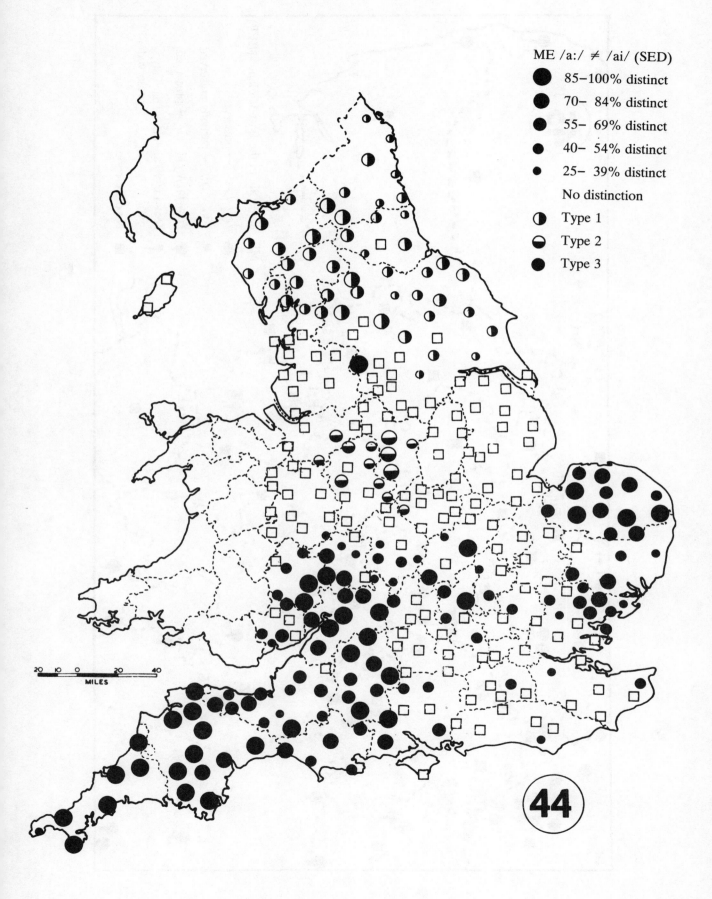

ME /a:/ ≠ /ai/ (SED)

● 85–100% distinct
● 70– 84% distinct
● 55– 69% distinct
● 40– 54% distinct
• 25– 39% distinct

No distinction

◐ Type 1
⊖ Type 2
● Type 3

MILES
20 10 0 20 40

44

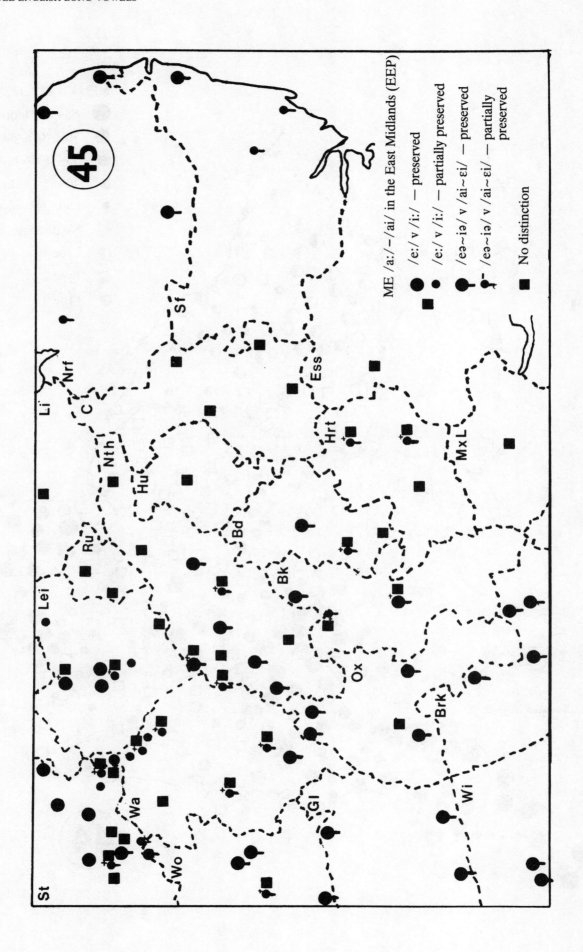

ME /a:/-/-/ai/ in the East Midlands (EEP)

/e:/ v /i:/ — preserved

/e:/ v /i:/ — partially preserved

/eə~iə/ v /ai~ɛi/ — preserved

/eə~iə/ v /ai~ɛi/ — partially preserved

No distinction

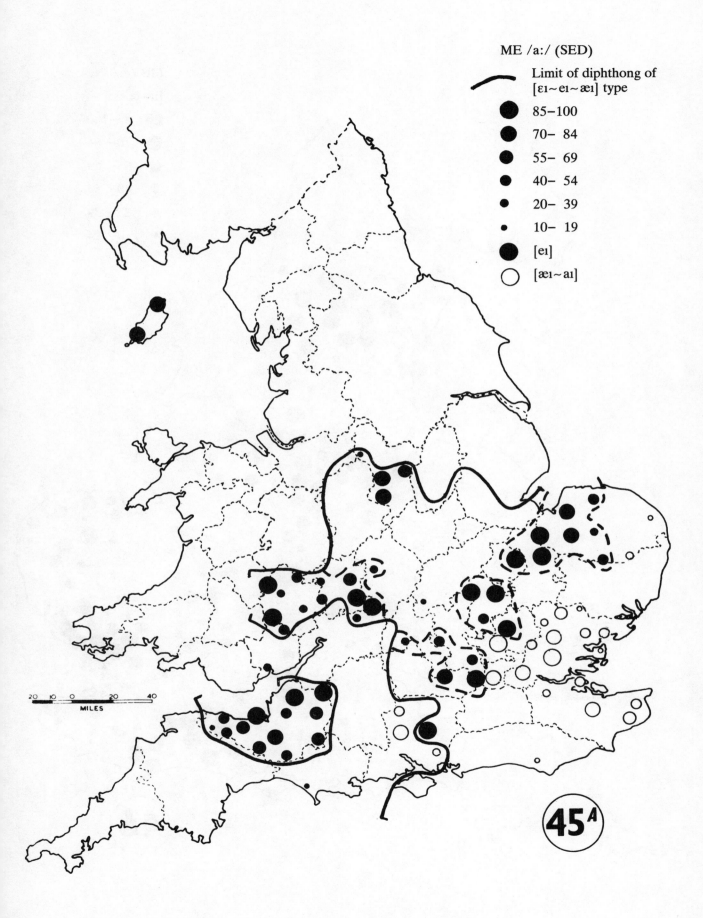

ME /aː/ (SED)

Limit of diphthong of
[ɛɪ ~ eɪ ~ æɪ] type

85–100
70– 84
55– 69
40– 54
20– 39
10– 19
[eɪ]
[æɪ ~ aɪ]

20 10 0 20 40
MILES

45ᴬ

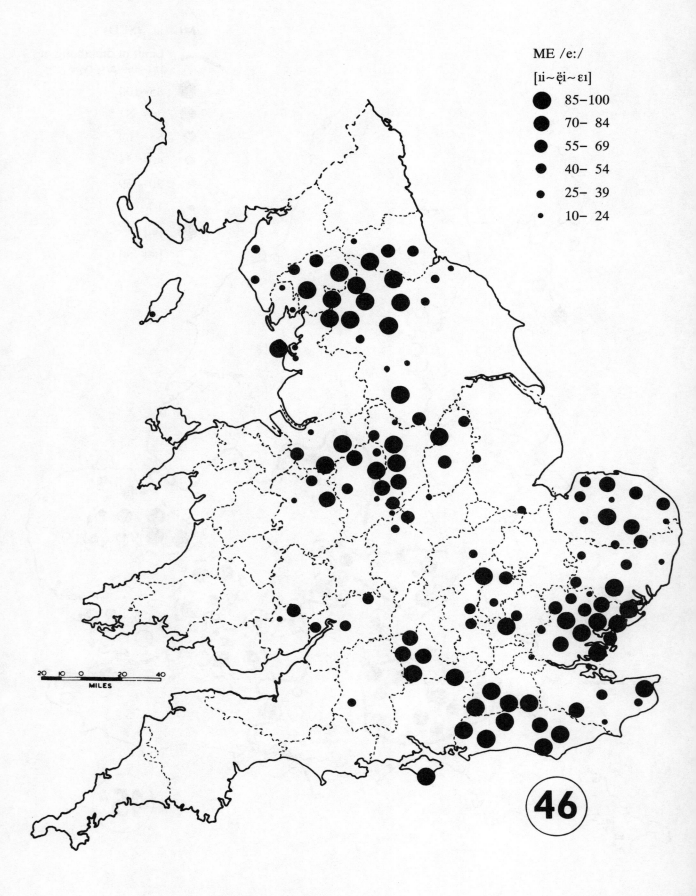

ME /e:/

[ɪi~ ëi~ ɛɪ]

● 85–100
● 70– 84
● 55– 69
● 40– 54
• 25– 39
· 10– 24

46

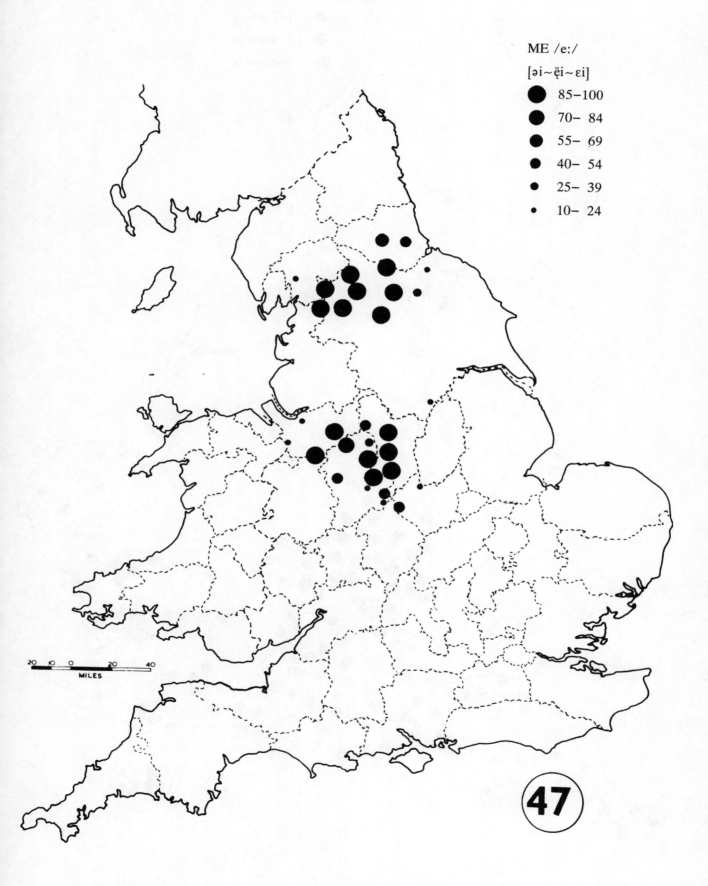

ME /eː/

[əi~ëi~ɛi]

- ⬤ 85–100
- ⬤ 70– 84
- ⬤ 55– 69
- ● 40– 54
- ● 25– 39
- • 10– 24

MILES

47

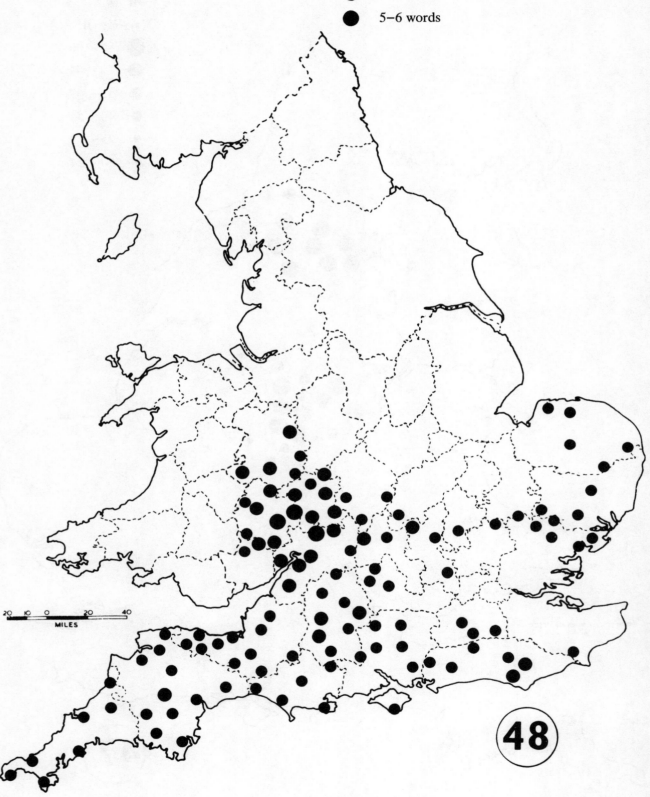

ME /e:/ Shortening to /ɪ/ in *between, creep, feed, feet, field, geese, keep, teeth, weed.*

● 1–2 words

● 3–4 words

● 5–6 words

MILES

48

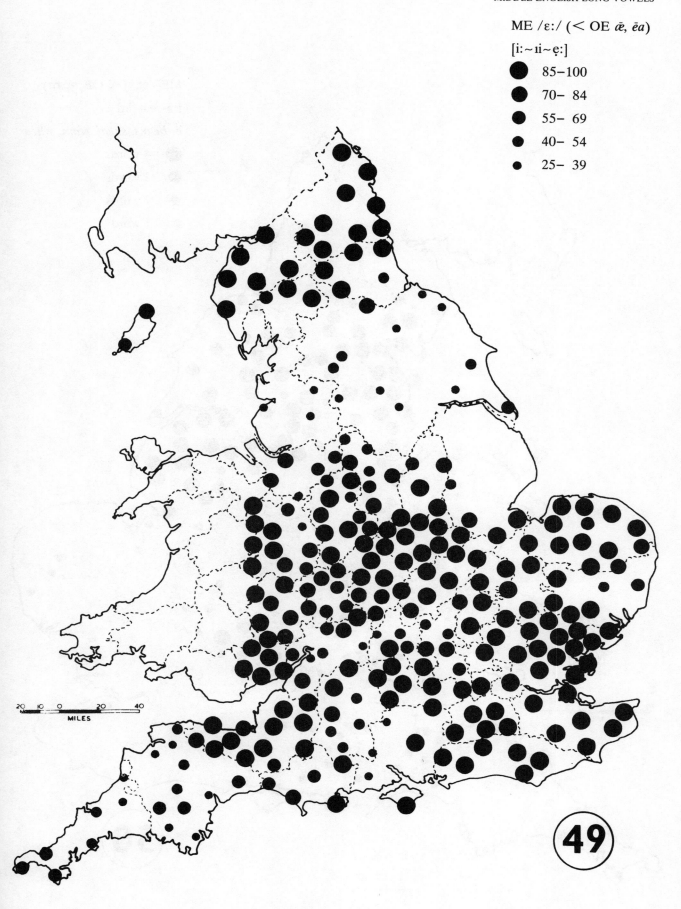

ME /ɛ:/ (< OE *ǣ, ēa*)

[i:~ɪi~ẹ:]

- ● 85–100
- ● 70– 84
- ● 55– 69
- ● 40– 54
- • 25– 39

MILES

20 10 0 20 40

49

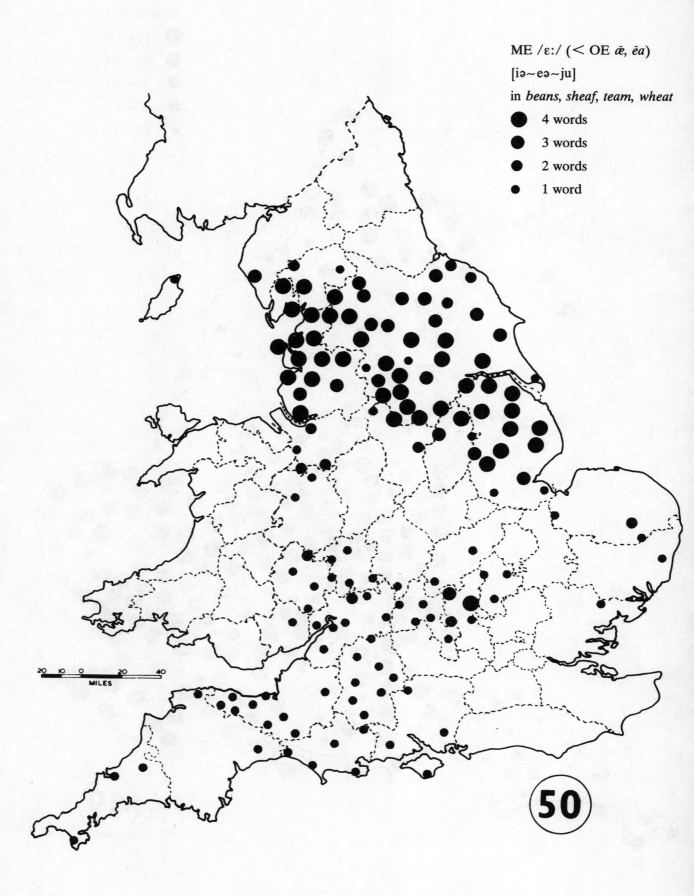

ME /ɛ:/ (< OE *ǣ, ēa*)

[iə~eə~ju]

in *beans, sheaf, team, wheat*

● 4 words

● 3 words

● 2 words

● 1 word

50

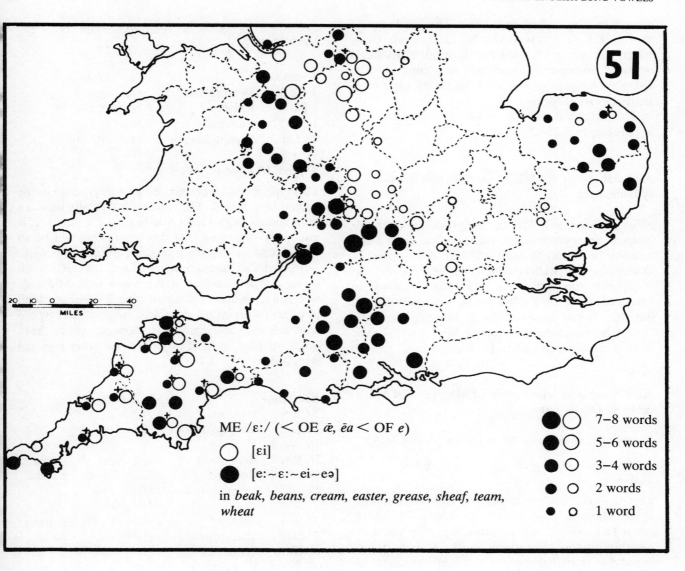

ME /ɛ:/ (< OE ǽ, ēa < OF e)

○ [ɛi]

● [e:~ɛ:~ei~eə]

in *beak, beans, cream, easter, grease, sheaf, team, wheat*

MILES

●○	7–8 words
●○	5–6 words
●○	3–4 words
●○	2 words
●○	1 word

3.22 Rising diphthongs

(a) /jɒ~jʌ~jə/ This type has been discussed at 3.20. Map 53 shows that the type is mainly concentrated in the Cotswolds though the development in initial position is a little more widespread.

(b) /jɛ/ Map 52 shows the distribution of the rising diphthong /jɛ/. It occurs in the West from Lancashire to Devon. In the north and west of its range it is conditioned by a preceding /d/ (and historically by a preceding /t/ or /s/) whilst in Wiltshire it occurs after /b/. The development in initial position is a much more widespread phenomenon occurring as far south as Devonshire and as far north as west Yorkshire. It is worth remarking that /jɛ/ has frequently merged with the preceding sound to give the respective affricate (for example /dʒɛd/ *dead*, /tʃɛm/ *team*).

The development of rising diphthongs parallels the development of rising diphthong for ME /a:/ in the northern dialects and it is likely that the two analogous developments are the result of a common trend, both sounds being affected at the /ɛ:/ stage. The opposite trend — towards ingliding diphthongs — was also present in Lancashire and Cheshire and other Western dialects. There were thus contrasting types existing in late Middle English in these dialects — /ɛə~eɛ́/. Because of the way in which they arose as prosodic variants, it is likely that they continued for some time in the same function.[41] At some stage, the rising type became generalised in initial position in the more northerly dialects (Cheshire and south Lancashire) and after /d/ whereas in other positions /ɛiə~iə/ was generalised. As late as 1886 Darlington records /tɛiəm/ beside /tʃɛm/ for *team* for South Cheshire indicating some variation in usage even at that late date.[42]

3.23 Shortening of ME /ɛ:/ (Map 54)

Map 54 shows the areas in which a long vowel is preserved in *dead, deaf* and *head.* The tendency to shorten ME /ɛ:/ is seen as a Midland development which has not reached the North or north Midlands or west Somerset, Devonshire or Cornwall. The rising diphthongs of the west Midlands have been treated as short forms.

The structural position of ME /ɛ:/ is considered at paragraphs 3.25–3.29.

3.24 ME /ɛ:/ (< eME /e/ lengthened in open syllables) (ę̄)

ME /ɛ:/ from early ME /e/ lengthened in open syllables is generally merged with ME /ɛ:/ from other sources. In the north Midlands and also in parts of Derbyshire and Staffordshire, it has become [ɛɪ] and is distinct from ME /ɛ:/ from other sources. In Cheshire and north Derbyshire, it is partially distinct but here it has become [e:~i:] merging with ME /a:/. The structural position of ME /ɛ:/ (<eME /e/) is discussed in paragraph 3.29.

3.25 Structural relationship of ME /e:/ and ME /ɛ:/ (< OE ǣ, ēa)

Three types of contrast occur (Maps 56 and 56A).

Type 1 Long monophthong versus ingliding diphthong

This type is found from south Cumberland southwards through Lancashire, Yorkshire, Cheshire, north Derbyshire, north Nottinghamshire and Lincolnshire (except the extreme south). It is also found in parts of Buckinghamshire and north Somerset. A secondary type occurs in the Cotswolds and adjoining parts of the south west Midlands where the contrast is between a long monophthong and a rising diphthong (the latter developing from an earlier centring diphthong).

Examples		/e:/	/ɛ:/	
5 La 3	Yealand	/i:/	/ɪə/	
6 Y 16	Easingwold	/i:/	/ɪə/	
10 L 12	Sutterton	/i:/	/ɪə/	
26 Bk 2	Stewkley	/ᵊi/	/ɪə/	
7 Ch 5	Audlem	/ɛɪ/	/ɛɪə/	partial
24 Gl 5	Sherborne	/i:/	/jɷ/	systems

Type 2 Upgliding diphthong versus long monophthong

This type is restricted to a small area of east Cheshire, north and east Staffordshire and west Derbyshire. The contrast is somewhat confused by a tendency to merge under /ɛɪ/ or /i:/ but the

distinction is quite clearly preserved in south Derbyshire.[43]

Examples		/e:/	/ɛ:/
7 Ch 3	Swettenham	/ɛɪ/	/i:/
8 Db 6	Kniveton	/ɛɪ/	/i:/
12 St 5	Ellenhall	/ɛɪ/	/i:/
13 Lei 7	Sheepy Magna	/ɛɪ/	/i:/

Type 3 High versus low

This type might be considered an earlier stage in the evolution of type 2. The contrast is typically between long vowels, high versus low (e.g. /i:/ v /e:/). It is not really surprising that this contrast should be so widespread in the dialects since Standard English possessed this distinction until into the eighteenth century. The situation in the south west Midlands and Buckinghamshire, where type 3 contrasts tend to coexist with type 1 contrasts, suggests that type 3 contrasts are an innovation deriving either from Standard English itself or from some other regional standard.[44]

Examples		/e:/	/ɛ:/	
7 Ch 6	Hanmer	/i:/	/e:~e:ᵊ/	
11 Sa 5	Kinnersley	/i:/	/ę:/	
16 Wo 3	Hanbury	/i:/	/e:ɪ~ɛ:ɪ/	partial
16 Wo 7	Bretforton	/i:/	/ɛɪ/	partial
21 Nf 11	Reedham	/i:/	/ë:~ę̣ɪ/	partial
22 Sf 2	Mendlesham	/i:~ ᵊi:/	/ɛɪ/	
22 Sf 3	Yoxford	/i:/	/ę·ə/	partial
24 Gl 5	Sherborne	/i:/	/e:/	partial
26 Bk 1	Tingewick	/i:/	/ɛɪ/	
32 W 9	Whiteparish	/i:/	/e:/	
36 Co 1	Kilkhampton	/i:/	/ɛɪ/	
37 D 1	Blackawton	/i:/	/ɛɪ/	partial
39 Ha 5	Hambledon	/i:/	/e:/	

3.26 Mergers ME /e:/ = /ɛ:/

In most of the areas in which ME /e:/ and ME /ɛ:/ are merged, the merger is as /i:~ı̣:/. Significantly, this type is found in most of the South East and East Midlands and is clearly the origin of the Standard English merger. Areas of merger of the Standard English type also occur in north Cumberland and Westmorland, Durham and Northumberland where ME /ɛ:/ was 'squeezed' between ME /ai/ and ME /a:/ on the one hand and ME /e:/ on the other and also on the Welsh Border which in other respects tends to have a 'standardised' system. The /ë̩ɪ/ type also occurs in south Durham as the further development of /i:/.

ME /ɛ:/ (< OE ǣ, ēa)

[jɛ]

in *beans, dead, deaf, east, easter, head, heat*
Shaded localities show development after /d/

○ ●   4 words +

○ ●   3 words

○ ●   2 words

○ ●   1 word

●   Also [bj]

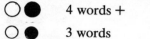
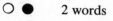

52

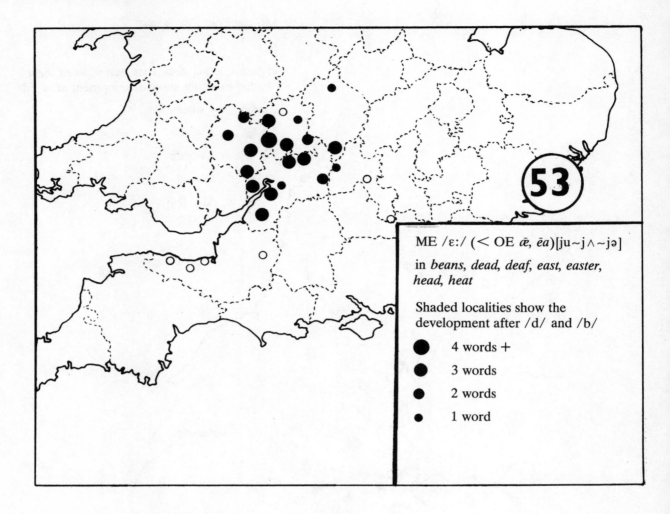

ME /ɛ:/ (< OE *ǣ, ēa*)[ju~j∧~jə]

in *beans, dead, deaf, east, easter, head, heat*

Shaded localities show the development after /d/ and /b/

● 4 words +

● 3 words

● 2 words

● 1 word

53

3.27 Structural relationship of ME /ɛ:/ (<OE ǣ, ēa) and ME /a:/

Most dialects follow Standard English in making a distinction between these two groups (see Map 57). In a number of dialects however, the two groups are merged reflecting perhaps the merger which prevailed in certain types of Standard English from approximately 1650 to the eighteenth century. In most of the South West (except Devon and Cornwall) and in the south Midlands, Ellis records a trend towards merger as [ɪə].[45] This type appears to be older than the later merger, much more common, as [e:]. Most likely the latter type was readily adopted in dialects which already had a merged phoneme albeit under a different phonetic type. The source of the substitution is probably Standard English or some local standardised dialect. The north Yorkshire merger as [ɪə] depends on the early (and rapid) fronting of ME /a:/ to merge with ME /ɛ:/ before developing an off-glide.

Examples

6 Y 15   Pateley Bridge   /ɪə/

7 Ch 1	Kingsley	/e:~i:/
7 Ch 6	Hanmer	/e:~e:ə/
22 Sf 2	Mendlesham	/ɛɪ/
24 Gl 6	Slimbridge	/e:/
32 W 4	Burbage	/e:/
39 Ha 5	Hambledon	/e:/

3.28 Structural relationship of ME /ai/ and ME /ɛ:/ (<OE, ǣ, ēa) (Map 58)

Two main areas show a merger of these two phonemes as a single structural unit. In Derbyshire, Cheshire and north and east Staffordshire the merger is as /i:/ presumably deriving from a monophthong of the [ɛ:] type (north Shropshire shows the merger at an earlier stage — /e:/). In Cheshire, this system is a secondary one, there being another probably older system which contrasts ME /ai/ and ME /ɛ:/.

The other area of merger (Devon) achieves the same structural effect by a quite different process, i.e. retention of ME /ai/ as /ɛɪ/ and the development of ME /ɛ:/ to a diphthong.[46]

ME /ɛ:/ (< OE ēa)

Unshortened forms in *dead, deaf, head*

● 3 words

● 2 words

● 1 word

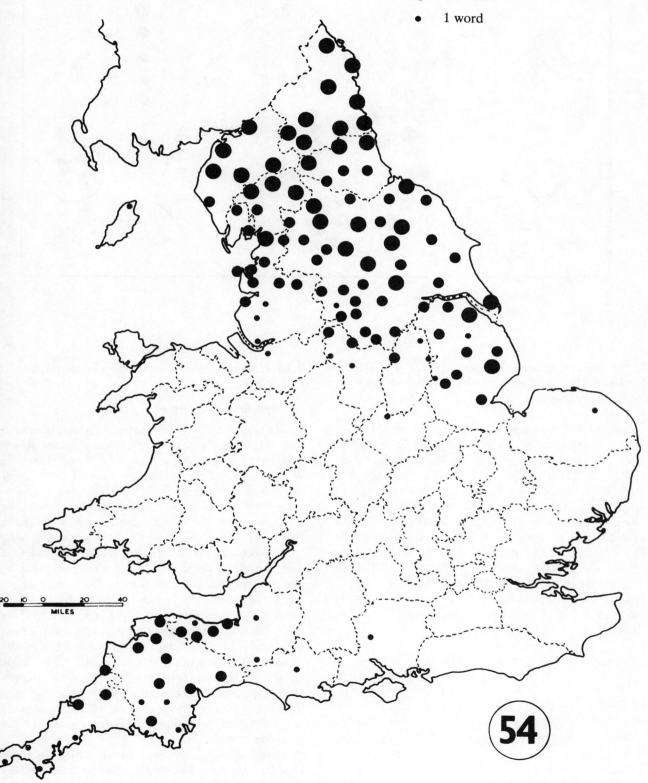

54

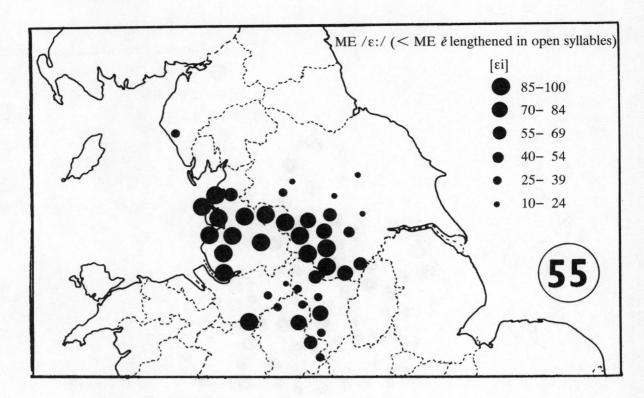

ME /ɛː/ (< ME ě lengthened in open syllables)

[ɛi]

● 85–100
● 70– 84
● 55– 69
● 40– 54
• 25– 39
· 10– 24

55

3.29 Structural relationship of ME /ɛː/ (< OE ǣ, ēa) and ME /ɛː/ (eME /e/ lengthened in open syllables) (Map 59)

Over most of England, the lengthening of eME /e/ in open syllables was followed by merger with ME /ɛː/. In an area of the north Midlands however, eME /e/ remains distinct from ME /ɛː/, the distinction being between an upgliding and an ingliding diphthong. This type of distinction persists in Lancashire and south Yorkshire and partially in north Derbyshire. In the rest of Derbyshire, north Staffordshire and east Cheshire, /ɛɪ/ < eME /e/ contrasts with a long close monophthong for ME /ɛː/ < OE ēa, ǣ. In west and mid Cheshire ME /ɛː/ < eME /e/ has merged with ME /aː/ and contrasts with ingliding diphthongs for ME /ɛː/ (< OE ǣ, ēa).

Examples		ME /ɛː/ (< OE ǣ, ēa)	ME /ɛː/ (< eME /e/)
5 La 7	Thistleton	/ɪə/	/ɛɪ/
6 Y 21	Heptonstall	/ɪə/	/ɛɪ/
7 Ch 4	Farndon	/əɪə/	/eː/ partial
7 Ch 5	Audlem	/ɛɪə/	/ɛɪ/
8 Db 1	Charlesworth	/ɪə/	/eː/
8 Db 6	Kniveton	/iː/	/ɛɪ/

3.30 General discussion of front vowel systems (Maps 59A, 59B)

(a) Synchronic structure

In all dialects ME /iː/ remains as a distinct phoneme and the differences in front vowel systems which arise in the dialects are concerned with the other ME vowels. ME had potentially five distinct front vowel phonemes, /iː/, /eː/, /ɛː/ (< OE ǣ, ēa), /ɛː/ (< eME /e/), /aː/ and /ai/, although outside the north and north central Midlands there were probably only four. The dialects show systems having from two to four phonemes but no dialect retains all five possible distinctions. On the other hand no dialect has merged all five phonemes. Standard English has a two phoneme system (System 1A) in which broadly (/eː/ = /ɛː/₁ = /ɛː/₂)/(/ai/ = /aː/). This system is not unexpectedly found in the South East and in west Cornwall and the Isle of Man. Quite surprisingly it is also usual in a wide belt of the Midlands from Shropshire to Cambridge and as far north as Nottingham. The separation of the two areas by a different system in the south east Midlands is noteworthy. Other two phoneme systems occur in the north west Midlands.

Three phoneme systems are the most common type but are quite clearly recessive in Northumberland and Durham and in Essex. System 2B is the most widespread relying on the retention of ME /ai/

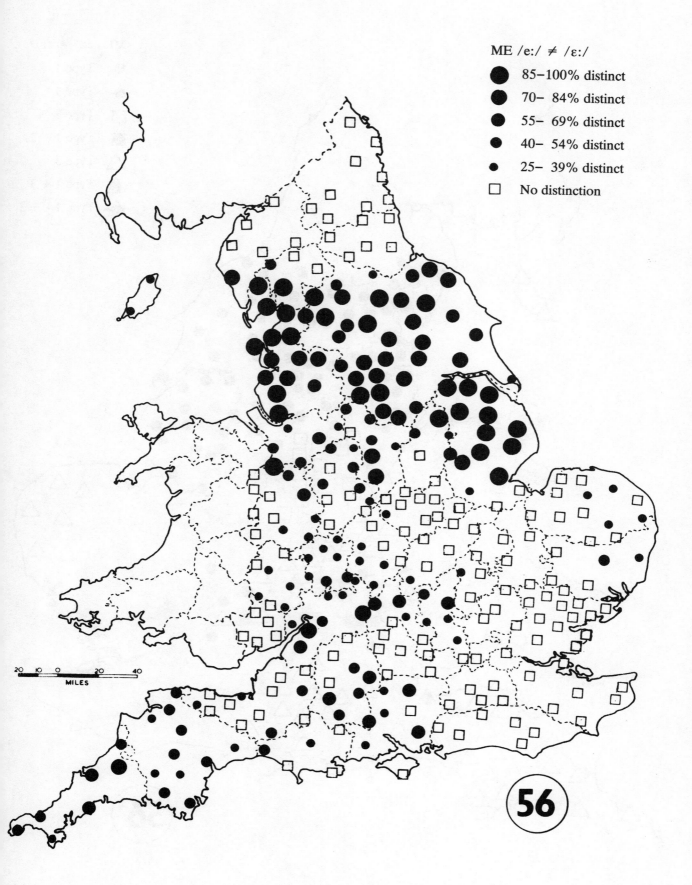

ME /e:/ ≠ /ɛ:/

● 85–100% distinct
● 70– 84% distinct
● 55– 69% distinct
● 40– 54% distinct
• 25– 39% distinct
□ No distinction

56

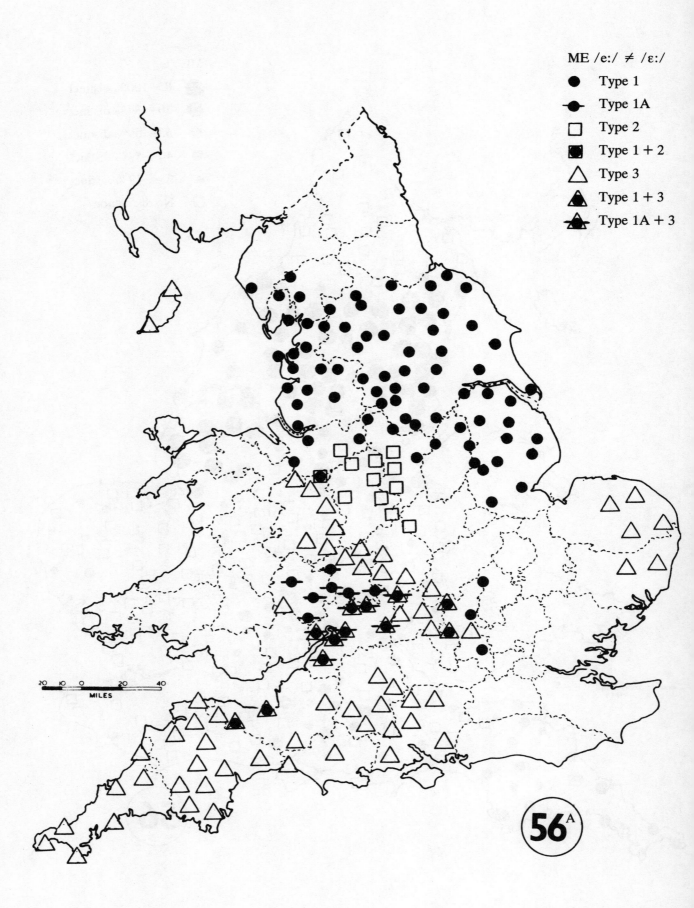

ME /e:/ ≠ /ɛ:/
●   Type 1
⬤   Type 1A
☐   Type 2
▣   Type 1 + 2
△   Type 3
▲   Type 1 + 3
◮   Type 1A + 3

MILES
20 10 0   20   40

56ᴬ

as a distinct phoneme and appears to be eliminating other phonemic systems in the South and South West. System 2A which shows a pattern ($/a:/ =$ $/ai/$) $\neq$ ($/e:/ \neq$ ($/\varepsilon:/_1$) $= /\varepsilon:/_2$) is clearly extending its range into east Yorkshire from Lincolnshire.

Four phoneme systems are restricted to Lancashire, west Yorkshire, the Yorkshire Dales and south Lakeland, the commonest system depending on a retention of ME $/\varepsilon:/_1$ ($<$ eME $/e/$) as a separate phoneme. Parts of north Buckinghamshire retain a four phoneme system at a secondary level and probably this type was formerly more widespread.

(b) Diachronic consideration of the front vowel systems

(i) Northern systems

Examples	/a:/	/ɛ:/	/e:/	/ai/
1 Nb 5 Wark	/ɪə/	/iː/	/iː/	/eː/
2 Cu 5 Hunsonby	/ɪa/	/iː/	/iː/	/ɛː/
4 We 4 Staveley	/ea/	/ɪə/	/iː/	/eː/
6 Y 7 Astrigg	/ɪə/	/ɪə/	/iː/	/eː/

These systems rely on the early monophthongisation of ME $/ai/$ and early raising of ME $/a:/$. Raising appears to have led to merger with ME $/\varepsilon:/$ where ME $/a:/$ became an ingliding diphthong. In the far North ME $/\varepsilon:/$ did not develop to an ingliding diphthong and was identified with ME $/e:/$.

(ii) North Midland systems (south Yorkshire and Lancashire)

Examples	/a:/	/ɛ:/₁	/ɛ:/₂	/e:/	/ai/
5 La 9 Read	/eː/	/ɪə/	/ɛɪ/	/iː/	/eː/
6 Y 21 Heptonstall	/eː/	/ɪə/	/ɛɪ/	/iː/	/ɛɪ/
6 Y 26 Thornhill	/eː/	/ɪə/	/ɛɪ/	/iː/	/eː/

These systems agree with Northern systems in showing the monophthongisation of ME $/ai/$.[47] They show the early diphthongisation of ME $/\varepsilon:/_1$ and the development of ME $/\varepsilon:/_2$ to upgliding $/\varepsilon\iota/$.

(iii) East Midland systems (Lincolnshire, north Nottinghamshire, east Yorkshire (partial))

Example	/a:/	/ɛ:/	/e:/	/ai/
10 L 7 Swaby	/ɛə/	/ɪə/	/iː/	/ɛə/

These systems agree with the north Midland systems in showing the merger of ME $/a:/$ and ME $/ai/$ but agree with the northern systems in showing a common development of ME $/\varepsilon:/$ whatever its origin.

(iv) North-west Midland systems (mid/west Cheshire, north west Derbyshire)

Examples	/a:/	/ɛ:/₁	/ɛ:/₂	/e:/	/ai/
7 Ch 4 Farndon	/eː/	/ɪə/	/eː/	/iː/	/eː/ (partial)
8 Db 1 Charlesworth	/eː/	/ɪə/	/eː/	/iː/	/eː/

This group of dialects, though far from uniform, shows the merger of ME $/ai/$ and ME $/a:/$ and the development of an ingliding diphthong for ME $/\varepsilon:/_1$ agreeing in these respects with the north Midland dialects. The group also shows the merger of ME $/\varepsilon:/_2$ with ME $/a:/$ indicating (probably) early raising of ME $/a:/$ in this area. My own researches in central Cheshire tend to confirm the SED position but show a system of the following type:[48]

/iː/	$<$	ME /a:/
/iː/	$<$	ME /ɛ:/₂
/ɛɪə/	$<$	ME /ɛ:/₁
/ɛɪ/	$<$	ME /e:/
/iː/	$<$	ME /ai/

Structurally this system is indistinguishable from the peripheral north west Midland system which SED shows. The phonetic realisations are consistent with an overlay of features more typical of Staffordshire/Derbyshire dialect but the underlying structure shows that the resemblance is only superficial.

(v) Mid Midland (east Cheshire, east Staffordshire, mid and south Derbyshire)

Examples	/a:/	/ɛ:/₁	/ɛ:/₂	/e:/	/ai/
7 Ch 3 Swettenham	/eː/	/iː/	/iː~ɛɪ/	/ɛɪ/	/iː/
8 Db 6 Kniveton	/eː/	/iː/	/ɛɪ/	/ɛɪ/	/iː/
12 St 2 Mow Cop	/ɛɪ/	/iː/	/iː~ɛɪ/	/ɛɪ/	/iː/
12 St 6 Hoar Cross	/ɛɪ/	/iː/	/ɛɪ/	/ɛɪ/	/iː/

This set of systems shares the separate development of ME $/\varepsilon.\!/_1$ with the north Midland. Otherwise it does not seem to fit very well with its neighbours and indeed there are a number of difficulties in the way of any consistent historical development. $/\varepsilon\iota/$ represents ME $/a:/$ by a very recent change in Staffordshire and the older system was probably the same as the current Derbyshire system. The dialects have clearly moved one stage beyond Standard English and the systems derive probably from an earlier system having the following form:

*$/\varepsilon:/$	$<$	ME /a:/
*$/\varepsilon\iota/$	$<$	ME /ɛ:/₂
*$/e:/$	$<$	ME /ɛ:/₁
*$/i:/$	$<$	ME /e:/
*$/e:/$	$<$	ME /ai/

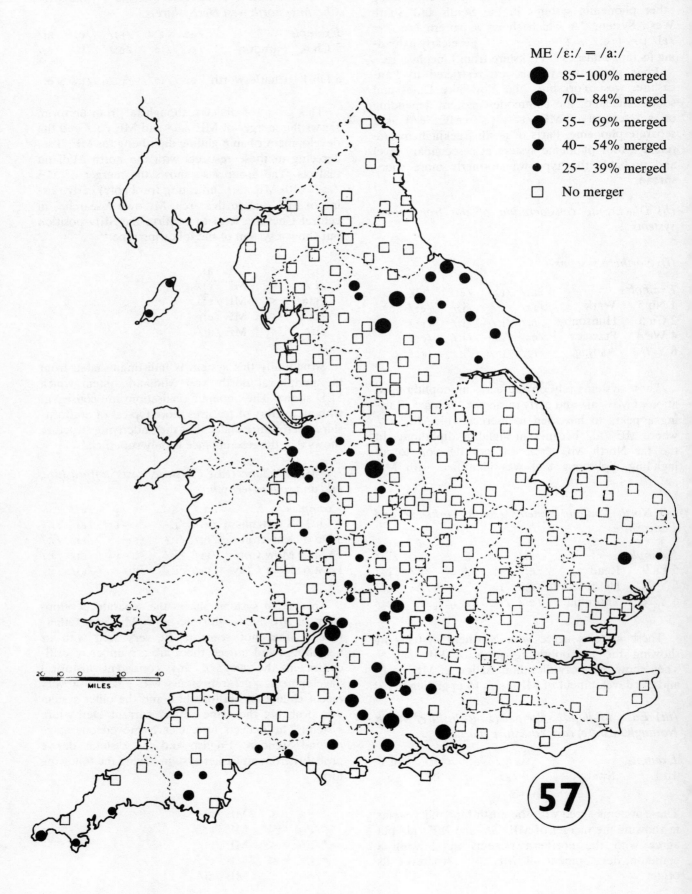

ME /ɛ:/ = /a:/

● 85–100% merged
● 70– 84% merged
● 55– 69% merged
● 40– 54% merged
• 25– 39% merged
□ No merger

MILES

57

It is difficult to see how ME /ɛ:/ < eME /e/ could avoid merging with ME /ai~ɛ:/ on the one hand and ME /a:/ on the other hand. The absence of any merger means that the development of a monophthong to represent ME /ai~ɛ:/ must be put back to a very early date, the assumption being that by the time eME /e/ was lengthened, ME /ai~ɛ:/ had already become [e:]. The present advanced development supports an earlier rapid evolution. An alternative equally tenable view is that the current system does not derive from a single ancestor but rather its origin is to be found in some Midland koine of the early Modern period. Standard English in one of its early forms does show the merger of ME /ai/ and ME /ɛ:/ and distinguishes ME /a:/. This system appears to antedate the later merger of ME /ai/,[49] ME /ɛ:/ and ME /a:/. The earlier merger is reflected in Derbyshire and Devon dialect whilst the later type is fairly frequent in Shropshire and the merger of ME /ɛ:/ and ME /a:/ is common in central southern England.[50]

(vi) South midland (north Shropshire)

Examples		/a:/	/ɛ:/	/e:/	/ai/
11 Sa 5	Kinnersley	/e:/	/e:/	/i:/	/e:/
7 Ch 6	Hanmer	/e:/	/e:/	/i:/	/e:/

This type of system supposes the development of a monophthong for ME /ai/, merger with ME /a:/ and raising to merge with ME /ɛ:/. The merger of ME /a:/ and ME /ɛ:/ appears in Gloucestershire, south Wiltshire and Hampshire and sporadically throughout the west Midlands (see Map 57). As a relic form the merger of ME /a:/ and ME /ɛ:/ occurs in East Anglia and formerly was spread further afield.[51] Although this may just be evidence that this type of system arose over a wide area, it is more likely in view of the older systems which persist in the same areas that it is modelled on Standard English or on a standardised dialect which had adopted the Standard English type.

(vii) Southern systems (north Buckinghamshire)

Example		/a:/	/ɛ:/	/e:/	/ai/
26 Bk 2	Stewkley	/eə/	/ɪə/	/i:/	/ɛɪ/

This type presents no problems of development. ME /ai/ remains as a diphthong and both ME /ɛ:/ and ME /a:/ become ingliding diphthongs. This system appears to be the oldest system in southern England appearing in relic form in east Somerset, Gloucestershire, Wiltshire and parts of Oxfordshire. (In east Somerset, Gloucestershire and Wiltshire the system shows a variant in which ME /ɛ:/ and ME /a:/ are merged as /ɪə/.)[52]

(viii) Mid-southern (Hampshire, Wiltshire and Gloucestershire)

Examples		/a:/	/ɛ:/	/e:/	/ai/
32 W 7	Sutton Veny	/e:/	/e:/	/i:/	/ai/
24 Gl 6	Slimbridge	/e:/	/e:/	/i:/	/ɛɪ/
39 Ha 5	Hambledon	/e:/	/e:/	/i:/	/ai/

(ix) Devon

Example		/a:/	/ɛ:/	/e:/	/ai/
37 D 6	South Zeal	/e:/	/ɛɪ/	/i:/	/ɛɪ/

(x) General southern

Examples		/a:/	/ɛ:/	/e:/	/ai/
21 Nf 8	Gooderstone	/eɪ/	/ɪi/	/ɪi/	/æɪ/
32 W 1	Ashton Keynes	/e:/	/i:/	/i:/	/ɛɪ/
38 Do 4	Portesham	/e:/	/i:/	/i:/	/ai/

All of these systems show the retention of ME /ai/ as a diphthong but in other respects it is impossible to postulate any common system intermediate between these systems and Middle English. Probably none of these systems descend directly from local ME systems but rather from local forms of early Standard English. The Devon system represents the earliest type of standardised system. The mid-southern system is intermediate and the general southern is the most recent type.

It is possible to conclude that the pronunciation of ME /a:/ and ME /ɛ:/ as ingliding diphthongs was marked out as a dialectal pronunciation at an early date and that pronunciation types with a long monophthong of the [e:~ɛ:] type were socially more acceptable. Pronunciation of ME /ai/ as a diphthong was a feature of Standard English until 1650 (albeit conservative) however and it seems to have been retained widely in the South though it does merge with ME /a:/ in a number of areas. The substitution of a long monophthong for ME /ai/ is likely to have met some resistance since the loss of the contrast with ME /a:/ would have resulted. On the other hand the change to long monophthongs for ME /a:/ and ME /ɛ:/ was a simple phonetic change since they were already phonemically merged in many parts of the South.

3.31 ME /e:r/ and ME /ɛ:r/ (ẹr, ẹ̈r)

The contrast between /ɪə/ and /ɛə/ carries a small structural load in Standard English and it is not surprising that some dialects have merged the two phonemes so that ME /e:r/, ME /ɛ:r/ and ME /a:r/ have a common descendant. The merger is /ɛə~eə/ in Norfolk, north Suffolk, north Cambridgeshire and north Hertfordshire.

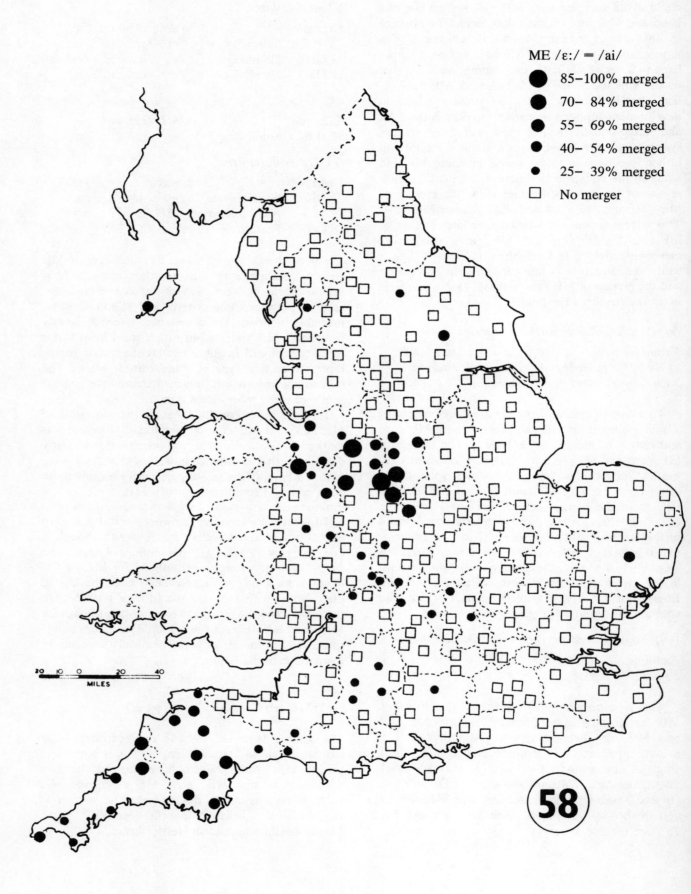

ME /ɛ:/ = /ai/

● 85–100% merged
● 70– 84% merged
● 55– 69% merged
• 40– 54% merged
• 25– 39% merged
□ No merger

58

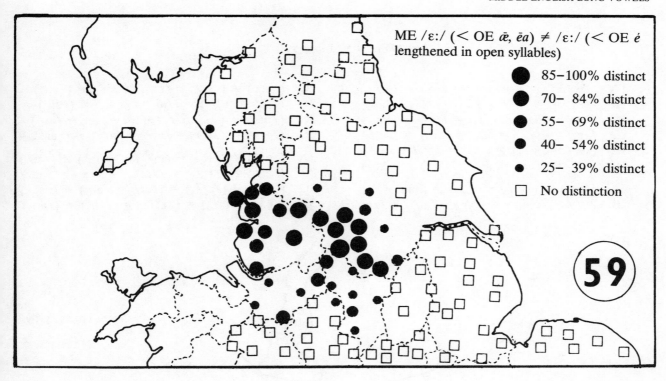

ME /ɛ:/ (< OE ǣ, ēa) ≠ /ɛ:/ (< OE é lengthened in open syllables)

- ● 85–100% distinct
- ● 70– 84% distinct
- ● 55– 69% distinct
- ● 40– 54% distinct
- • 25– 39% distinct
- ☐ No distinction

59

3.32 ME /o:/ (ǫ)

Already in Middle English the northern development of ME /o:/ had diverged from the midland and southern types and seems to have become centralised. The two areas are to be considered separately.

3.33 Non-northern dialects fronting of ME /o:/ (Map 61)

ME /o:/ is fronted in an area extending from south Lancashire to East Anglia and in a separate enclave in Devon. In Devon, south Lancashire and Cheshire it is fully fronted to /ʏ:/. In Cheshire, Norfolk and Devon fronting is related probably to the raising of ME /ɔ:/ to /ǫ:~u:/. In Derbyshire and east Staffordshire, ME /ɔ:/ is also raised but ME /o:/ becomes a diphthong /ɛɷ/.

3.34 Shortening of ME /o:/ (Maps 62–64)

This is discussed at paragraph 2.18. Shortening has been most complete in the south Midland and East Anglian areas where ME /o:/ has been more frequently shortened than retained as a long vowel. The North and north Midlands are the most conservative regions and here ME /o:/ is retained as a long vowel in most contexts.

3.35 Development of /ɷɪ/ in the north Midlands (Map 65)

ME /o:/ becoms /ɷɪ/ in west and south Yorkshire. This is a positional development before front consonants. It does not occur before /k/ or finally.[53] It does occur before /l/ since in these dialects this has a fronted point of articulation in most positions. The development is unlikely but not unique (see 3.47). The most likely development would be to *[ɷə] but in these dialects ME /ɔ:/ becomes /ɷə/ so that a change to /ɷɪ/ preserves the phonemic contrast. The change is to be dated before 1450 on the evidence of placename spelling.[54] SED does not record /ɷɪ/ from Sheffield but my own observations suggest that it does occur in northern parts of the city as a relic form.

3.36 Northern dialects (Maps 66–67)

In the northern dialects ME /o:/ was fronted during the late ME period. The oldest type of dialect pronunciation is of the /ɪɷ/ type often with the stress on the second element (Map 67). Over most of the area, there is no merger with ME /iu/ which has the stress on the first element. Most frequently the second element has been weakened and the stress shifted to the first element to give /ɪə/ especially in medial and final position (Map 66). Some areas retain /jɷ/ initially but develop /ɪə/ medially and finally (i.e. in positions of less stress). In final position the schwa has been dropped in the Tyneside area and merger with ME /e:/ results (/di:/ do).

Key to Maps 59A and 59B

1A $(/e:/ = /\varepsilon:/_1 = /\varepsilon:/_2 \neq (/ai/ = /a:/)$
1B $(/e:/ = /a:/) \neq (/\varepsilon:/_1 = /\varepsilon:/_2 = /ai/)$
1C $(/e:/ = /a:/ = /\varepsilon:/_2) \neq (/\varepsilon:/_1 = /ai/)$
1D $(/\varepsilon:/_1 = /\varepsilon:/_2 = /ai/ = /a:/) \neq (/e:/)$
1E $(/e:/ = /\varepsilon:/_1) \neq (/a:/ = /\varepsilon:_2/ = /ai/)$
1F $(/e:/ = /\varepsilon:/_1 = /\varepsilon:/_2 = /ai/) \neq (/a:/)$

2A $(/e:/) \neq (/\varepsilon:/_1 = /\varepsilon:/_2) \neq (/ai/ = /a:/)$
2B $(/e:/ = /\varepsilon:/_1 = /\varepsilon:/_2) \neq (/ai/) \neq (/a:/)$

2C $(/e:/) \neq (/\varepsilon:/_1 = /\varepsilon:/_2 = /ai/) \neq (/a:/)$
2D $(/e:/ = /\varepsilon:/_2) \neq (/ai/ = /\varepsilon:/_1) \neq (/a:/)$
2E $(/e:/) \neq (/\varepsilon:/_1) \neq (/\varepsilon:/_2 = /a:/ = /ai/)$
2F $(/e:/) \neq (/\varepsilon:/_1 = /\varepsilon:/_2 = /a:/) \neq (/ai/)$

3A $(/e:/) \neq (/\varepsilon:/_1 = /\varepsilon:/_2) \neq (/a:/) \neq (/ai/)$
3B $(/e:/) \neq (/\varepsilon:/_1) \neq (/\varepsilon:/_2) \neq (/a:/ = /ai/)$
3C $(/e:/) \neq (/\varepsilon:/_1) \neq (/\varepsilon:/_2 = /ai/) \neq (/a:/)$
3D $(/e:/ = /\varepsilon:/_2) \neq (/\varepsilon:/_1) \neq (/ai/) \neq (/a:/)$

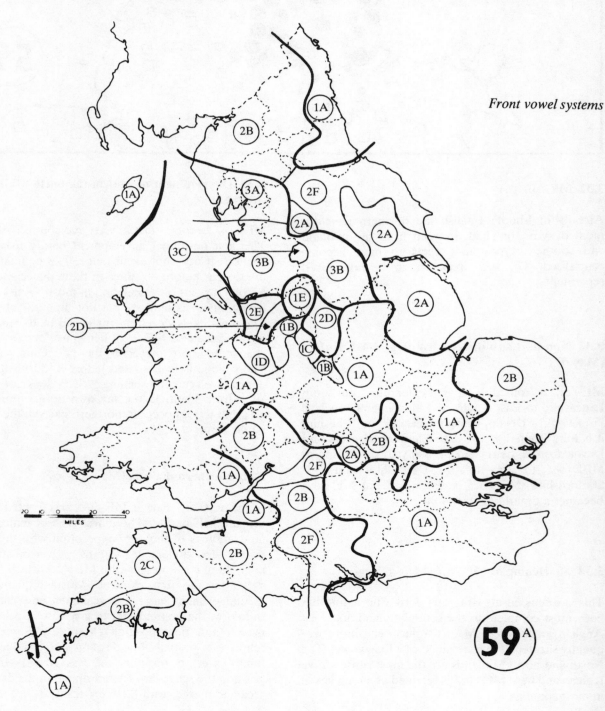

Front vowel systems

59ᴬ

Secondary systems

○	1a	△	2c
⊖	1b	>	2d
⬙	1c	∨	2e
♀	1d	<	2f
⚥	1e	⊓	3a
⊕	1f	⊐	3b
∧	2a	⊟	3c
⋀	2b	⊔	3d

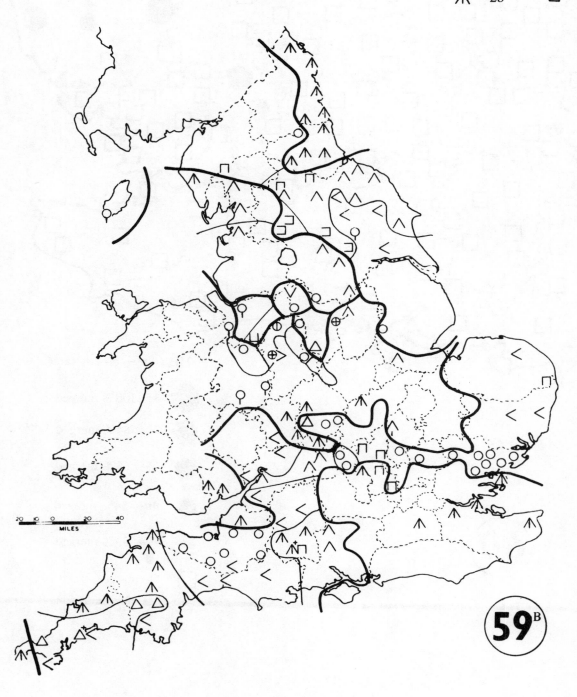

59ᴮ

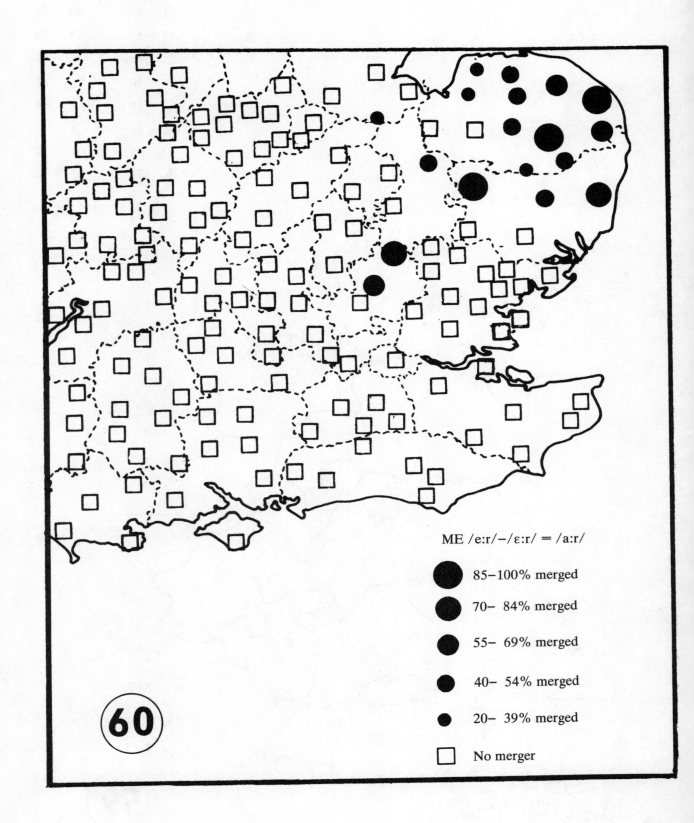

ME /e:r/−/ɛ:r/ = /a:r/

● 85−100% merged

● 70− 84% merged

● 55− 69% merged

● 40− 54% merged

• 20− 39% merged

☐ No merger

60

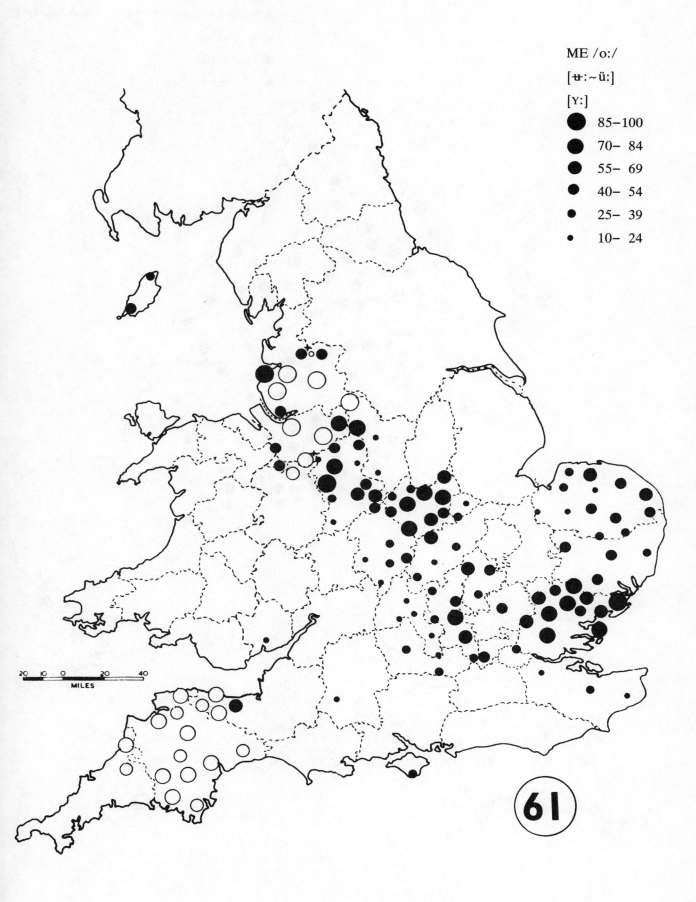

ME /o:/

[ʉ:~ü:]

[ʏ:]

● 85–100

● 70– 84

● 55– 69

● 40– 54

• 25– 39

• 10– 24

MILES

61

ME /oː/

Retention of long vowel in *crook, hook, look*

● 3 words

● 2 words

● 1 word

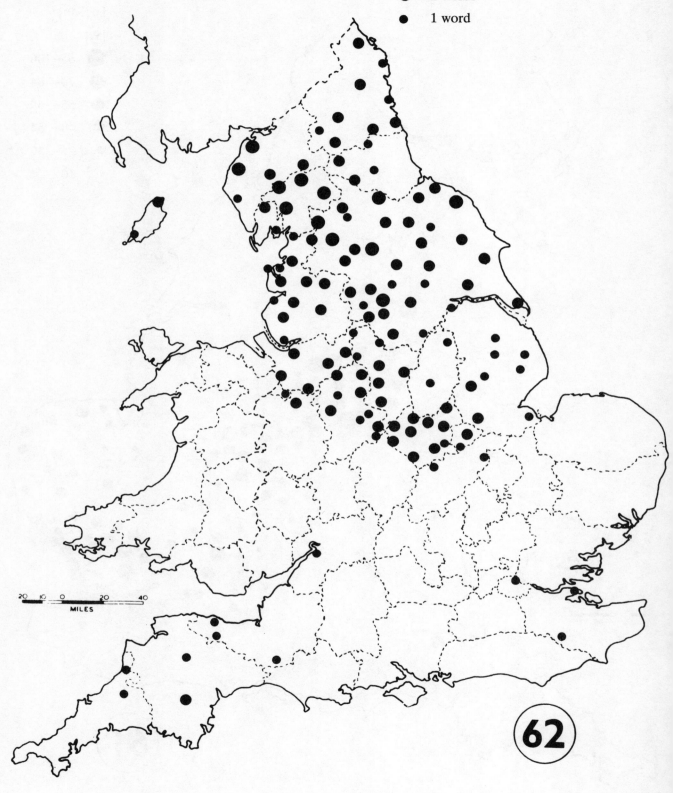

62

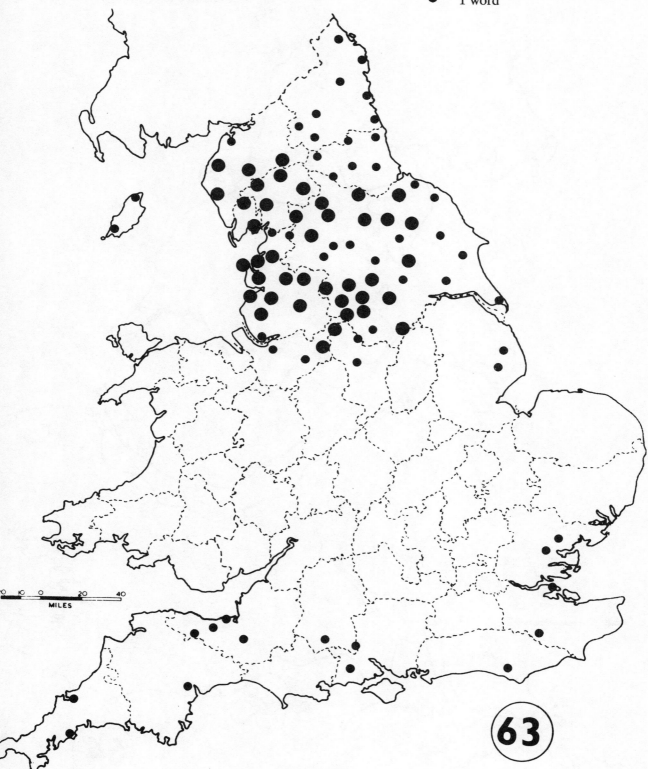

ME /oː/

Retention of long vowel in *foot, soot*

● 2 words

• 1 word

MILES

63

ME /o:/

1. Limits of shortening in *tooth* etc. (Map 17)
2. Limits of retained long vowel in *took* etc. (Map 58)
3. Limit of retained long vowel in *foot* etc. (Map 59)

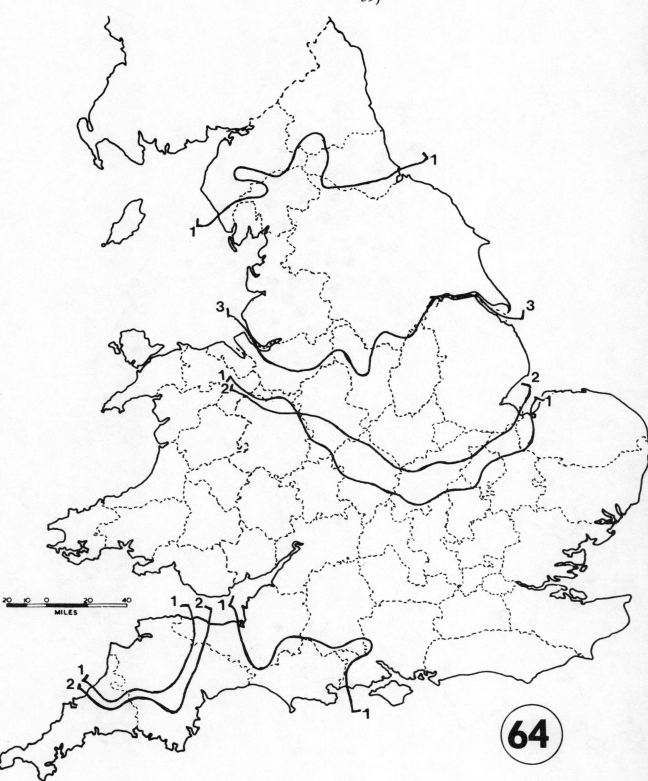

MILES

64

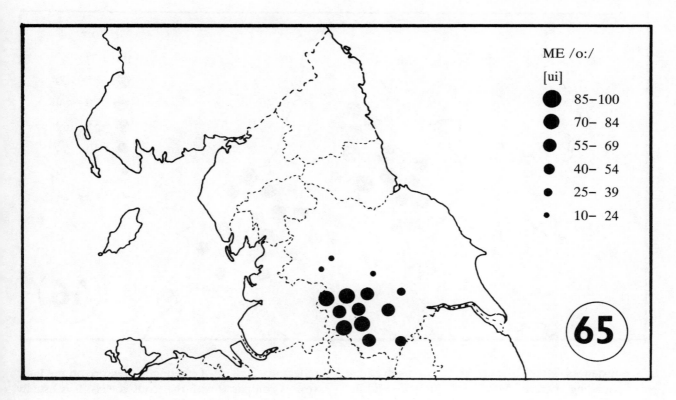

ME /o:/

[ui]

● 85–100

● 70– 84

● 55– 69

● 40– 54

• 25– 39

· 10– 24

65

3.37 ME /ɔ:/ (< OE ā) (ǭ)

In the northern dialects ME /ɔ:/ did not develop from OE ā and the probability is that OE had a fronted type *[a:] which remained in ME and was merged with ME /a/ lengthened in open syllables. It is useful to consider the developments of NME /a:/ from both origins to see the extent to which they remain merged (see paragraph 3.46 and Maps 79–83). In the remaining dialects the assumption is that OE ā was a long low back vowel which was subsequently raised in ME.

3.38 Non-northern developments – Ingliding diphthongs (Maps 68–69)

ME /ɔ:/ tended to develop to an ingliding diphthong in many dialects paralleling the evolution of ingliding diphthongs to represent ME /ɛ:/. In the dialects of mid Lancashire, west Yorkshire and Lincolnshire this development occurs in all positions. In south Lancashire and Cheshire it only takes place before a following dental (primarily /t/, /d/, /θ/, and /n/). Ingliding diphthongs are relic types in the South and it is difficult to be certain whether the development is conditioned in these areas. Although the type is receding in southern England, it is clear that in the northern dialects ingliding diphthongs are spreading from the north Midlands and supplanting forms derived from NME /a:/.

3.39 Non-northern developments – Rising diphthongs (Maps 70–71)

Comparisons can be drawn between the development of rising diphthongs to represent ME /ɔ:/ and the development of /jɛ/ to represent ME /ɛ:/. In some ways they are parallel developments but the geographical distribution differs.[55] A distinction must be drawn between ME /ɔ:/ in initial position (forms /wɒ wɤ wʌ wə/) and ME /ɔ:/ in medial position (forms /wɤ wʌ wə/).

(a) Initial position (Map 71)

This is a very widespread development but primarily a western and south western change. This agrees with the development of ME /ɛ:/. The likelihood is that all the types have developed from a [uɔ́(:)] form which arose by stressing of the onset to the long vowel. [wɒ] represents shortening at an early stage whereas [wɤ~wʌ~wə] suggests that raising to [wo:] occurred followed by shortening and lowering.[56,57]

(b) Medial position (Map 70)

These forms parallel the development of ME /ɛ:/ to /jɤ jʌ/ and occur in much the same areas of the south west Midlands though the evidence tends to suggest that there was formerly a wider distribution. The development has taken place after /b/, /p/, /k/ and /t/. Probably the type descends from /ɤə/ with subsequent stress-shift but it is also likely that in

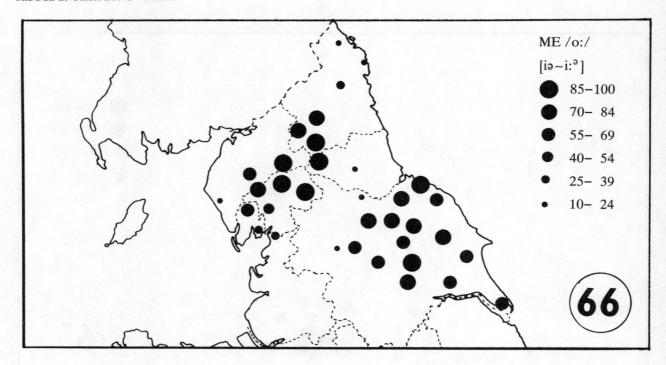

ME /o:/

[iə~i:ᵊ]

● 85–100
● 70– 84
● 55– 69
● 40– 54
• 25– 39
· 10– 24

66

some instances (after /b/ and /p/), /w/ evolved by over-rounding before ME /ɔ:/ in the Middle English period and was subsequently raised to */wo:/ and then shortened and sometimes lowered as in initial position (see note 55).

3.40 Non-northern developments –Long monophthongs (Map 72)

These forms occur in the north west Midlands where they are positional developments and also in the Welsh Border counties, in the south western counties of Wiltshire, Hampshire, Dorset, Gloucestershire and Somerset and in west Cornwall. The type is recessive throughout most of its range but the sprinkling of forms in the northern counties shows that in this area it is the type which is taking the place of forms descended from ME /a:/. In the South and parts of the South West it appears that long monophthongs have supplanted earlier ingliding diphthongs.

3.41 Fronting of ME /ɔ:/ (Map 73)

ME /ɔ:/ is fronted to /ø:/ in east Northumberland where it contrasts with /œ:/ which appears for ME /o/. This type is descended from an early Modern English *[o:].

3.42 Raising of ME /ɔ:/

Raising of ME /ɔ:/ to /u:/ is relatively infrequent

reflecting the lack of phonemic pressure on the back vowels compared with the front vowels. It is usually associated with an advanced pronunciation for ME /o:/. Raising is found in Devon and to a lesser extent in Hampshire and Wiltshire and also in Cheshire, where ME /ɔ:/ varies between [o̝:] and [u̜:]. In both Devon and Cheshire ME /o:/ is fronted to /ʏ:/. Raising occurs to a lesser extent in East Anglia but rarely reaches /u:/.

3.43 Raising of ME /ɔ:/ and later fronting (Map 74)

In east Cheshire and parts of north Staffordshire and Derbyshire ME /ɔ:/ is fronted to /ü:/. This change appears to be a conditioned one before dentals agreeing with the conditioned change to /ʏə/ in similar positions in south Lancashire and Cheshire. Possibly /u:/ represents an earlier ingliding diphthong which has lost its second element.[53]

3.44 Shortening of ME /ɔ:/ (Map 75)

The shortening of ME /ɔ:/ is primarily an East Anglian development presumably from an earlier *[o:] type. /ɷ/ ocurs most frequently alongside /ʌ/ and /o/, the latter of dubious structural status. This would suggest that the shortening has taken place gradually over a fairly lengthy period. /ʌ/ forms represent the earliest shortenings and /o/ forms the most recent. The so-called 'East Anglian short o' does not merge with ME /u/ or shortened ME /o:/ but seems to be a structural compromise between /ɷ/ and /oɷ/.

98

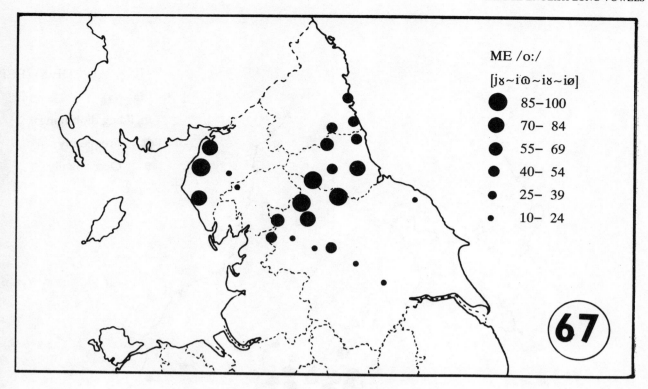

ME /oː/

[jɤ~iɷ~iɤ~iø]

● 85–100

● 70– 84

● 55– 69

● 40– 54

• 25– 39

• 10– 24

67

3.45 Upgliding diphthongs (Maps 76–78)

Upgliding diphthongs seem to be recent innovations wherever they occur. EEP (Map 76) shows that in the late nineteenth century /oɷ~ɔɷ/ occurred in the central and eastern Midlands often alongside older /ɷə/. Probably the type arises partially by analogy with ME /ɔu/ which is usually retained as a diphthong in the South and in the east Midlands. The link is made through Standard English or a prestige dialect based on Standard English in which both ME phonemes were merged. The present distribution of the upgliding diphthongs shows that they are usual throughout the Midlands and in Norfolk (Map 77). The fringe area along the South Coast indicates that this type is recessive in the Home Counties. In the north Midlands the material suggests that upgliding diphthongs are replacing older /oː/ or /ɷə/.

Within the South East ME /ɔː/ is usually an upgliding diphthong with an unrounded or neutral onset and in some dialects the first element is being fronted with resultant pressure on the local developments of ME /uː/ (/ɛɷ~ɛ̈ɷ/). Historically this is a very recent newcomer. EEP records the /ʌɷ/ type only in London. Standard English itself has a range of forms from older conservative [oɷ~öɷ] to advanced [ɛɷ] though the commonest is [əɷ].

3.46 Northern developments (Maps 79–82)

In the northern dialects OE /aː/ is merged with ME /a/ lengthened in open syllables (see Maps 36–37 and discussion at 3.8–3.9).

In initial position rising diphthongs occur throughout the northern area (Map 80) but they appear in medial position only in southern and central Cumberland and Westmorland and in mid Durham and Tyneside (Maps 79, 81 and 82 — compare Maps 36–37). In other areas /ɪə/ is found as for ME /aː/ from other sources. Map 83 shows the extent of the preservation of the merger between ME /aː/ < eME /a/ lengthened in open syllables and NME /aː/ < OE ā. The contrast is strongly preserved only in the central areas from the Yorkshire Dales north to the Cheviots. In the Tyneside and south Durham areas and in north Lancashire and east Yorkshire, the retention of the merger is minimal, a distinction having been introduced by the adoption of north Midland types for ME /ɔː/.

3.47 ME /ɔː/₂ (< eME /o/ lengthened in open syllables) (ǭ)

In most English dialects ME /ɔː/ from early ME /o/ lengthened in open syllables is merged with ME /ɔː/ from other sources. However, over most of

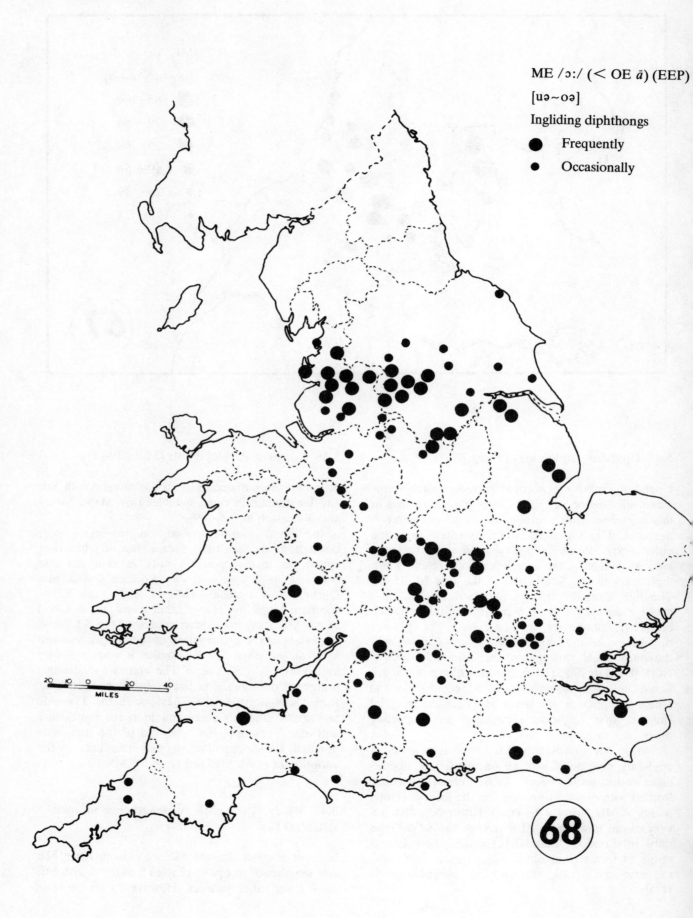

ME /ɔː/ (< OE ā) (EEP)

[uə~oə]

Ingliding diphthongs

●   Frequently

•   Occasionally

MILES

68

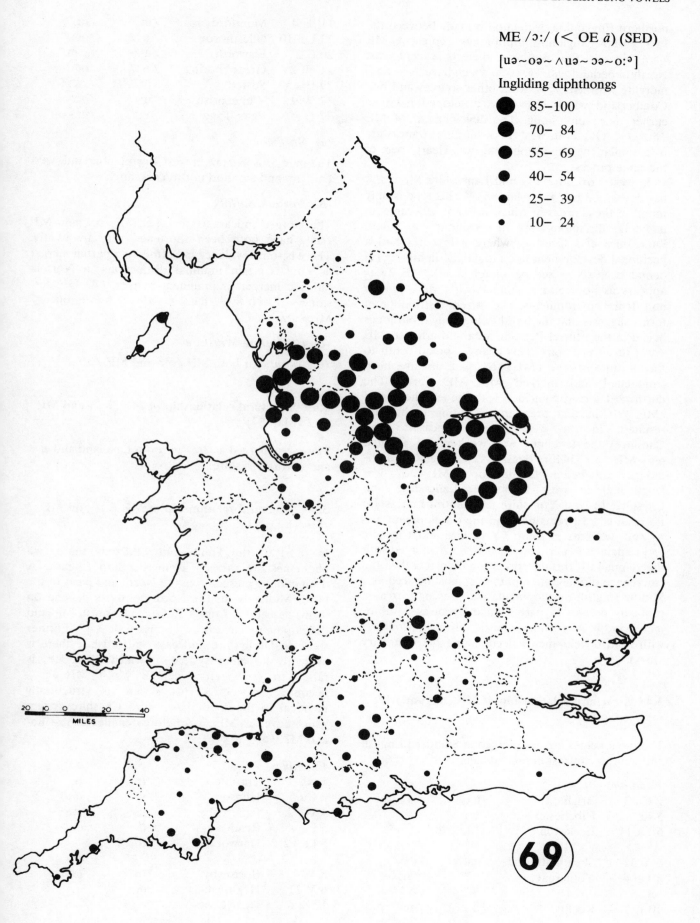

ME /ɔ:/ (< OE ā) (SED)

[uə~oə~ ∧uə~ɔə~oːə]

Ingliding diphthongs

●   85–100
●   70– 84
●   55– 69
•   40– 54
·   25– 39
·   10– 24

69

northern England, a distinction is made between the two groups. Ingliding diphthongs represent ME /ɔ:/₂ in all the northern dialects except east Northumberland and Tyneside which have /ø:~øə/, merging with ME /ɔ:/ from other sources and mid Cumberland which has /wɒ/ developed from an earlier rising diphthong. The development of ME /ɔ:/₁ (< OE ā) in west Yorkshire and Lancashire to a similar ingliding diphthong was clearly part of the same process.

In west Yorkshire and mid Lancashire ME /ɔ:/₂ has developed to /ɔɪ/ (Map 85).[59] This type is only found in those areas in which ME /ɔ:/₁ became an ingliding diphthong in all positions. In south Lancashire and Cheshire where ME /ɔ:/₁ had a positional development to an ingliding diphthong (in dental contexts — see paragraph 3.38), ME /ɔ:/₂ appears as /o:/ and is merged with ME /ɔ:/₁ in non-dental environments. The current distribution of forms suggests that the trend to ingliding diphthongs began in the central Pennine area and affected ME /ɔ:/₁ in all positions. This change spread south to Lincolnshire where eME /o/ had already been lengthened and merged with ME /ɔ:/₁. The northward spread coincided with the lengthening of eME /o/ in that area and ingliding diphthongs resulted. In the west (south Lancashire and Cheshire) the tendency was weaker and affected only ME /ɔ:/₁ before dentals. After ingliding diphthongs had begun to develop, eME /o/ was lengthened in west Yorkshire, Lancashire and Cheshire. In west Yorkshire and central Lancashire no residual [ɔ:] remained and the development was to /ɔɪ/ whereas in south Lancashire and Cheshire [ɔ:] remained in part and the new /ɔ:/₂ merged with this remnant. If this interpretation is correct then the emergence of ingliding diphthongs must be seen as a Middle English development. The present /ɔɪ/ area probably derives in part from indigenous developments and in part from linguistic diffusion (doublets with both developments occur along the boundary areas).

3.48 Structural relationship of ME /o:/ and ME /ɔ:/₁ (Map 86)

These phonemes are not merged in Standard English and tend to contrast in most dialects.

Examples		/o:/	/ɔ:/₁
2 Cu 3	Brigham	/ɪɷ/	/ɪa~ea/
5 La 8	Ribchester	/ʏ:/	/ɷə/
5 La 11	Eccleston	/ᵚu:~ᵚü:/	/ɷə/ — /o:/
6 Y 31	Skelmanthorpe	/ɷɪ/	/ɷə/
8 Db 4	Youlgreave	/ɛᵚ/	/ᵚü:/ — /o:ᵚ/
10 L 3	Keelby	/u:/	/ɷə/

11 Sa 4	Montford	/u:/	/o:/
13 Lei 10	Ullesthorpe	/ʉ:/	/oɷ/
20 C 2	Elsworth	/u:/	/ʌɷ/
21 Nf 2	Great Snoring	/ʉ:/	/oɷ/
29 Ess 5	Stisted	/ü:/	/ʌɷ/
32 W 9	Whiteparish	/u:/	/o:/
37 D 8	Peter Tavy	/ʏ:/	/u:~o:/

(a) Northern

The merger is as /ɪə/ in west Northumberland, west Durham and east and north Yorkshire.

(b) Norfolk/Suffolk

The merger appears as /ɷ/, i.e. ME /o:/ and ME /ɔ:/₁ have both been shortened very frequently. There is some evidence in Suffolk of a partial merger as /ü:/. Certain minimal distinctions in Norfolk indicate merger or imminent merger. (At Gooderstone — 21 Nf 8 — /ɷu/ < ME /o:/ and /ou/ < ME /ɔ:/₁)

(c) Hampshire/Wiltshire

/u:/ occurs for both ME /o:/ and ME /ɔ:/₁.

3.49 Structural relationship of ME /o:/₁ and ME /ɛ:/ (Map 87)

These are merged as /ɪə/ in south Lakeland and east and north Yorkshire.

3.50 Structural relationship of ME /ɔ:/ and ME /ɔ:/₂ (Map 88)

In most of the South and Midlands these two phonemes are merged as in Standard English. A distinction is preserved in the North and parts of the north Midlands. In the North contrasts depend on forms descended from ME /a:/. The north Midland developments have been discussed at 3.47. Further south in Derbyshire and east Staffordshire there is evidently an older system in which ME /ɔ:/₁ is raised to /ü:/ before dentals whilst ME /ɔ:/₂ becomes /o:~oɷ/. This system is structurally identical to the south Lancashire/Cheshire system which develops ME /ɔ:/₁ before dentals to /ʏə ~ üə/ and ME /ɔ:/₂ to /o:/.

Examples		/ɔ:/₁	/ɔ:/₂
1 Nb 3	Thropton	/ɪə/	/ø:/
2 Cu 5	Hunsonby	/ɪə/	/ɷə/
4 We 2	Patterdale	/ɪa/	/ɷə/
5 La 9	Read	/ɷə/	/ɒɪ/
5 La 12	Harwood	/o:/ + /ʏə/	/o:/
6 Y 9	Borrowby	/ɪə/	/ɷə/
6 Y 21	Heptonstall	/ɷə/	/ɒɪ/
12 St 6	Hoar Cross	/ɷ:/	/oɷ/

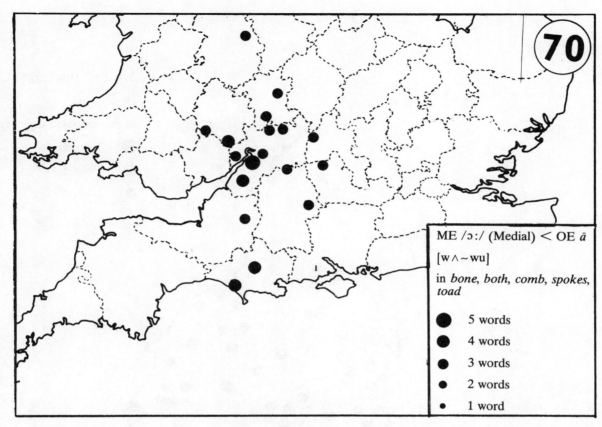

Map 70 legend:

ME /ɔː/ (Medial) < OE ā

[wʌ ~ wu]

in *bone, both, comb, spokes, toad*

- ● 5 words
- ● 4 words
- ● 3 words
- ● 2 words
- · 1 word

3.51 ME /oːr/, /ɔːr/, /or/ (ǭr, ǫr, or)

Maps 89–91 show the relationship of these three groups though the conclusions are tentative in view of the small sample of material available and the likelihood of differing ME ancestral types.

Standard English tends to merge all three ME phonemes into a single phoneme /ɔː/. In more conservative types of Standard English, a distinction (not always corresponding to the ME distinction) is maintained between /uə/, /ɔə/ and /ɔː/.

The dialects show widely differing developments. The retention of raised types for ME /oːr/ is generally recessive (northern and south western — see Map 89).

Merger of all three phonemes is found in south Staffordshire, north Warwickshire and east Leicestershire and also in Surrey, south Kent, Sussex and east Hampshire. Much of the North of England preserves a distinction between the three ME phonemes as do north west Somerset, Wiltshire, north Derbyshire and Cheshire (Maps 90–91).

Examples		ME /oːr/	ME /ɔːr/	ME /or/
1 Nb 3	Wark	/uːr/	/eːr/	/or/
2 Cu 5	Hunsonby	/ɷə/	/ɔː/	/ɔː/
5 La 12	Harwood	/ʏːr/	/oːr/	/or/
6 Y 6	Muker	/iuə/	/ɷə/	/or/
6 Y 18	Spofforth	/ɷə/	/ɷə/	/ɔː/
7 Ch 4	Farndon	/üə/	/oə/	/ɔː/
10 L 9	Scopwick	/ɷə/	/ɷə/	/ɔə/
11 Sa 7	All Stretton	/oːr/	/oːr/	/or/
13 Lei 3	Seagrave	/ɔː/	/ɔː/	/ɔː/
15 He 4	Checkley	/oːr/	/oːr/	/ar/
17 Wa 1	Nether Whitacre	/ɔː/	/ɔː/	/ɔː/
18 Nth 3	Little Harrowden	/oə/	/oə/	/ɔː/
20 C 1	Little Downham	/oə/	/oə/	/ɔː/
21 Nf 2	Great Snoring	/ɔə/	/ɔə/	/ɔː/
22 Sf 5	Kersey	/ɔə/	/ɔə/	/ɔː/
24 Gl 3	Bream	/oɷr/	/oɷr/	/ɑr/
26 Bk 2	Stewkley	/uːr/	/uːr/	/or/
28 Herts 1	Therfield	/oə/	/oə/	/ɔə/
29 Ess 5	Stisted	/ɔə/	/ɔə/	/ɔː/
31 So 4	Coleford	/uːr/	/oɷr/	/or/ + /ar/
32 W 3	Avebury	/uːr/	/or/ + /oːr/	/ar/
34 Sr 2	East Clandon	/or/	/or/	/or/
35 K 1	Stoke	/oə/	/oə/	/ɔː/
36 Co 2	Altarnum	/uːr/	/uːr/	/or/ + /ar/
36 Co 7	Mullion	/uə/	/uə/	/or/
37 D 7	Kennford	/uːr/	/uːr/	/or/
38 Do 1	Handley	/oːr/	/or/	/ar/
39 Ha 5	Hambledon	/uːr/	/uːr/	/ar/
40 Sx 1	Warnham	/or/	/or/	/or/

103

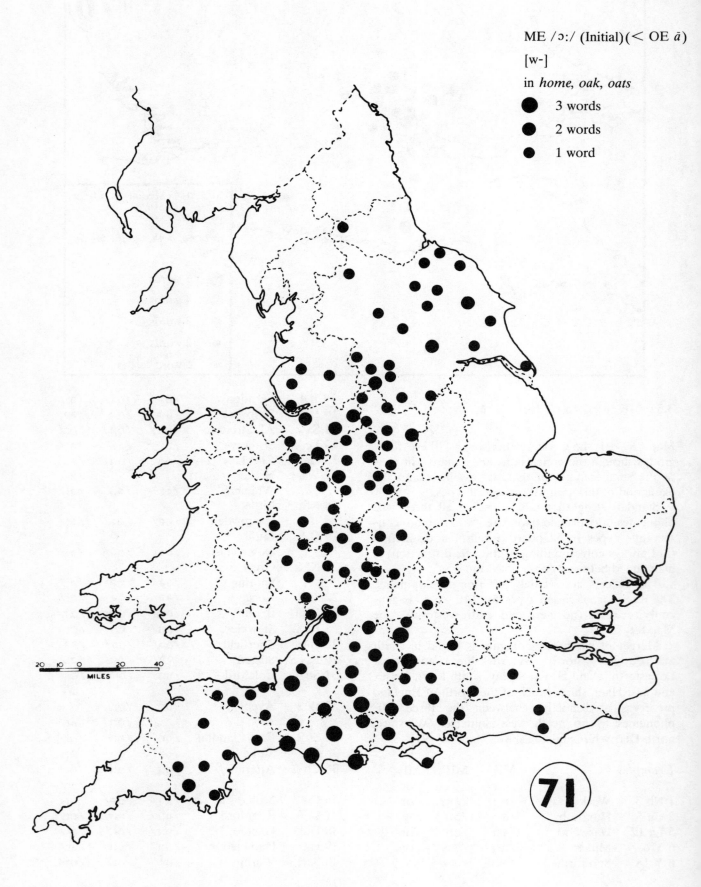

ME /ɔ:/ (Initial)(< OE ā)

[w-]

in *home, oak, oats*

● 3 words

● 2 words

• 1 word

71

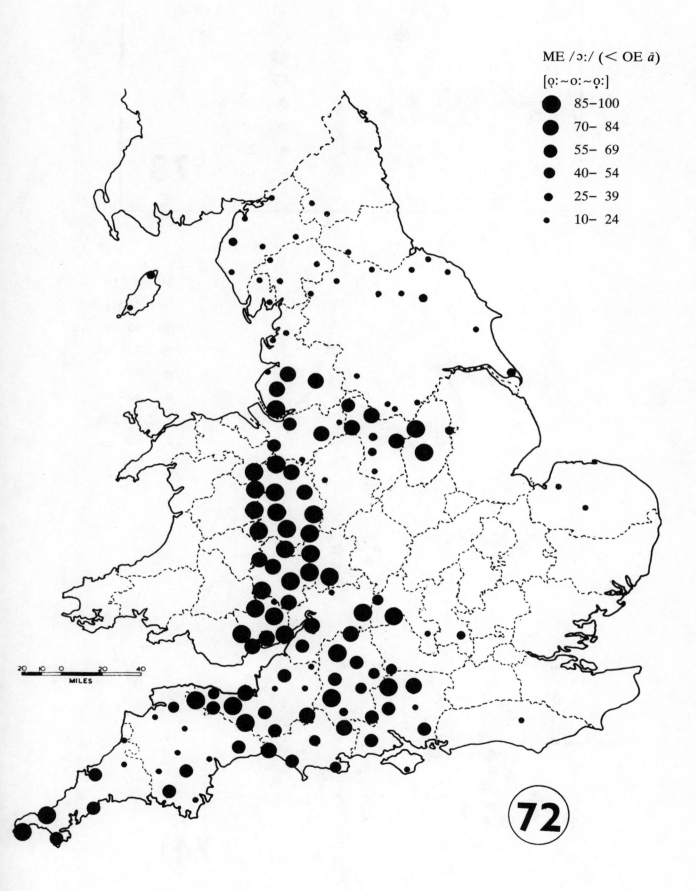

ME /ɔ:/ (< OE ā)

[o̞:~o:~ǫ:]

● 85−100
● 70− 84
● 55− 69
● 40− 54
● 25− 39
· 10− 24

72

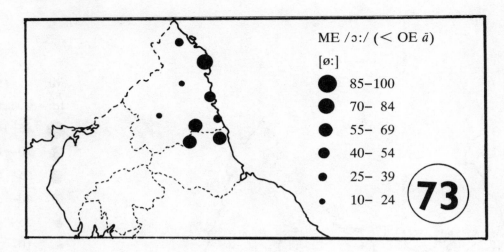

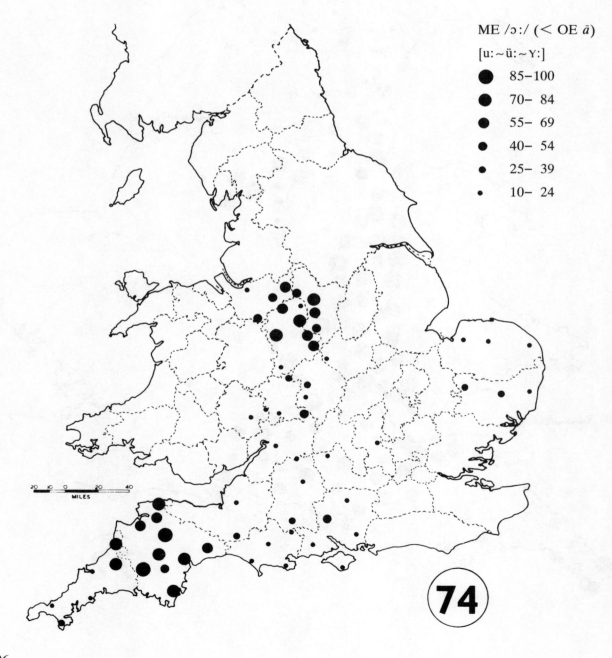

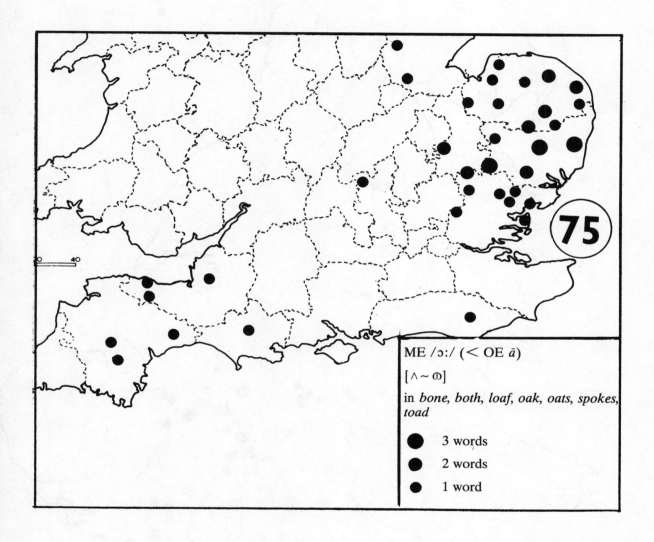

ME /ɔː/ (< OE ā)

[ʌ ~ ɒ]

in *bone, both, loaf, oak, oats, spokes, toad*

● 3 words

● 2 words

● 1 word

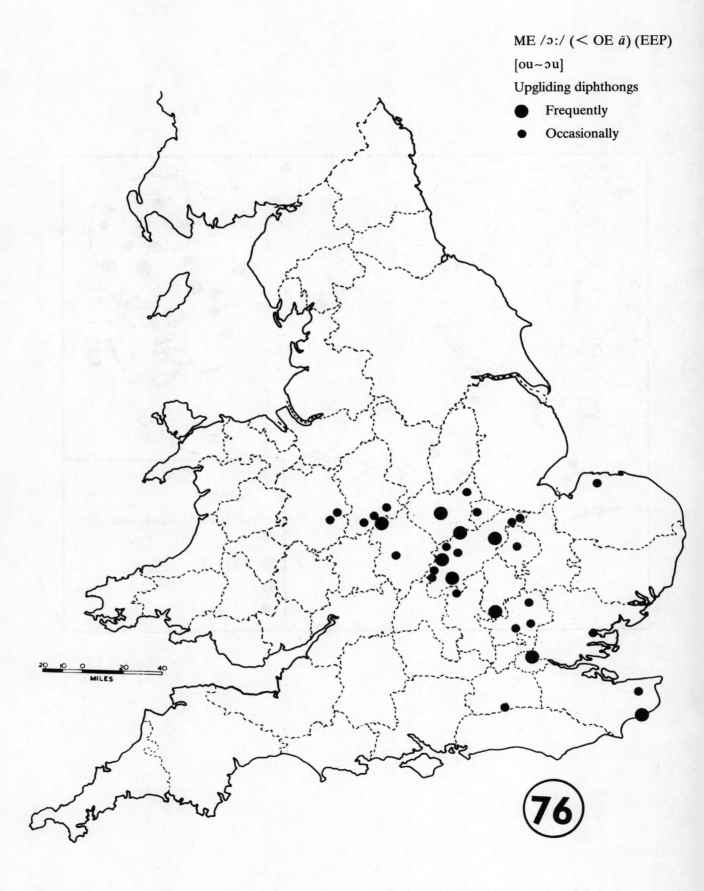

ME /ɔː/ (< OE ā̆) (EEP)

[ou~ɔu]

Upgliding diphthongs

● Frequently

● Occasionally

⟨76⟩

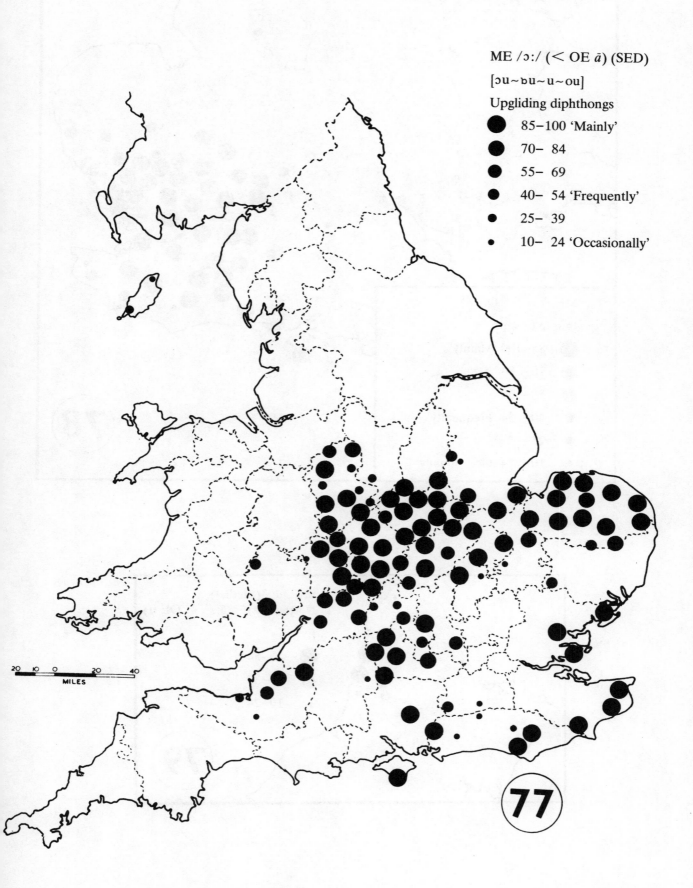

ME /ɔː/ (< OE ā) (SED)

[ɔu~ɒu~u~ou]

Upgliding diphthongs

● 85–100 'Mainly'
● 70– 84
● 55– 69
● 40– 54 'Frequently'
● 25– 39
● 10– 24 'Occasionally'

MILES

77

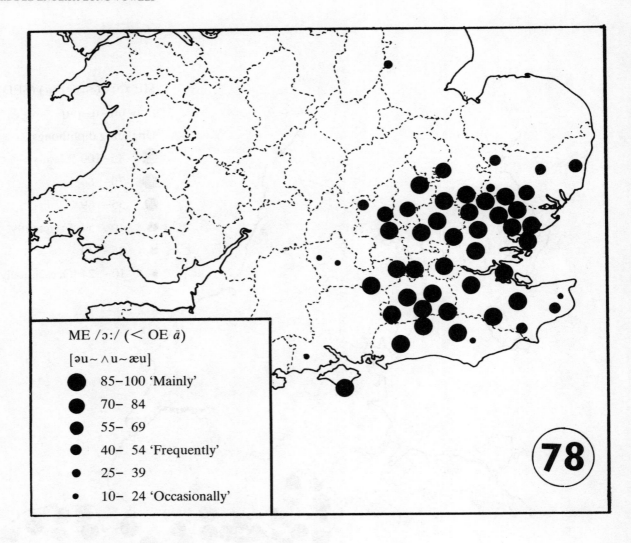

ME /ɔ:/ (< OE ā)

[əu~ ʌu~æu]

- ● 85–100 'Mainly'
- ● 70– 84
- ● 55– 69
- ● 40– 54 'Frequently'
- • 25– 39
- · 10– 24 'Occasionally'

78

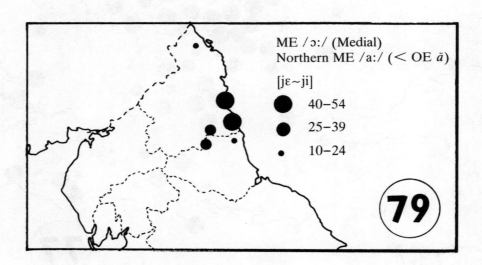

ME /ɔ:/ (Medial)
Northern ME /a:/ (< OE ā)

[jɛ~ji]

- ● 40–54
- ● 25–39
- · 10–24

79

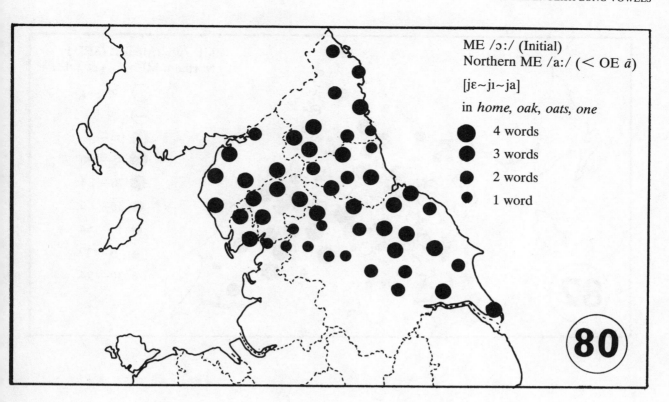

ME /ɔ:/ (Initial)
Northern ME /a:/ (< OE ā)

[jɛ~jɪ~ja]

in *home, oak, oats, one*

⬤ 4 words

● 3 words

● 2 words

• 1 word

80

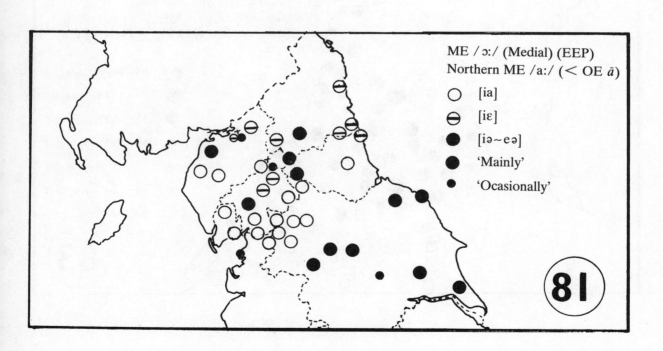

ME /ɔ:/ (Medial) (EEP)
Northern ME /a:/ (< OE ā)

◯ [ia]

⊖ [iɛ]

⬤ [iə~eə]

● 'Mainly'

• 'Ocasionally'

81

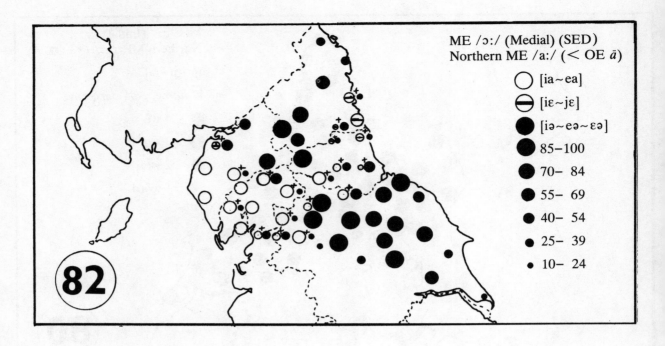

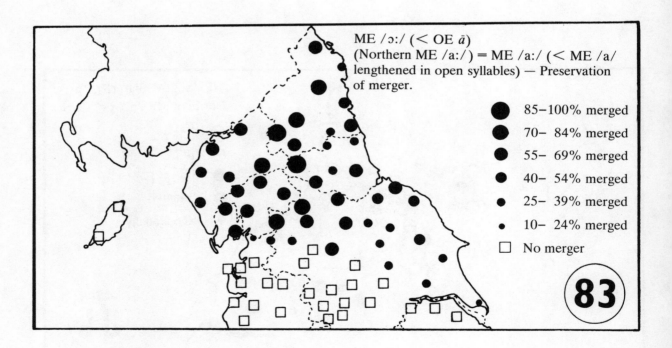

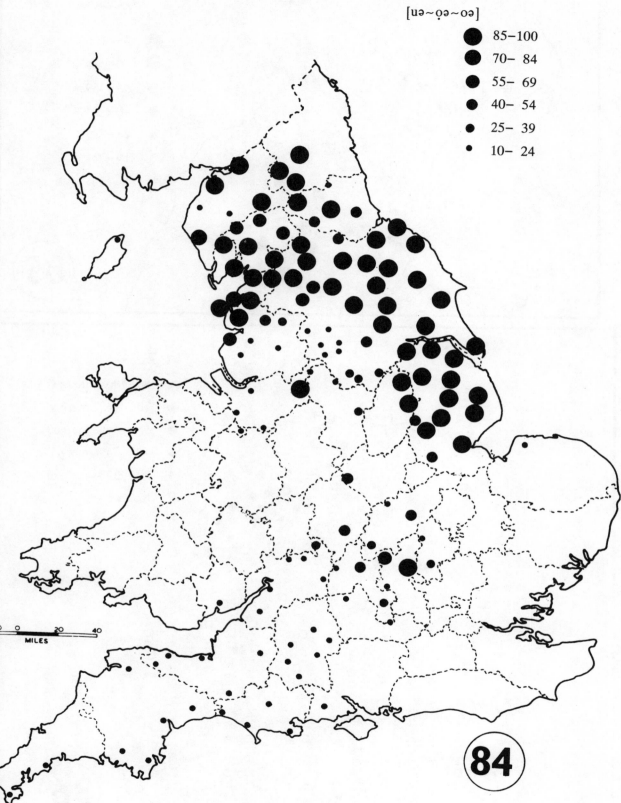

ME /ɔ:/ (< ME /o/ lengthened in open syllables)

[uə~ọə~oə]

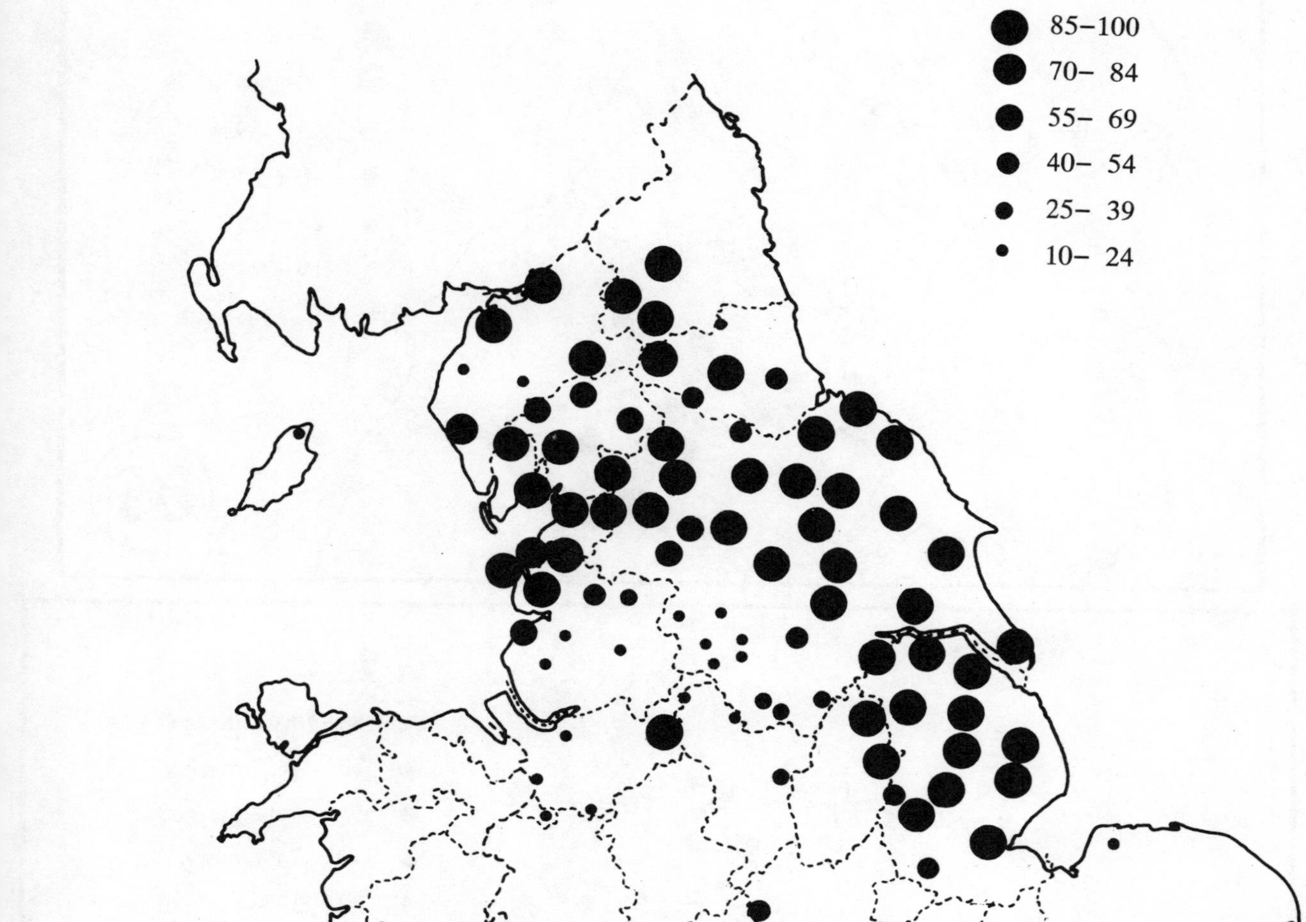
85–100
70– 84
55– 69
40– 54
25– 39
10– 24
20 10 0 20 40
MILES
84

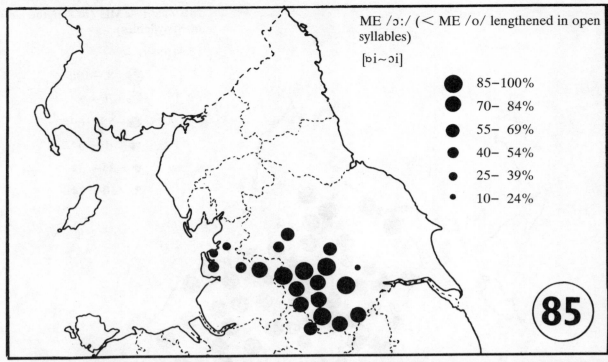

ME /ɔ:/ (< ME /o/ lengthened in open syllables)

[ɒi~ɔi]

- ● 85–100%
- ● 70– 84%
- ● 55– 69%
- ● 40– 54%
- • 25– 39%
- • 10– 24%

85

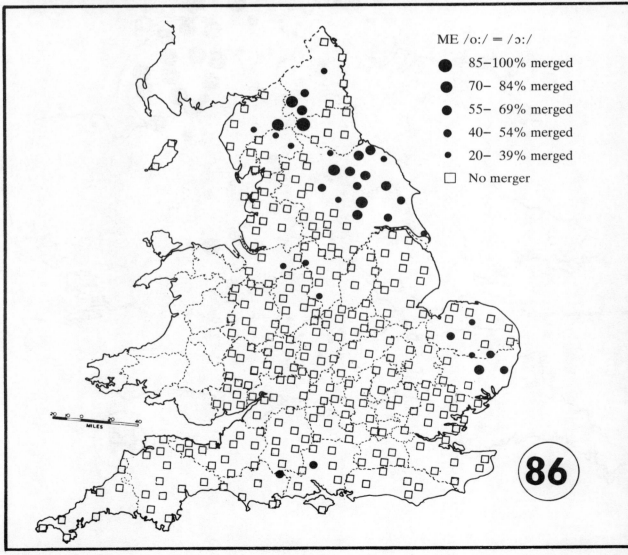

ME /o:/ = /ɔ:/

- ● 85–100% merged
- ● 70– 84% merged
- ● 55– 69% merged
- • 40– 54% merged
- • 20– 39% merged
- □ No merger

86

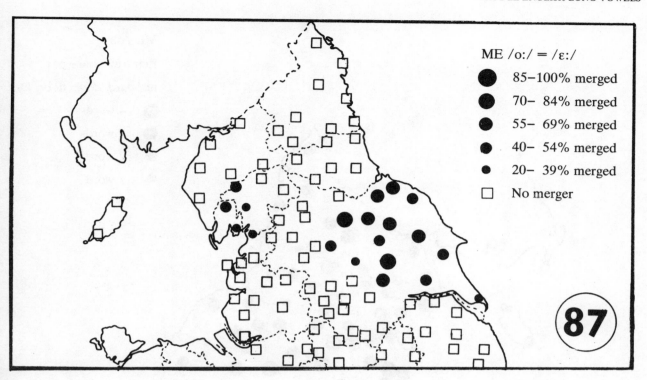

ME /o:/ = /ɛ:/

- ● 85–100% merged
- ● 70– 84% merged
- ● 55– 69% merged
- ● 40– 54% merged
- • 20– 39% merged
- ☐ No merger

87

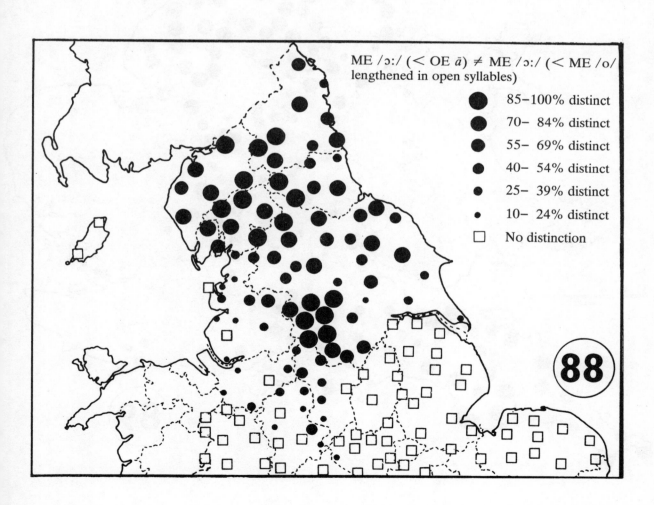

ME /ɔ:/ (< OE ā) ≠ ME /ɔ:/ (< ME /o/ lengthened in open syllables)

- ● 85–100% distinct
- ● 70– 84% distinct
- ● 55– 69% distinct
- ● 40– 54% distinct
- • 25– 39% distinct
- • 10– 24% distinct
- ☐ No distinction

88

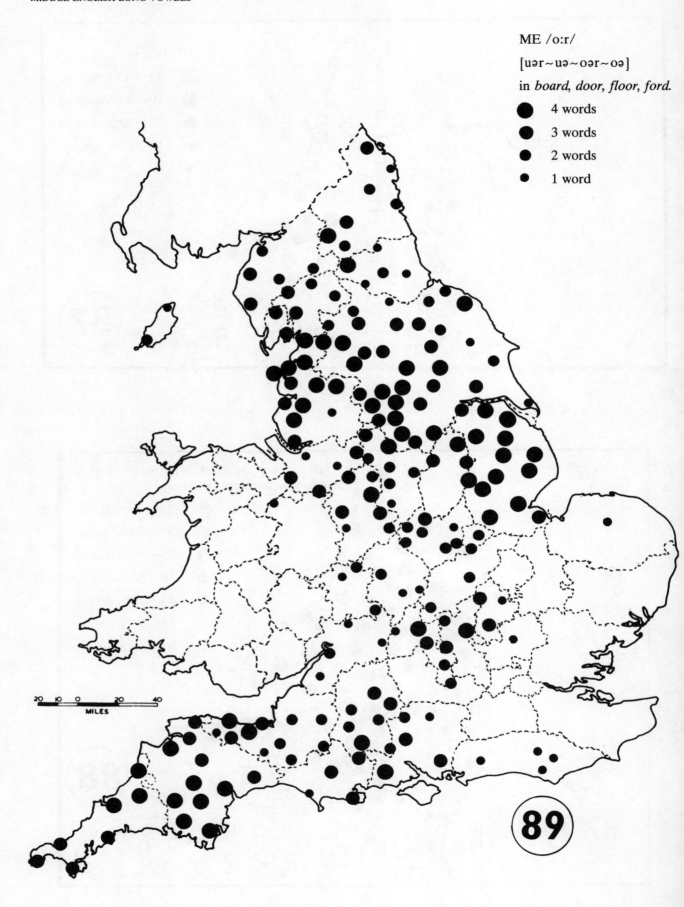

ME /oːr/

[uər~uə~oər~oə]

in *board, door, floor, ford.*

● 4 words

● 3 words

• 2 words

· 1 word

89

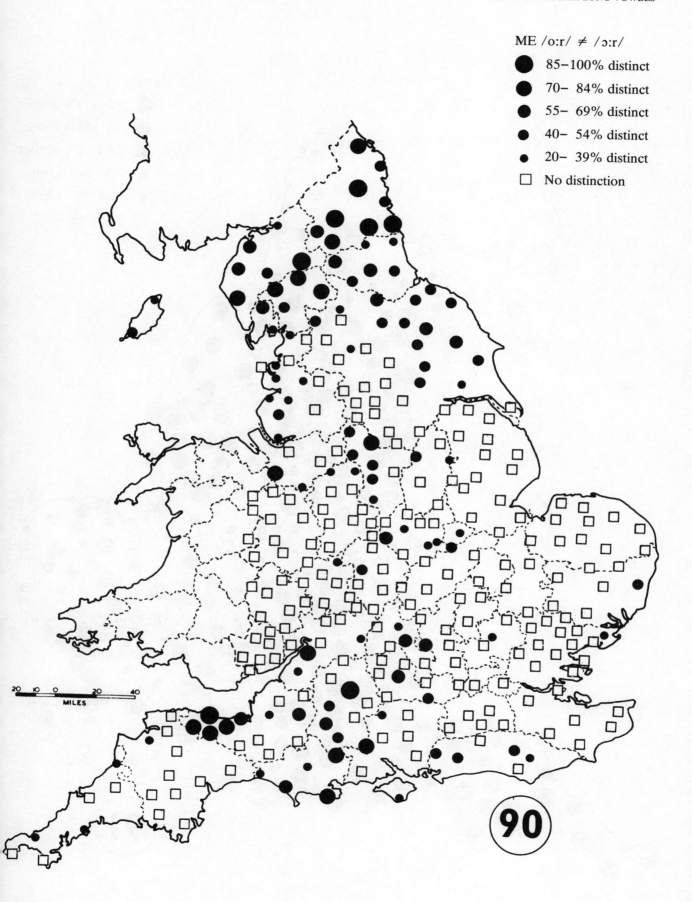

ME /oːr/ ≠ /ɔːr/

● 85–100% distinct
● 70– 84% distinct
● 55– 69% distinct
● 40– 54% distinct
• 20– 39% distinct
□ No distinction

MILES

90

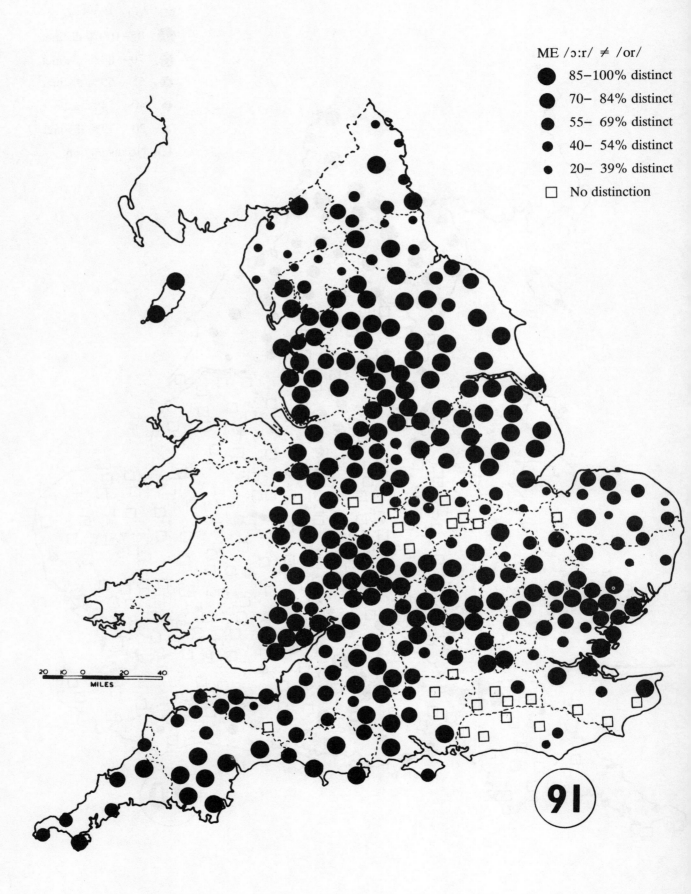

ME /ɔːr/ ≠ /or/

● 85–100% distinct
● 70– 84% distinct
● 55– 69% distinct
• 40– 54% distinct
· 20– 39% distinct
□ No distinction

91

MILES

20 10 0 20 40

NOTES

1. Mencken, 1963, pp. 463, 470.

2. Orton, 1933, para. 107.

3. A similar split in the development of ME /i:/ following /w/ is reported for Naunton (Gloucestershire). The development there presupposes a merger with ME /ui/. This may also account for the Cheshire pronunciation but more likely it is the result of merger with ME /e:/. Barth, 1968, paras. 83, 97.

4. SED records [ᾶɪ] from Sheffield but the usual pronunciation nowadays is [aɪ~a·ɪ] though [ɑɪ] may be heard from older working class males.

5. See also Barth, 1968, para. 55 where the sound is transcribed [oɷ].

6. Kurath and Lowman, 1970, pp. 4–6 indicate that the feature was more extensive in Lowman's field recordings from 1936–37.

7. Dobson, 1968, vol. I, p. 142.

8. [ɛɷ~æɷ] areas are separated from the [u:] region in the North by forms of the [aɷ] type. Within the [u:] region there are forms showing centralised onsets [ᵊu:~ᵚu:]. These forms can be seen as transitional between [u:] and [ɛɷ].

9. Samuels, 1972, p. 43.

10. See also Ellis, 1887, p. 427 where [aɪ] is also reported for north east Derbyshire.

11. Samuels, 1972, para. 2.5.

12. The loss of final unstressed schwa and the lengthening of short vowels in open syllables clearly had dramatic effects on the stress and tempo of all types of English.

13. Ellis, 1889, pp. 563 et seq.

14. Ellis, 1889, p. 43.

15. Ellis, 1889, p. 497 records [ɛə] for ME /a:/ from the marshland area bordering Lincolnshire (Snaith, near Goole).

16. Ellis, 1889, p. 397.

17. Dean, 1962, para. 58, comes down in favour of 'traditional [ɪə]' in all positions in north Yorkshire. He sees [ja] as a later importation from the north where it is regular. This is a tenable view but if it is correct [ja] has certainly been helped in its spread by suprasegmental features.

18. Orton, 1933, paras. 364-371.

19. Dobson, 1968, para. 229, note 1. 'It would follow of course that in these dialects ME ẹ̄ had become [e:], ME ę̄ [i:] and ME i [əɪ] before 1450 and in the NW Midlands perhaps before 1425 but such a conclusion dos not seem to conflict with other evidence on dialectal developments.'

20. Patchett in TYDS 1981, pp. 24 et seq.

21. Dobson, 1968, para. 229.

22. Ekwall, 1951, Ekwall, 1956.

23. Dobson, 1968, pp. 147 et seq.

24. The continuing influence of the Midland dialects cannot be doubted. [æ] < ME /a:/ is a distinctly old-fashioned type in RP where it has been displaced by [a] most likely from the central Midlands.

25. Dobson, 1968, para. 228, note 5, where spellings are quoted showing mergers in the fifteenth century.

26. Ellis, 1889, p. 226.

27. It is possible that so-called Cockney before this date did not reflect typical spoken usage but rather a conventional 'literary' dialect.

28. Ellis, 1889, p. 226.

29. Samuels, 1972, para. 2.5.

30. Ellis, 1889, p. 80*.

31. See DeCamp, 1969, pp. 355-368.

32. In Northumberland there is a positional development [ĕɪ~ɛ̆ɪ] appearing in final position only.

33. See SED III.6.1 SHEEP and VII.3.1 WEEK. In *week* the short vowel may be due to the failure of lengthening of ME /i/ to ME /e:/.

34. OE $\bar{æ}_1$ (< Primitive Germanic $\bar{æ}$) becomes $\bar{e}$ in non-West Saxon dialects but remains in West Saxon. By the late OE period it appears to have spread to parts of the south Midlands and East Anglia. OE $\bar{æ}_2$ remains everywhere except in Kentish where it becomes $\bar{e}$. There was therefore a basis for vacillation between /e:/ and /ɛ:/ in ME.

35. Dobson, 1968, para. 107.

36. This [ɪɷ] type is actually recorded by SED at 18 Nth 5 occasionally and frequently at 5 La 12. In the dialects of the north-west and south-west Midlands there appear to be three vowels in unstressed syllables: /ɪ/, /ə/ and /ɷ/, whereas elsewhere there are only two: (/ɪ/ and /ə/). /ɷ/ typically occurs in conjunction with an element of secondary stress (e.g. Cheshire ['ɡɹɪndlˌstɷn] *grindstone* and ['ˈkaɷˌmɷn] *cowman*). It is suggested that [ɪɷ] and hence [jɷ~jʌ] arose when stress began to be shifted to the second element eventually giving a rising diphthong. The west Midlands has other examples of stress-shifting. For example, the development of OE $\bar{e}aw$ to /jɔɷ/ in the Cotswolds (see 4.13). Also to be noted is the curious form [fjɔf] *flea* recorded from Shropshire (and by me in Cheshire) which seems to arise from a non-Anglian OE *flēah* with shift of stress. Probably the form [ʃɔf] *sheaf* (< OE *scēaf*) should also in part be attributed to this process.

37. Cheshire /ɛɪə/ represents the further development of earlier /ɪə/.

38. Ellis, 1889, pp. 55, 67.

39. See Barth, 1968, para. 78.4. The following forms occur for Naunton dialect:

< ME /ɛ:/ /bjʌn/ *bean*, /bjʌst/ *beast*, /bjʌt/ *beat*, /tʃʌp/ *cheap*, /tʃʌt/ *cheat*, /dʒjʌθ/ *death*, /dʒjʌd/ *dead*, /jʌzi/ *easy*, /jʌt/ *heat*, /jʌd/ *head*, /jʌp/ *heap*, /ljʌd/ *lead*, /ljʌn/ *lean*, /mjʌn/ *mean*, /ʃʌv/ *sheaf*.
< ME /a:/ /kjʌk/ *cake*, /gjʌm/ *game*, /gjʌt/ *gate*, /ʃʌk/ *shake*, /ʃjʌm/ *shame*, /ʃʌv/ *shave*.

40. Devon represents an innovative area in the South West and has done since the ME period. (e.g. the unrounding of ME /y:/ occurs earlier in Devon than in the rest of the South West.)

41. Darlington, 1886, p. 40. Whether these were in free variation or conditioned by context is uncertain. There is no conditioning today. Perhaps some idea of the former use of the two types can be seen in the contrasting use of the word *seam*. This is /si:m/ in isolation but forms the compound /ˈʃɛmrɪpt/ *seam-ripped* referring to a shoe with its sole hanging loose (Cheshire).

42. The /jɛ/ type is absent in the [jɷ~jʌ] areas of the Cotswolds, though there is some overlap along the fringes of the area. It is very unlikely that [jɷ~jʌ] descend from [jɛ] but it is quite likely that the development of rising diphthongs from earlier [ɪə~ɪɷ] deprived the rising diphthong /jɛ/ of its function and it subsequently fell out of use in these areas.

43. Ellis, 1889, pp. 424-447, gives a much clearer picture of contrast.

44. Kökeritz takes a similar view with regard to the Suffolk dialect, supposing that /e:/ types for ME /ɛ:/ have been introduced directly from Standard English. Dobson sees the variation between /e:/ and /i:/ as the result of the raising of ME /ɛ:/ to /e:/ in certain positions (Dobson, 1968, para. 106, note 3).

45. See for example Ellis, 1889, pp. 54 et seq. (Wiltshire), pp. 66 et seq. (Gloucestershire). Barth, 1968, records [jʌ] for both ME /ɛ:/ and ME /a:/ in some words (Naunton, Gloucestershire).

46. For evidence of the merger in Standard English see Dobson, 1968, para. 228.

47. With the exception of Upper Calderdale.

48. Anderson, 1977, vol. 2, p. 22.

49. Dobson, 1968, para. 228.

50. A system which merges ME /a:/, ME /ɛ:/ and ME /ai/ as /i:/ overlies the older system in Cheshire.

51. Ellis, 1889, pp. 248-254 gives evidence of the merger in Cambridgeshire, Rutland and north Northamptonshire.

52. Ellis, 1889, pp. 44-84. In some cases the merger is only shown by the presence of rising diphthongs [jɷ~jʌ] for both ME /a:/ and ME /ɛ:/. In isolative position /e:/ ocurs for both ME /a:/ and ME /ɛ:/.

53. In this position merger with ME /iu/ has taken place in some parts of west Yorkshire.

54. Smith, 1961, et seq. Note especially the following spellings: Vol. I, p. 164 — *boethes* (1452). Vol. III, p. 97 *lez Boethes* < OE (Scandinavian) *bōð* 'booth'.

55. Standard English has /wʌn/ *one* but no [jɛ] types.

56. Raising after /w/ occurs in *two, who*.

57. Development of rising diphthongs is clearly a late ME process (Brunner, 1963, para. 13D−1). The form *whom* 'home' occurs in a ME text of the fifteenth century in Cheshire and in wills of the Tudor period from the same county (see Anderson, 1977, para. 3.17.1).

58. I have recorded [dü:] as a variant of a more common [düə] *door* in Cheshire.

59. There is evidence for west Yorkshire at an early date and the placename spellings tend to suggest that /ɔi/ spread at a later date from the west Yorkshire area into south Yorkshire and the Doncaster area and north into the Keighley area.

4

Middle English Diphthongs

4.1 ME /ai/ (ai) (Maps 92, 94)

The development of a monophthong to represent ME /ai/ is largely a northern and north Midland development extending as far south as Shropshire. In parts of the East from south east Northumberland to Lincolnshire the long monophthong has become an ingliding diphthong (see 4.2). In parts of the central Midlands, notably Staffordshire, an upgliding diphthong has been reintroduced under the influence of a local type of Standard English. ME /ai/ has ceased to be a diphthong in mid Oxfordshire (see 3.13 for a suggested explanation). No diphthongs are found in Monmouthshire or in west Cornwall but in these two areas the long monophthong represents both ME /ai/ and ME /a:/ and is to be attributed to the late arrival of English in these areas. ME /ai/ is usually a close monophthong /i:/ (probably a further development of /e:/) in east and south Cheshire, north and east Staffordshire, west Derbyshire and fringe areas of Leicestershire (Map 94). This is a recessive type which at the time of EEP extended into northern Warwickshire and well into western Leicestershire (see Map 43).

4.2 Ingliding diphthongs (Map 93)

There has been a strong tendency to develop ingliding diphthongs to represent ME /ai/ in much of north eastern England from south Northumberland to south Lincolnshire. In the North East (Northumberland, Durham), a closer type /ẹə~ɪə/ is tending to be generalised for ME /ai/ and for ME /a:/.

4.3 Upgliding diphthongs (Map 95)

Although closer types occur, the major forms are of the [ɛɪ~æɪ~aɪ] type representing retention of the phonetic form of the ME type. Retention is associated with the dialects of the South and south Midlands (together with the Upper Calder valley in west Yorkshire and the Isle of Man). In Leicestershire and south Staffordshire /ɛɪ/ is a relatively

recent substitution for older long monophthongs.

For a discussion of the structural position of ME /ai/ see paragraphs 3.12, 3.28.

4.4 ME /ɔu/ (ọu)

The developments of ME /ɔu/ are quite complicated due to the differing origins of the phoneme and the structural results are correspondingly complex.

4.5 ME /ɔu/ (< OE āw) (Maps 96A–96C)

In the dialects of northern England the unrounded type was retained and merged with ME /au/ (Map 96A). This positional retention of OE ā as an unrounded type is clearly more extensive than the retention in isolative position (see Maps 79–82). The presence of /ɔ:/ in the South West is probably due to the unrounding of ME /ɔu/ to ME /au/ related to the general unrounding of ME /o/ to /ɑ/. The development does not always lead to the merger of ME /au/ and ME /ɔu/ especially in final position (see Map 14).[1]

In the West and South West ME /ɔu/ was monophthongised and remains as such merging in varying degrees with ME /ɔ:/ (Map 96B). The presence of a front rounded vowel in Northumberland is due to an intrusion from Standard English.

Over most of southern England and central and eastern areas, ME /ɔu/ appears as a diphthong (Map 96C). This may represent a retention of the ME type but often the diphthong is the result of a very recent south eastern phonetic innovation which has affected merged ME /ɔ:~ɔu/.

4.6 Late ME /ɔu/ < eME /ɔ:ld/,[2] /ol/, /oxt/[3]

In these groups many dialects developed late ME /ɔu/ which either merged with ME /ɔu/ or had a separate development because ME /ɔu/ had already become a monophthong.

For example:

7 Ch 1 *Kingsley*

		ME /oxt/				
/ɛu/	<	ME /ɔːld/	/o:/	<	ME /ɔu/
		ME /ol/			

By contrast:

10 L 14 *Lutton*

		ME /oxt/
		ME /ɔːld/
/ɔu/	<	ME /ol/
		ME /ᴜɔ/

4.7 Structural relationship of ME /ɔː/ (< OE ā) and ME /ɔu/ (< OE āw) (Map 97)

Two broad areas of contrast are evident, a northern — east Midland — East Anglian area and a south western area centered on the Cotswolds. In fact the Lincolnshire and East Anglian contrasts should be seen as related most closely to the south western type. The northern contrasts depend on the development of OE āw to /au/ and in some dialects on the retention of OE ā as NME /a:/. The southern contrast is maximally /uə/ versus /ɔu/ but this is rarely found, the most common distinction being /o:/ versus /ɔu/. The two phonemes are tending to be merged as diphthongs for ME /ɔː/ spread.[4] Along the edge of this merger zone the contrast seems to be /ou/ versus /ɔu/ — clear evidence of the marginal nature of the contrast in these areas.

Examples of contrasts

			ME /ɔː/ (NME /a:/)	ME /ɔu/ (NME /au/)
1	Nb 3	Thropton	/ɪə/	/a:/
2	Cu 5	Hunsonby	/ɪə/	/ɔ:/
3	Du 2	Ebchester	/ø:/	/a:/
5	La 2	Cartmel	/ea/	/a:/
5	La 9	Read	/ɷə/	/ɔ:/
5	La 12	Harwood	/ʏə/ + /o:/	/o:/
6	Y 10	Helmsley	/ɪə/	/ɔ:/
6	Y 21	Heptonstall	/ɷə/	/ɔ:/
7	Ch 4	Farndon	/üə/ + /o:/	/o:/
8	Db 6	Kniveton	/ü:/ + /o:/	/o:/
10	L 2	Swaby	/ɷə/	/ɔ:/
10	L 12	Sutterton	/ɷə/	/ɔɷ/
15	He 4	Checkley	/o:/	/æɷ/
16	Wo 5	Earls Croome	/o:/	/aɷ/
17	Wa 5	Aston Cantlow	/oɷ/	/ɒɷ/
18	Nth 3	Little Harrowden	/oə/	/ɔɷ/
21	Nf 4	Grimston	/ou/	/ɒɷ/
22	Sf 2	Mendlesham	/ü:/ + /ʌɷ/	/aɷ/ + /ʌɷ/

24	Gl 3	Bream	/oɷ/	/ɒɷ/
25	O 2	Steeple Aston	/ɷə/	/ɔɷ/
31	So 6	Stogursey	/o:/	/oɷ/
37	D 7	Weare Gifford	/o:~u:/	/ɔ:/
38	Do 1	Handley	/u:/ + /o:/	/o:/

Examples of mergers

11	Sa 6	Chirbury	/o:/
12	St 7	Lapley	/oɷ/
13	Lei 8	Goadby	/oɷ~ɔɷ/
18	Nth 1	Warmingham	/äɷ~ɒɷ/
20	C 2	Elsworth	/ʌɷ/
29	Ess 9	Tiptree	/ʌɷ/
33	Berks 4	Inkpen	/oɷ~ɔɷ/
39	Ha 4	Alresford	/oɷ~ɔɷ/

4.8 Structural relationship of ME /au/, /ɔu/ and late ME */ɔu/ < eME /oxt/, /ɔːld/, /ol/ (Maps 98A, 98B)

Two major systems arise: those dialects which have three contrasts and those which have only two as in Standard English (see Maps 98A and 98B). The Standard English contrast is of the 1E type and this is very frequent in the South and in the central Midlands. System 1A is the usual northern type reflecting forms which have NME /au/ as their origin. System 1B is a transitional type found in a band from mid Lancashire to mid Lincolnshire. It shares the northern development of OE āw to ME /au/ and contrasts this phoneme with the later secondary ME*/ɔu/. System 1D is intermediate between the north Midlands system 1B and the Standard system 1E. In this system ME /au/ becomes /ɔ:/ but ME /ɔu/ (including secondary ME */ɔu/) becomes /ɔu/. The system requires retention of ME /ɔu/ without change. The present concentration of the system in two relic areas indicates that it is recessive but there is ample evidence throughout the east Midlands that it once had a much wider distribution. The shrinking of the system is due to the spread of forms for ME /oxt/ which had ME /axt/ (and subsequently /auxt/), i.e. southern types. Type 1G is marginal in the South West and shows the merger of ME /au/, /ɔu/, /oxt/ (southern /au/?) as /ɔ:/ contrasting with ME /ɔːld/, /ol/ as /o:/.

The systems showing three contrasts are concentrated in the North West. System 2A shows (typically):

/ɔ:/	<	ME /au/
/o:/	<	ME /ɔu/
/ɛu~ɔu/	<	Secondary ME */ɔu/

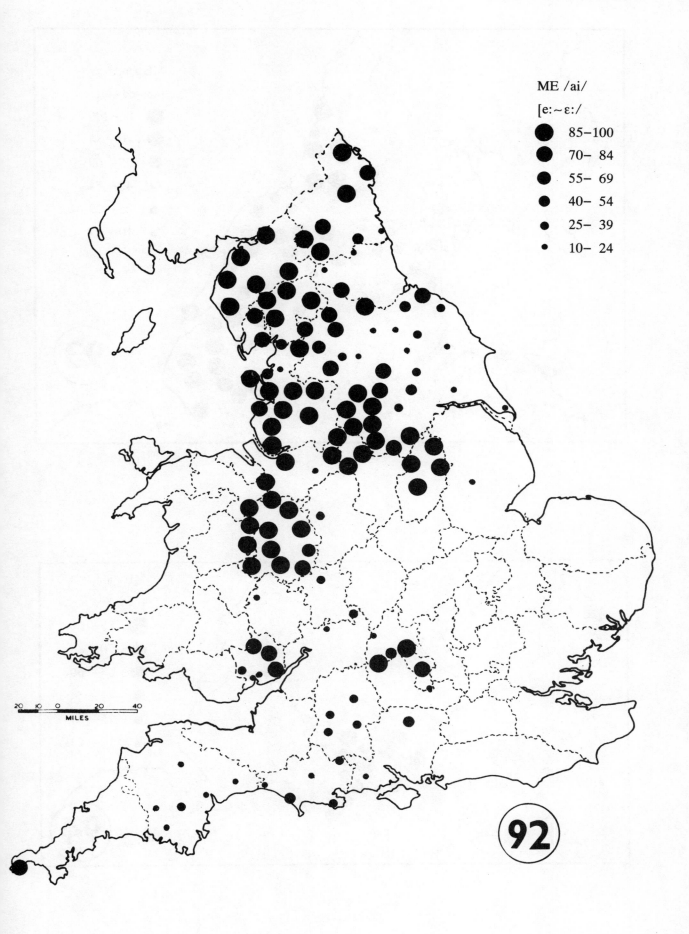

ME /ai/

[e:~ɛ:/

● 85–100
● 70– 84
● 55– 69
● 40– 54
• 25– 39
· 10– 24

92

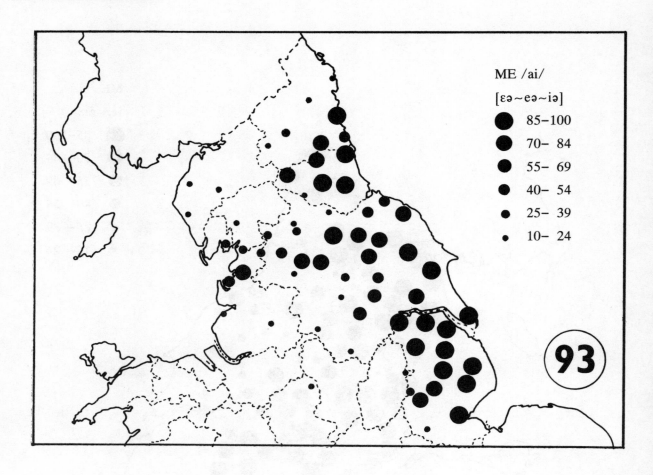

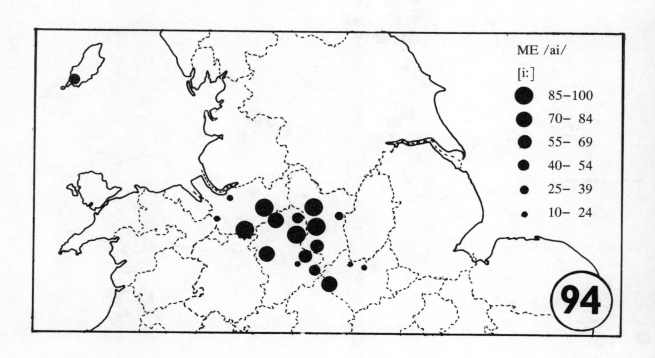

This suggests that ME /ɔu/ was monophthongised before the end of the ME period in this area, certainly before the later ME /ɔu/ developed. Systems 2B and 2C both represent types which show modifications in the direction of the Standard system — 1E .

4.9 ME /iu/ (iu)

Three types of development are to be found.
(a) Retention of a diphthong in all positions.
(b) Loss of diphthong in certain contexts together with reinterpretation of the diphthong as /j/ plus long vowel.
(c) Loss of diphthong in all positions.

4.10 Retention of a diphthong (Map 99)

Retention of ME /iu/ as a diphthong is largely a northern and eastern feature but the diphthong is retained in west Monmouthshire and west Cornwall.

4.11 Loss of diphthong in certain contexts (Map 100A)

The diphthong becomes a long monophthong in most positions and is reinterpreted as /j/ + /u:/ in remaining positions (after /n/, /t/ and sometimes /s/). There is thus a partial merger with ME /o:/ (see 4.14 and Map 103). This accords with the Standard English development which looks to be atypical of the South East region and follows rather the central Midlands. The differences which arise between Standard English and these dialects are distributional, e.g. many dialects drop /j/ after /s/ as Standard English is tending to do in certain words. A further development which is quite widespread is a tendency to affrication, /tj/ and /dj/ becoming /tʃ/ and /dʒ/ respectively.

4.12 Loss of diphthong in all positions (Map 100B)

Map 100B shows the areas in which ME /iu/ is no longer a diphthong. This map needs to be considered in conjunction with Map 100A. /iu/ is lost in all positions in much of Norfolk and Suffolk as well as in a wide belt of central England from mid Staffordshire through Warwickshire, Northamptonshire and Buckinghamshire to Surrey, east Sussex and Kent. ME /iu/ appears as /ʏ:/ in all positions in Devon and north Cornwall as a separate innovation. The widespread distribution of the monophthongal type helps to explain its presence in many types of American English.

4.13 ME /ɛu/ (ęu)

ME /ɛu/ is generally merged with ME /iu/ but this is not the case in Lancashire or west Yorkshire (Map 101). Here it remains as /ɛɷ/. In the Cotswolds, such forms as /fjaɷ/ few do not show retention of the independent phoneme but rather derive from late Old English forms which shifted stress which developed via ME /ɔu/ (< OE eắw) (Map 102). The word ewe (SED III.6.6) is a special case and shows stress-shifted forms in many dialects.

4.14 Structural relationship of ME /iu/ and ME /o:/ (Map 103)

Most of northern England retains a contrast which depends on the retention of ME /iu/ as a diphthong.

Examples

			ME /o:/	ME /iu/
1	Nb 1	Haltwhistle	/ɪə/	/ɪu/
2	Cu 2	Abbeytown	/ɪɷ/	/ɪu/
3	Du 2	Ebchester	/ɪɷ ~ jɤ/	/ɪu/
3	Du 3	Wearhead	/ɪə/	/ɪu/
5	La 6	Pilling	/u:/	/ɪu/
6	Y 20	Nafferton	/u:/ + /ɪə/	/ɪɷ/ + /ju:/
6	Y 26	Thornhill	/ɷɪ/	/ɪu/
7	Ch 1	Kingsley	/ʏ:/	/ɪʏ ~ /jʏ:/
10	L 9	Scopwick	/u:/	/ɪu/
29	Ess 4	Henham	/u:/	/ɪu/

Over much of the South and the west Midlands there is a partial merger with ME /o:/ and because of the reinterpretation of the diphthong as a sequence of two phonemes, the /iu/ phoneme as a structural unit is effectively lost.

4.15 Merger of ME /iu/ and ME /o:/

ME /iu/ is merged with ME /o:/ in:
(a) North west Yorkshire (as /iu/)
(b) Norfolk and Suffolk (as /əü ~ ü:/)
(c) Northampton, Buckinghamshire, Surrey and Kent (as /ü: ~ u:/)
(d) Devon and east Cornwall (as /ʏ:/)

4.16 ME /ɔi/, /ui/ (ME oi, ui)

Map 104 is a tentative summary of the phonemic status of ME /ɔi ~ ui/ in relation to ME /i:/. There are broadly four areas of contrast covering northern England and east England as far as Norfolk, the Welsh Border, the South East and the South West.

125

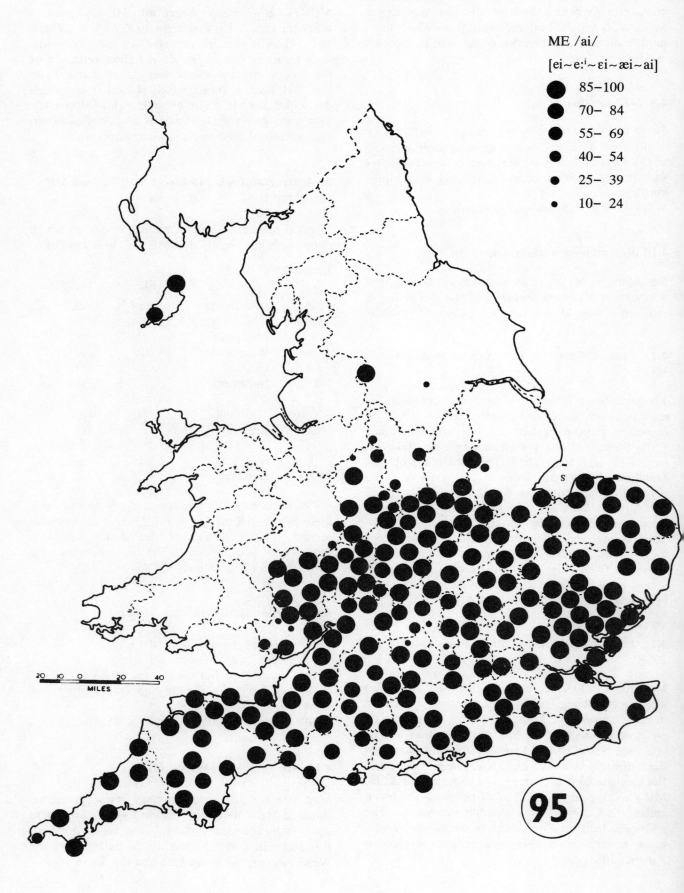

ME /ai/

[ei~e:ⁱ~ɛi~æi~ai]

● 85–100

● 70– 84

● 55– 69

● 40– 54

• 25– 39

· 10– 24

95

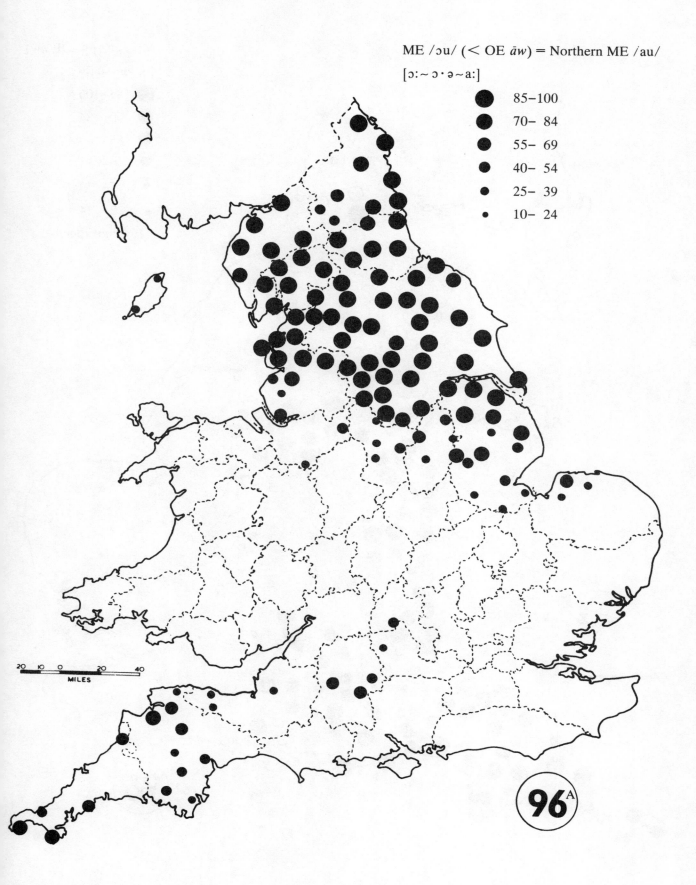

ME /ɔu/ (< OE āw) = Northern ME /au/

[ɔ:~ ɔ·ə~a:]

● 85–100
● 70– 84
● 55– 69
● 40– 54
● 25– 39
● 10– 24

96ᴬ

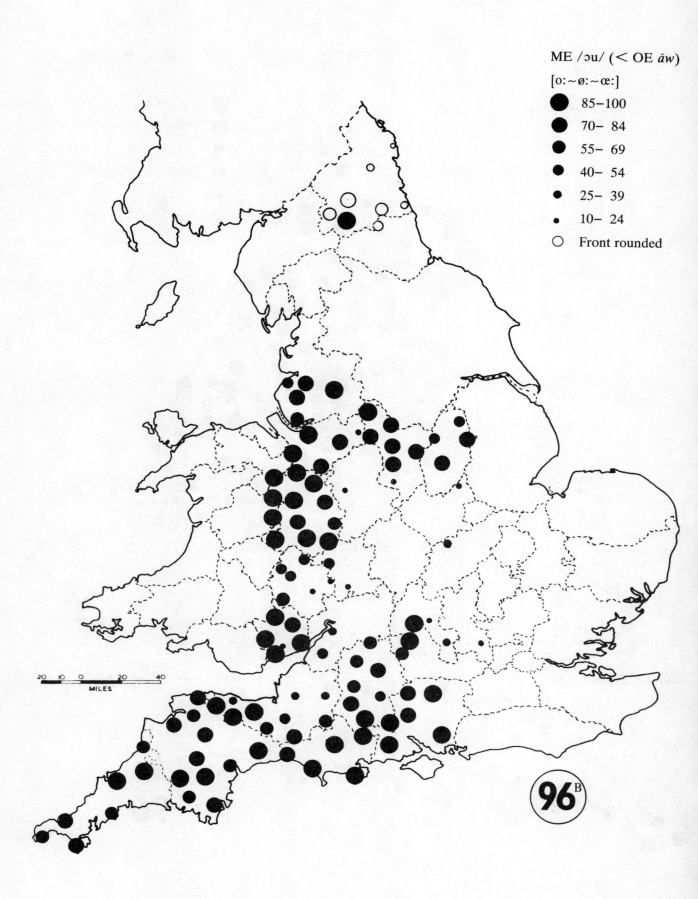

ME /ɔu/ (< OE āw)

[o:~ø:~œ:]

● 85–100
● 70– 84
● 55– 69
● 40– 54
• 25– 39
· 10– 24
○ Front rounded

96ᴮ

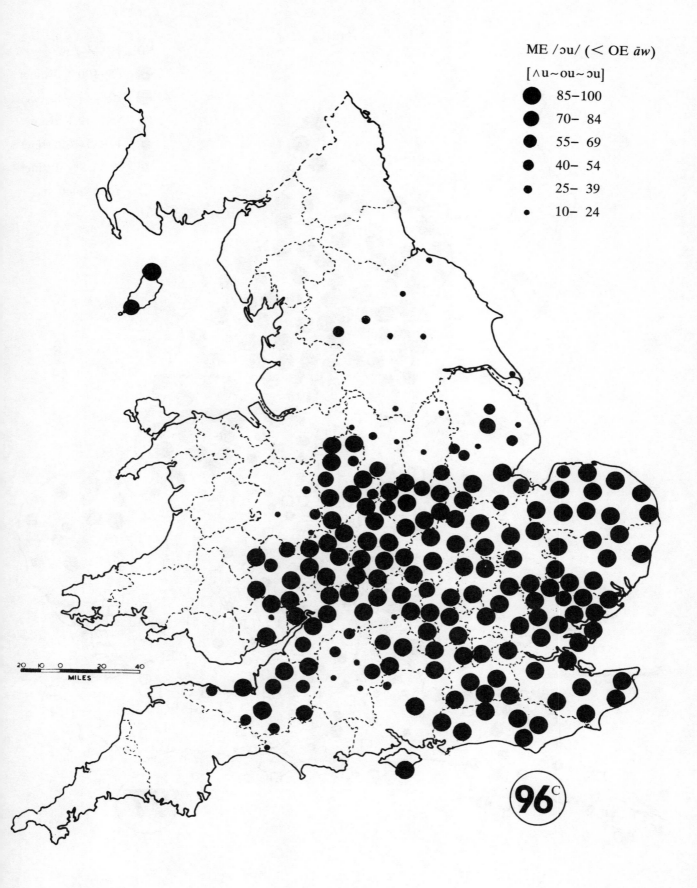

ME /ɔu/ (< OE āw)

[ʌu~ou~ɔu]

● 85–100
● 70– 84
● 55– 69
● 40– 54
• 25– 39
· 10– 24

96ᶜ

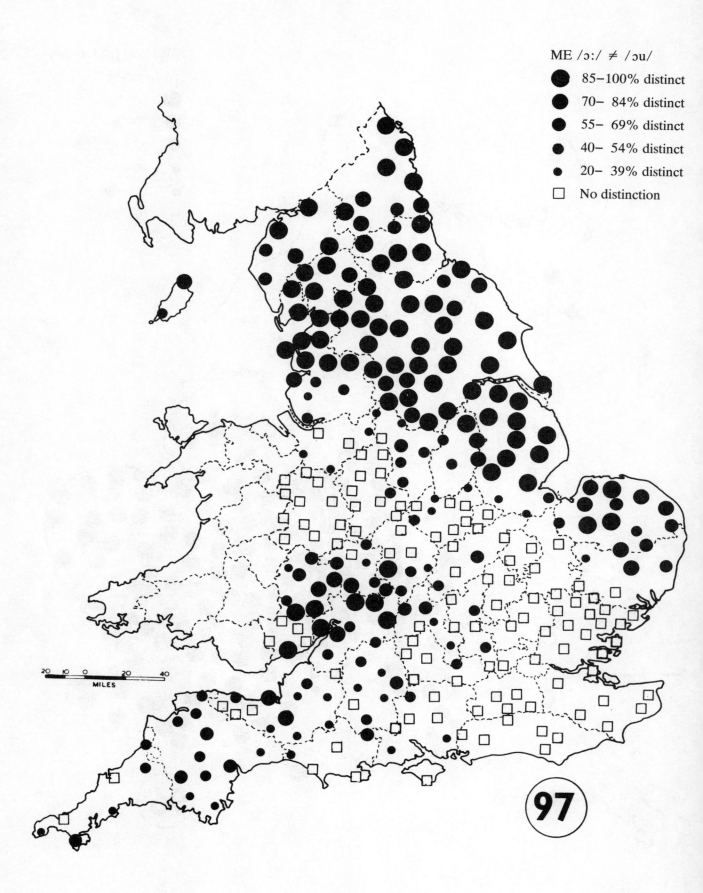

ME /ɔ:/ ≠ /ɔu/

- ● 85–100% distinct
- ● 70– 84% distinct
- ● 55– 69% distinct
- ● 40– 54% distinct
- ● 20– 39% distinct
- □ No distinction

97

Structural relationship of ME

/au/,   /ɔu/,   /oxt/,   /ɔ:ld/,   /ol/

(1)   (2)   (3)   (4)   (5)

Secondary Systems

○	1A	1=2=4 / 3=5
⊖	1B	1=2 / 3=4=5
⊕	1C	1=2=5 / 3=4
⦷	1D	1 / 2=3=4=5
⟜○	1E	1=3 / 2=4=5
⊖	1F	1=2=3=4 / 5
⊕	1G	1=2=3 / 4=5
Γ	2A	1 / 2 / 3=4=5
□	2B	1=3 / 2=5 / 4
⊔	2C	1=3 / 2 / 4=5

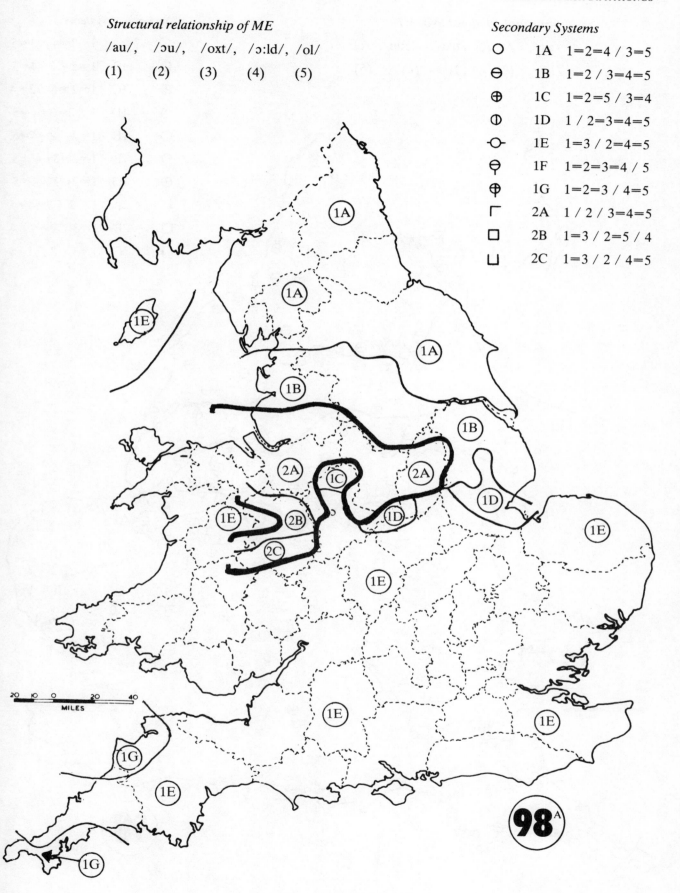

Structural relationship of ME

/au/, /ɔu/, /oxt/, /ɔːld/, /ol/

(1)   (2)   (3)   (4)   (5)

Secondary Systems

O	1A	1=2=4 / 3=5
⊖	1B	1=2 / 3=4=5
⊕	1C	1=2=5 / 3=4
⦶	1D	1 / 2=3=4=5
⦵	1E	1=3 / 2=4=5
⨁	1F	1=2=3=4 / 5
⊕	1G	1=2=3 / 4=5
⌐	2A	1 / 2 / 3=4=5
☐	2B	1=3 / 2=5 / 4
⊔	2C	1=3 / 2 / 4=5

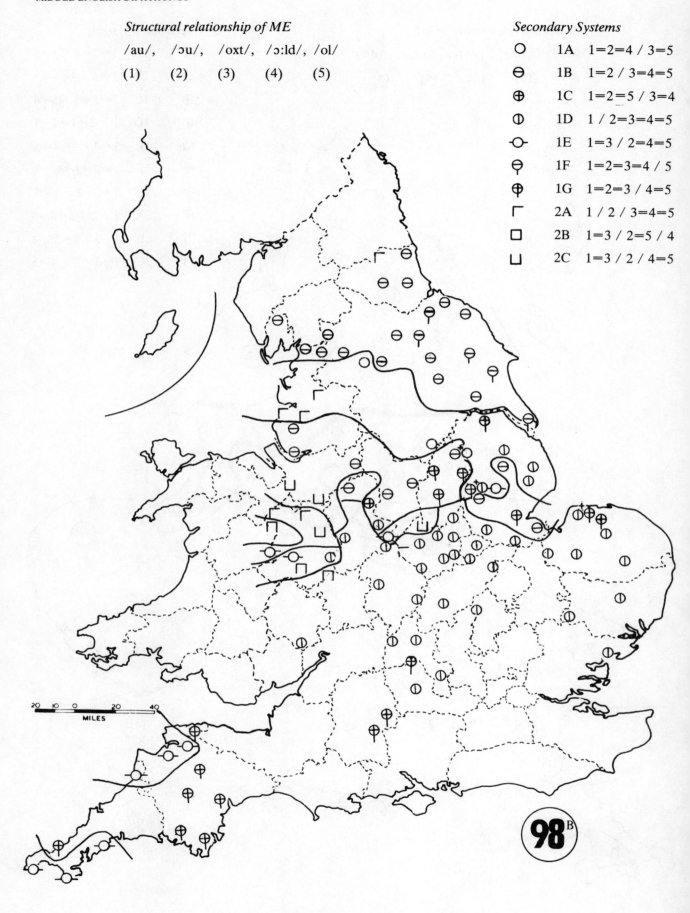

98ᴮ

132

ME /iu/

[iu]

in *new, suet, suit, tune, Tuesday*

● 85–100

● 70– 84

● 55– 69

● 40– 54

• 20– 39

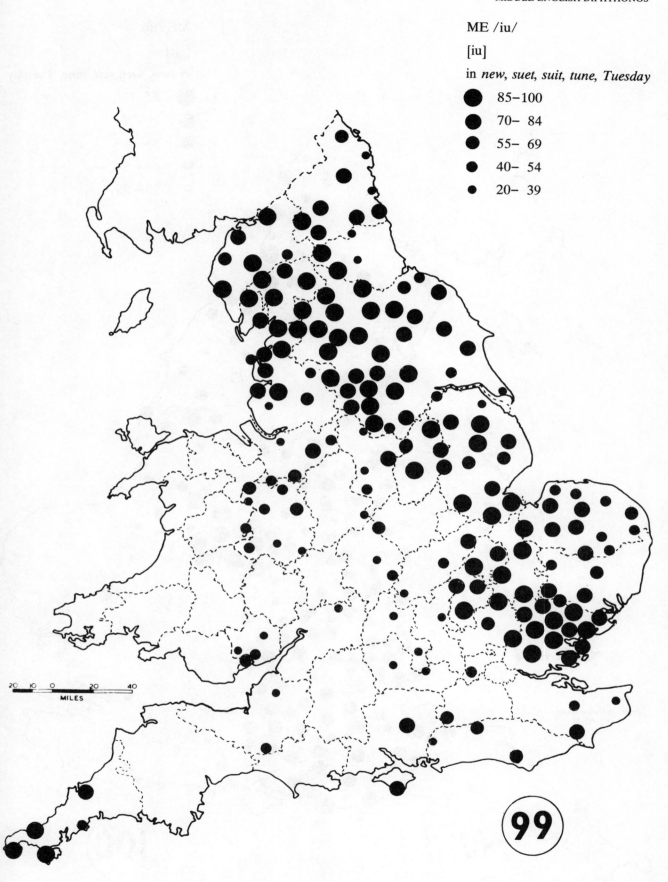

MILES

99

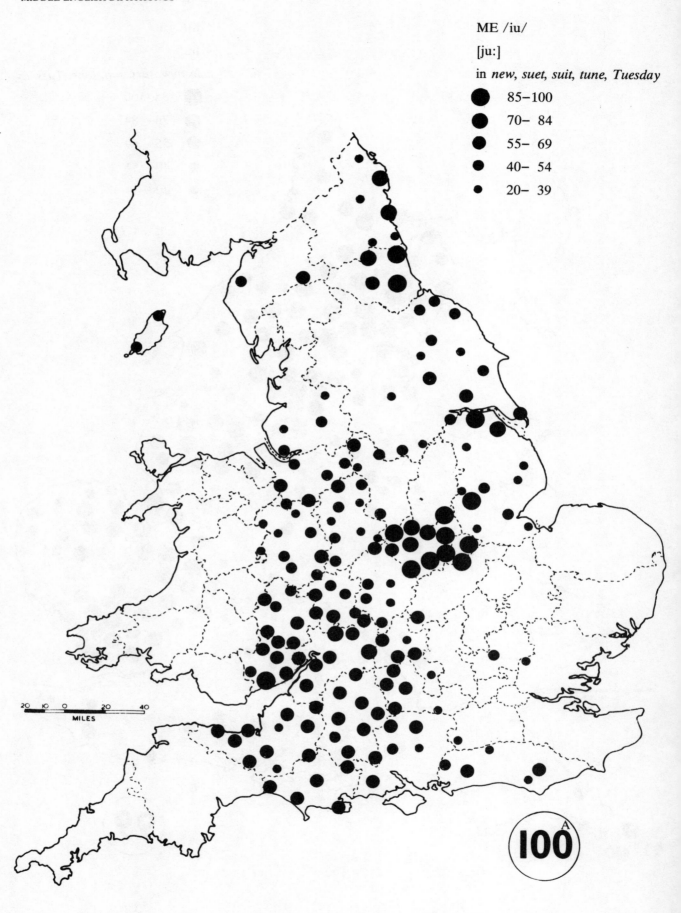

ME /iu/

[ju:]

in *new, suet, suit, tune, Tuesday*

- 85–100
- 70– 84
- 55– 69
- 40– 54
- 20– 39

100 A

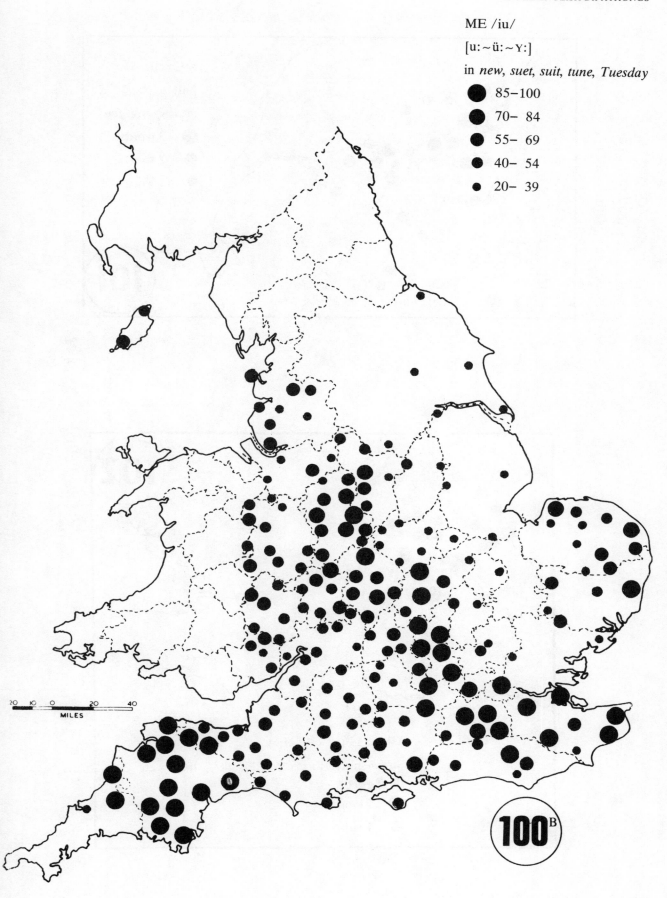

ME /iu/

[uː ∼ üː ∼ ʏː]

in *new, suet, suit, tune, Tuesday*

● 85–100

● 70– 84

● 55– 69

● 40– 54

• 20– 39

100ᴮ

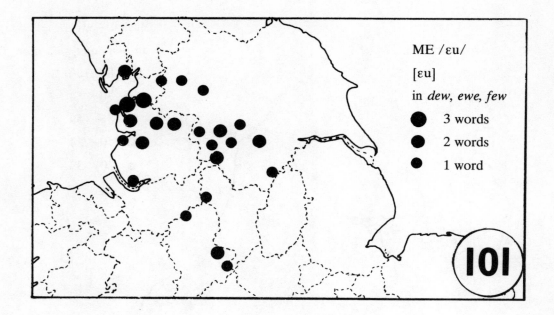

ME /ɛu/

[ɛu]

in *dew, ewe, few*

● 3 words

● 2 words

• 1 word

101

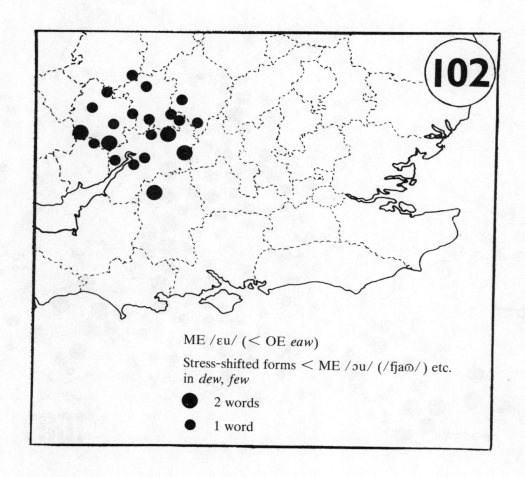

102

ME /ɛu/ (< OE *eaw*)

Stress-shifted forms < ME /ɔu/ (/fjaʊ/) etc.
in *dew, few*

● 2 words

• 1 word

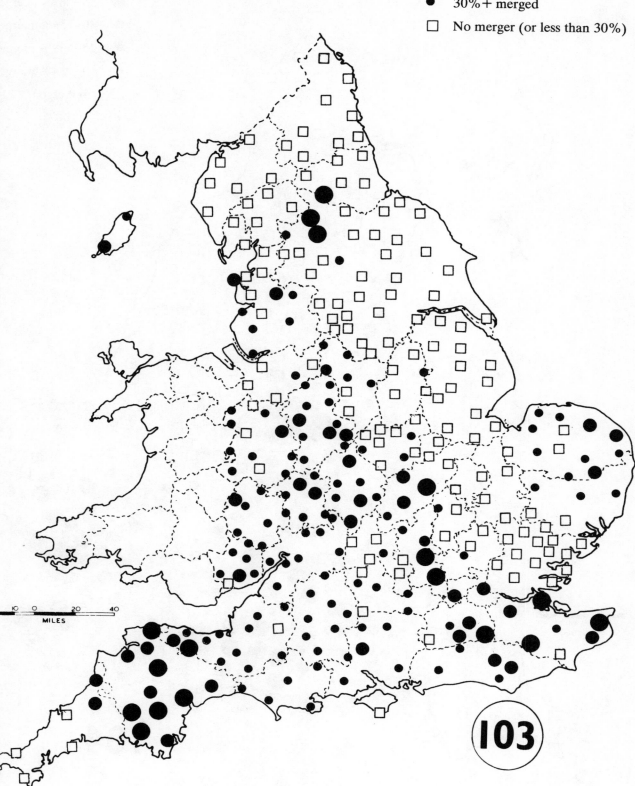

ME /iu/ = /oː/

● 70%+ merged

● 50%+ merged

• 30%+ merged

□ No merger (or less than 30%)

MILES

103

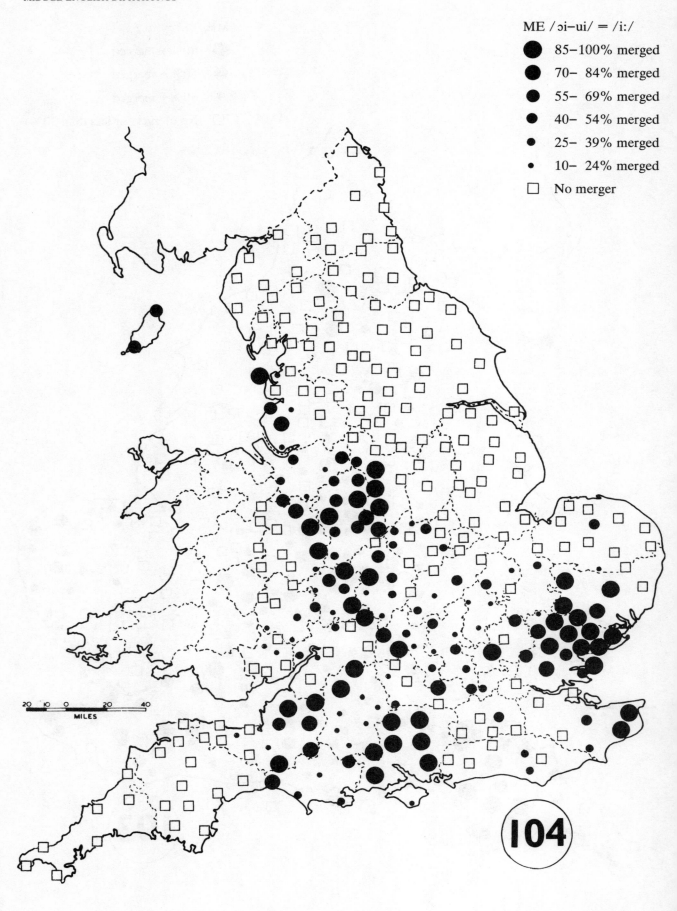

ME /ɔi–ui/ = /iː/

● 85–100% merged
● 70– 84% merged
● 55– 69% merged
● 40– 54% merged
● 25– 39% merged
· 10– 24% merged
□ No merger

104

Examples of contrasts

		/ɔi~ui/	/i:/
1 Nb 1	Lowick	/ɔɪ/	/ɛɪ/
4 We 3	Soulby	/ɒɪ/	/aɪ/
5 La 8	Ribchester	/ɔɪ/	/aɪ/
5 La 12	Harwood	/ɛɪ/	/a:/
6 Y 9	Borrowby	/ɔɪ/	/aɪ/
6 Y 34	Sheffield	/ɒɪ/	/ɑɪ/
7 Ch 3	Swettenham	/ɛɪ/	/ɑɪ/
10 L 12	Sutterton	/ɔɪ/	/ɑɪ/
11 Sa 4	Montfond	/ɒɪ/	/ɛɪ/
11 Sa 9	Clun	/ɒɪ/	/aɪ/
18 Nth 2	Welford	/oɪ/	/ɑɪ/
21 Nf 8	Gooderstone	/ɔɪ/	/ʌɪ/
34 Sr 2	East Clandon	/ɒɪ/	/ɑɪ/
36 Co 5	Gwinear	/ʌɪ/	/æɪ/
37 D 11	Blackawton	/ʌɪ/	/æ:/
40 Sx 3	Sutton	/ɒɪ/	/aɪ/

In most areas the contrast relies on ME /ɔi/ but probably the Devon and Cornwall type /ʌi/ descends from the /ui/. In these areas it is therefore unlikely that the development of ME /i:/ has been via *[ʌɪ] as in Standard English.

In Cheshire and south Lancashire and neighbouring parts of Derbyshire and Staffordshire the current type is descended from ME /ui/ but is not merged with ME /i:/.[6]

4.17 Mergers

The presence of a number of merger areas in the west Midlands, the South and East Anglia has to be seen in the light of the Standard English development. Up till the eighteenth century a merged type was usual in cultivated speech (derived from ME /ui/ and ME /i:/ merged at the *[ʌɪ] stage). From the eighteenth century /ɔi/ came to be reintroduced partly through doubtlets with ME / i/ but also with the support of spelling conventions. The dialects showing mergers frequently had the same development as Standard English but the persistence of the merger is no doubt due to the support of educated Standard English up to the eighteenth century. Some of the mergers represented in the SED material may be due to the development of ME /i:/ to /ɔɪ~ɒɪ/ to merge with ME /ɔi/. In the south west Midlands and in parts of the South, /w/ was developed after /p/ and /b/ absorbing the first element of the diphthong /ui/ and merging with ME /i:/, e.g. */puint/ > */pwi:nt/ > /pwʌint/.

Examples of mergers

5 La 13	Bickerstaffe	/ɑɪ/
7 Ch 6	Hanmer	/aɪ/
8 Db 6	Kniveton	/ɑɪ/
11 Sa 2	Prees	/aɪ/
11 Sa 8	Hilton	/ɒɪ~aɪ/
12 St 6	Hoar Cross	/ɒɪ/
16 Wo 6	Offenham	/ɒɪ/
21 Nf 5	Elmham	/ʌɪ/
22 Sf 5	Kersey	/ɔɪ/
29 Ess 5	Stisted	/ɔɪ/
39 Ha 2	Oakley	/ʌɪ/

NOTES

1. Brunner, 1963, para. 13, note 7.
2. Northern dialects: /au/ < OE *ald.*
3. Southern dialects: /au/ as in *daughter.*
4. For example Suffolk /ʌɪ̃/. On the other hand Norfolk seems to contrast /ou/ v /ɔɪ̃/.
5. See Anderson, 1978, for a detailed discussion of this development in relation to the dialects of the north west Midlands.
6. Dobson, 1968, paras. 252–263.

5

Middle English Consonants

5.1 Consonants

The consonant system shows much less variation than the vocalic system in all the English dialects. There are however a few well-marked structural differences and some distributional variations.

5.2 ME /f, s, θ/ in initial position

In Old English, voiceless and voiced consonants were in complementary distribution, the voiced allophone occurring in medial positions. In the southern dialects OE had voiced consonants /v, z, ð/ in initial position. In ME, long consonants were shortened which brought /f/ (< OE *ff*) into contrast with /v/ in medial position. Later, final /ə/ was lost resulting in contrasts appearing in final position, e.g. *life* versus *live*. The remaining initial contrast arose through the borrowing of words with initial /v/ or /z/ from French and also from the southern dialects (e.g. *vat, vetch, vixen*). In the southern dialects, the development was much the same in medial and final position. In initial position, the contrast arose by the arrival of loanwords from French with initial /f, s/. There appears to have been some resistance to the development of a contrast in initial position in some parts of the South West (Devon, Hampshire) where the loanwords developed initial voiced sounds by analogy with native words. Contrasts developed in Wiltshire, Somerset and Gloucestershire (Map 105–108). In initial position only /ð/ occurs in the southern dialects being frequently simplified to /d/ before /r/ (Maps 109–110).

5.3 Retention of /h/ (Map 111)

/h/ is retained in four main areas, the northern counties as far south as Westmorland and north west Yorkshire, the Isle of Man, East Anglia and in the south western counties of Somerset (except west Somerset), south Wiltshire and north Dorset. A sprinkling of forms in the South East suggests re-introduction from Standard English.

5.4 Retention of /hw/ (Map 112)

/hw/ has been voiced in all areas except Northumberland, north Cumberland and the Isle of Man. The Tyneside area shows a tendency to voice.

5.5 Loss of /v/ (Map 113)

ME /v/ becomes /w/ in East Anglia and also in east Buckinghamshire. The phenomenon is a relic wherever it occurs but clearly the distribution areas were continuous in the past.

5.6 Loss of /w/ (Map 114)

ME /w/ is lost by assimilation to a close back vowel in the west Midlands and the South West and as a relic form in East Anglia and the South East.

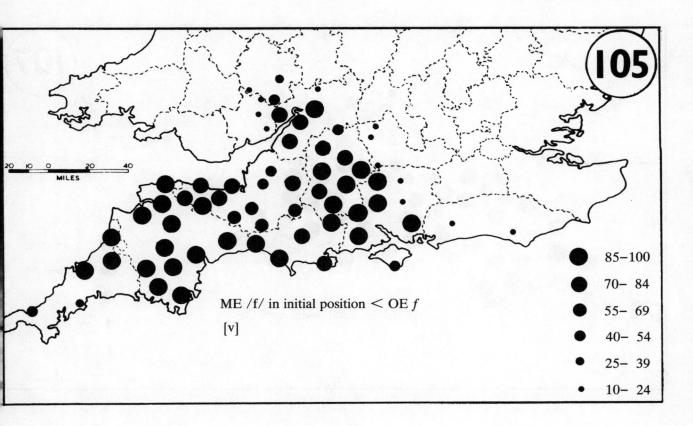

ME /f/ in initial position < OE *f*

[v]

85–100
70– 84
55– 69
40– 54
25– 39
10– 24

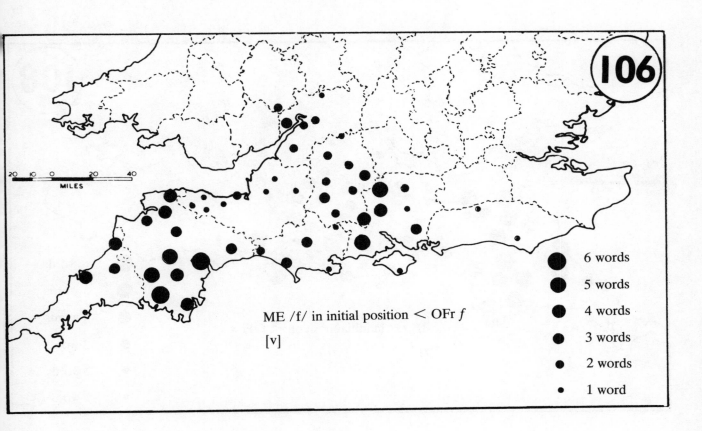

ME /f/ in initial position < OFr *f*

[v]

6 words
5 words
4 words
3 words
2 words
1 word

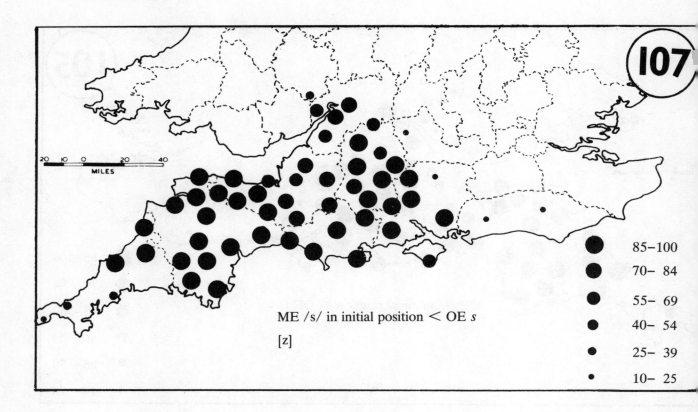

107

ME /s/ in initial position < OE *s*

[z]

- 85–100
- 70– 84
- 55– 69
- 40– 54
- 25– 39
- 10– 25

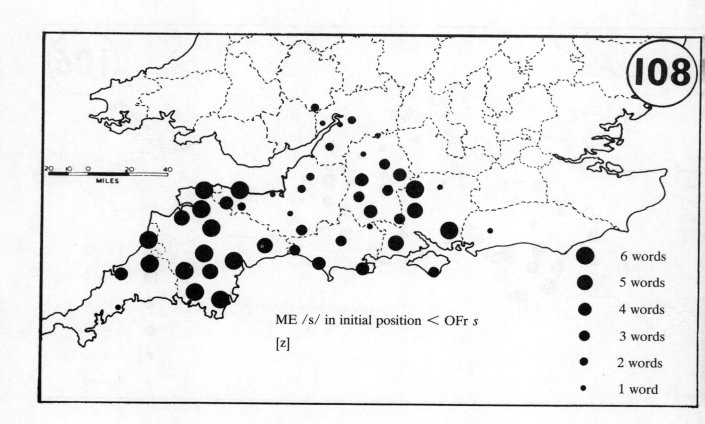

108

ME /s/ in initial position < OFr *s*

[z]

- 6 words
- 5 words
- 4 words
- 3 words
- 2 words
- 1 word

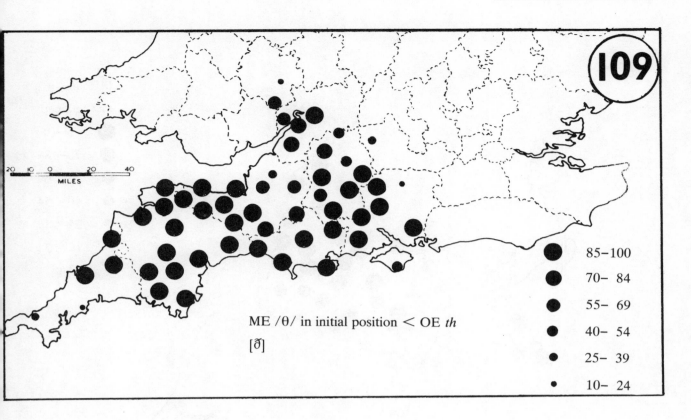

109

ME /θ/ in initial position < OE *th*
[ð]

● 85–100
● 70– 84
● 55– 69
● 40– 54
● 25– 39
• 10– 24

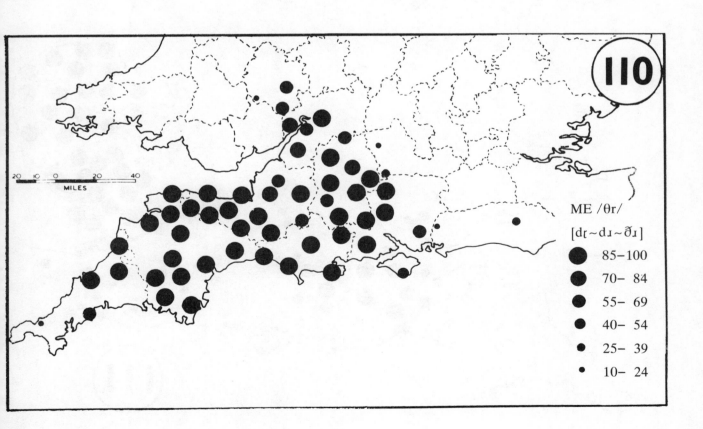

110

ME /θr/

[dɾ~dɹ~ðɹ]

● 85–100
● 70– 84
● 55– 69
● 40– 54
● 25– 39
• 10– 24

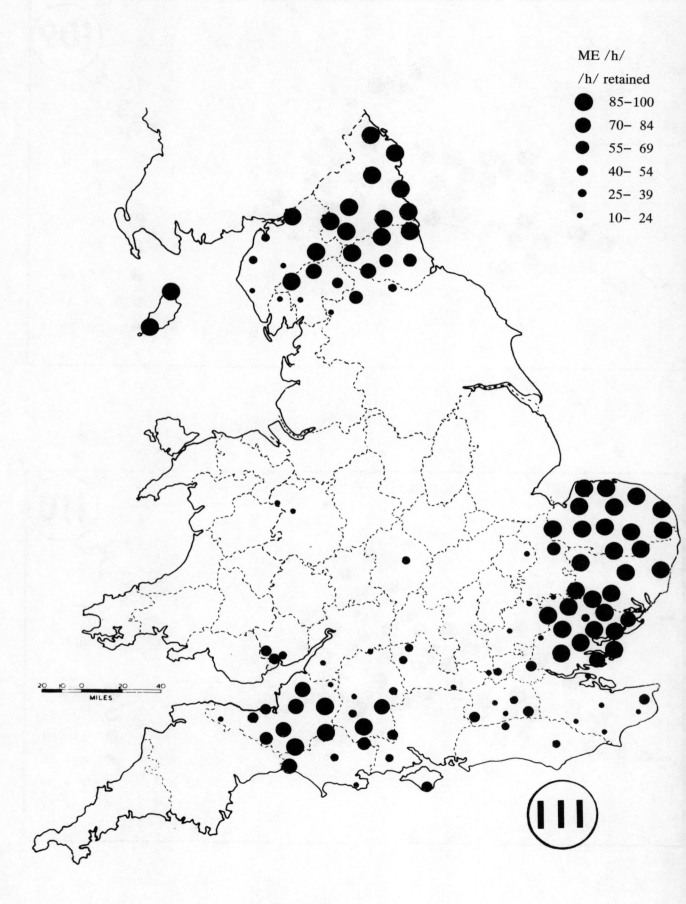

ME /h/
/h/ retained

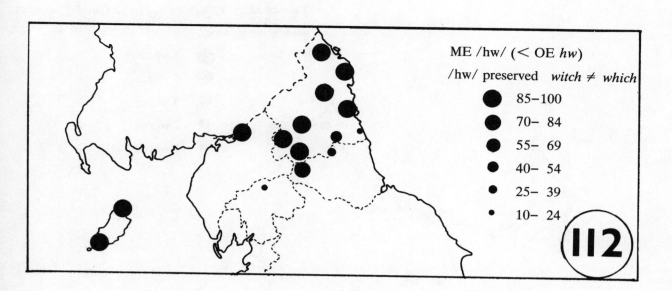

ME /hw/ (< OE *hw*)

/hw/ preserved   *witch ≠ which*

● 85–100
● 70– 84
● 55– 69
● 40– 54
● 25– 39
· 10– 24

112

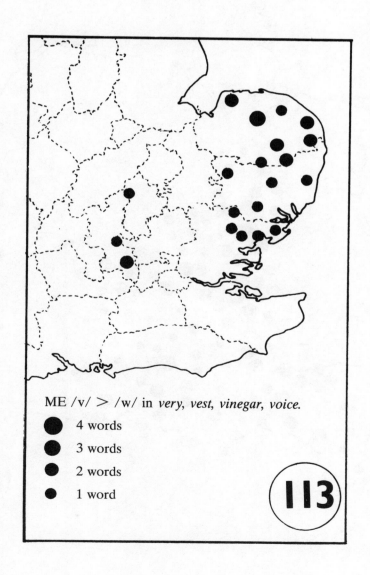

ME /v/ > /w/ in *very, vest, vinegar, voice.*

● 4 words
● 3 words
● 2 words
· 1 word

113

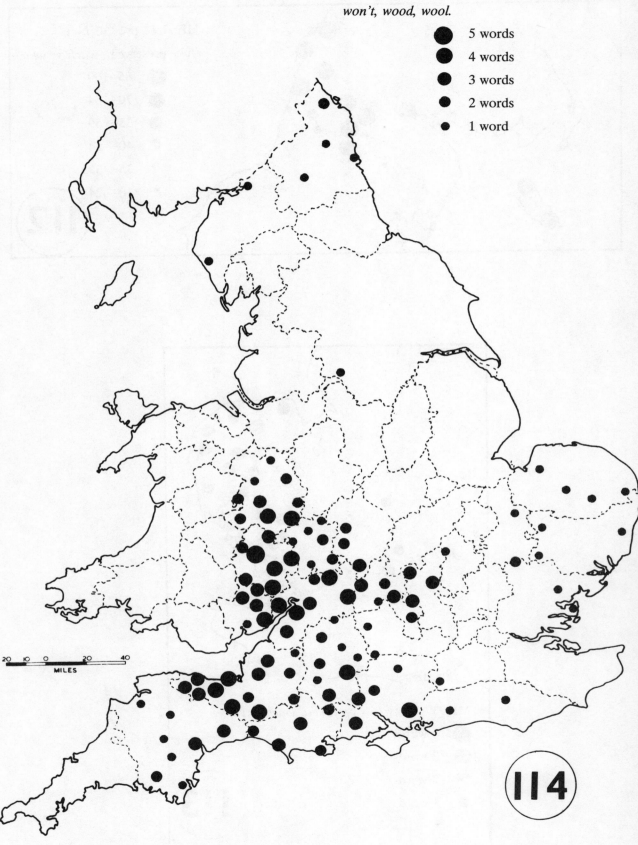

Loss of ME /w/ before /u/ in *unt* (mole), *woman*, *won't, wood, wool.*

● 5 words
● 4 words
● 3 words
● 2 words
• 1 word

20 10 0 20 40
MILES

114

Bibliography

Anderson, P.M. (1977) 'The dialect of Eaton-by-Tarporley (Cheshire), a descriptive and historical grammar', unpublished PhD thesis, University of Leeds

—— (1978) 'The development of ME *oi/ui* in the dialects of the north-west Midlands', *Journal of the Lancashire Dialect Society*, vol. 27, pp. 18-23

Barth, E. (1968) *The dialect of Naunton (Gloucestershire)*, Verlag P.G. Keller, Zurich

Brunner, K. (1963) *An outline of Middle English grammar*, translated by G.K.W. Johnston, Blackwell, Oxford

Chambers, J.K. and Trudgill, P. (1980) *Dialectology*, Cambridge University Press, Cambridge

Darlington, T. (1886) *The folk-speech of South Cheshire*, English Dialect Society, London

Dean, C. (1962) *The dialect of George Meriton's 'A Yorkshire dialogue'*, Yorkshire Dialect Society, Leeds

DeCamp, D. (1969) 'The genesis of Old English dialects — a new hypothesis'. In R. Lass (ed), *Approaches to English Historical Linguistics. An anthology*, Holt Rinehart and Winston, New York

Dobson, E.J. (1968) *English pronunciation 1500–1700*, 2nd edition, Oxford University Press, London

Ekwall, E. (1951) 'Two early London subsidy rolls', *Skrifter utgivna av Kung L. Humanistika Vetenskapsamfundet, i Lund*, University of Lund, Lund, 1951

—— (1956) *Studies in the population of medieval London*, Kungl. Vitterhets Historie och Antiquitels Akademiens Handlingar Filogisk — Filasofiska Serienz, Lund, 1956

Ellis, A.J. (1889) *On early English pronunciation*, part 5, Trubner and Co., London

Fries, C.C. and Pike, K.L. (1949) 'Coexistent phonemic systems', *Language* vol. 25, pp. 29-50

Hoeningswald, H.M. (1960) *Language change and linguistic construction*, University of Chicago Press, Chicago

Kolb, E. (1966) *Phonological atlas of the northern region*, Francke Verlag, Bern, 1966

Kökeritz, H. (1932) *The phonology of the Suffolk dialect*, Appelberg, Uppsala

Kurath, H. and Lowman, G.S. (1970) 'The dialectal structure of southern England: phonological evidence', *Publications of the American Dialect Society*, vol. 54

McDavid, R.I. (1979) 'Structural linguistics and linguistic geography'. In W.A. Kretschmar (ed), *Dialects in culture: Essays in general dialectology by Raven I. McDavid Jnr*, University of Alabama Press, Alabama, 1979

McIntosh, A. (1963) 'A new approach to Middle English Dialectology', *English Studies*, volume 44, pp. 1-11

Mencken, H.L. (1963) *The American language, (The fourth edition and the two supplements abridged with annotations and new material)*, R.I. McDavid (ed), Alfred A. Knopf, New York

Moore, S., Meech, S.B. and Whitehall, H. (1935) 'Middle English dialect characteristics and dialect boundaries: Preliminary report of an investigation based exclusively on localised texts and documents', *Essays and studies in English and comparative linguistics*, pp. 1-60, University of Michigan Press, University of Michigan, 1935

North, D. (1979) 'Some linguistic and cultural boundaries in South East England', *Transactions of the Yorkshire Dialect Society* part 79, vol. 14, pp. 8-37

Orton, H. (1933) *The phonology of a south Durham dialect*, Kegan Paul Trench, Trubner and Co., London

—— (1952) 'The isolative treatment in living north Midland dialects of OE *e* lengthened in open syllables in Middle English' *Leeds studies in English and kindred languages*, nos. 7-8, pp. 97-128

—— Sanderson, S. and Widdowson, J. (1978) *Linguistic atlas of England*, Croom Helm, London

Patchett, J.H. (1981) 'The dialect of Upper Calderdale', *Transactions of the Yorkshire Dialect Society*, part 81, vol. 15, pp. 24-37

Petyt, K.M. (1980) *The study of dialect*, Andrew Deutsch, London

Samuels, M.L. (1969) 'Some applications of Middle English dialectology'. In R. Lass (ed), *Approaches to English historical linguistics. An anthology*, Holt Rinehart and Winston, New York

—— (1972) *Linguistic evolution with special reference to English*, Cambridge University Press, Cambridge

Sapir, E. (1921) *Language: an introduction to the study of speech*, Harcourt, Brace and Co., New York

SED (1962) *Survey of English dialects*, H. Orton and E. Dieth (eds), E.J. Arnold, Leeds. *A — Introduction. B — Basic material vol. 1 Six northern counties and man*, H. Orton and W. Halliday (eds), *Vol. 2 The West Midlands*, H. Orton and M.V. Barry (eds), *Vol. 3 The East Midlands*, H. Orton and P.M. Tilling (eds). *Vol. 4 The Southern Counties*, H. Orton and M. Wakelin (eds)

Smith, A.H. (1961) *The placenames of the West Riding of Yorkshire*, Cambridge University Press, Cambridge

Stenton, F. (1971) *Anglo Saxon England*, Oxford University Press, London

Sternberg, T. (1851) *Dialect and folklore of Northamptonshire*, John Russell Smith, London, 1851

Trudgill, P. (1974) *The social differentiation of English in Norwich*, Cambridge University Press, Cambridge

Weinrich, U. (1974) *Languages in contact*, Mouton, The Hague

Wright, J. and Wright, E.M. (1925) *Old English grammar*, Oxford University Press, London

Wyld, H.C. (1927) *A short history of English*, Murray, London

Index of Words Used by ME Phoneme (with SED References)

ME /a/
apples IV.11.8
bat IV.7.7
cabbage V.7.18
carrots V.7.8
cat III.13.8/17
cattle III.1.3
flap VI.14.16
rabbits III.13.13
saddle I.5.6
scratching VI.1.2
shallow IV.1.5a
stack II.7.1
tag VI.14.26

ME /a/ + /s/, /f/, /θ/
ask IX.2.4
chaff II.8.5
grass II.9.1
last VII.2.2/6
laughing VIII.8.7; IX.2.14
past VII.5.4
pasture II.1.3
path IV.3.11
shaft I.7.7/2; I.9.4

ME /ar/ (including eME /er/)
arm VI.6.8
arse VI.9.2
cart I.9.3
farm I.1.3
harvest I.6.1
lard III.12.8

ME /o/
boggy IV.1.8
cocks II.9.12
collar I.5.3
dock II.2.8
dog III.13.1
fog VII.6.9
fox IV.5.11
frogs IV.9.6
hog III.8.8
holly VI.10.9
lop VI.12.5
pockets VI.14.15
pod V.7.12
pond IV.1.5
porridge V.7.1
stop (= stay) VII.5.2
top and tail II.4.3; V.7.23

ME /o/ + /s/, /f/, /θ/
broth V.7.20
coffin VIII.5.7
coughing VI.8.2
cross VIII.5.14
frost VII.6.6
loft I.3.18
off LX.2.13

ME /or/
corn II.5.1
fork I.7.9

forty VII.1.14
gorse IV.10.11
horse I.6.5
morning VII.3.10/11
north VII.6.25

ME /ol/
colt III.4.3
gold VII.7.10
mole IV.5.4
bowl (= scoop) V.9.9

ME /oxt/
aught (= anything) V.8.16
brought VII.1.11
daughter VIII.1.4/18
naught (= nothing) VII.8.14
ought IX.4.6/7

ME /u/
bull III.1.14
bullock III.1.16
bushes IV.10.5
butcher III.11.1; VIII.4.6
butter V.5.4
cut (= castrated) III.1.15
cousins VIII.1.15
dozen VII.1.10
drunk VI.13.11
duck IV.6.14
dust VII.6.1
hundred VII.1.15
hungry VI.14.9
must IX.4.11
put IX.3.3
some V.8.4
stubble II.1.2
sun IX.2.3
thunder VII.1.2
uncle VIII.1.2
us IX.8.1

ME /ur/
burnt V.6.7
churn V.5.5
curds V.5.8
curse VIII.8.9
durst IX.4.18
furrow II.3.1
girth I.5.8
furze (= gorse) IV.10.11
hurt VI.13.3
Thursday VII.4.3
turd II.1.6
turn II.9.11; VII.5.8
worms IV.9.1

ME /i:/
beside IX.2.5
five VII.5.6
ice VII.6.12
ivy IV.10.10
knife I.7.18
mine IX.8.5
rind III.12.6

scythe II.9.6
slide VIII.7.1
spider IV.8.9
time VII.3.16
tried VIII.8.4
white V.10.7
wife VIII.1.18/24
windpipe VI.6.5
wipe VI.5.3
writing VIII.6.6

ME /u:/
about VII.2.8
cow I.1.18; I.3.12; II.1.6; III.1.1
clouds VII.6.2
down VIII.3.3/6
drowned IX.9.6
house V.1.1
louse IV.8.1
mouse IV.5.1
mouth VI.5.1/2/3
ounce VIII.8.5
out IX.2.15
rooms V.2.4
snout III.9.1
south VII.6.25
thousand VII.1.16
trousers VI.14.13
without V.8.10(a)

ME /a:/
April VII.3.3
bacon III.12.4
baking-board V.6.5
braces VI.14.10
gable VI.1.5
gate IV.3.1/8
grave VIII.5.6
hames I.5.6
(boot)-laces VI.14.25
lane IV.3.13
mates VIII.4.1/2
naked VI.13.20
spade I.7.6
table V.8.12/14
trace-horse I.6.3

ME /ɛ:/ (< OE ēa, æ)
beans V.7.18
breast VI.8.5
leading (= carting) II.6.6
dead (body) VIII.5.7(a)
deaf VI.4.5
east VII.6.25
Easter VII.4.8/9
great IX.1.6
head VI.1.1
heat VI.13.6
peat IV.4.3
reach VI.7.15
sheaf II.6.3
sheath III.4.9
steep IV.1.11
teacher VIII.6.5

148

team I.6.1
wheat II.5.1

ME /ɛ:/ (< eME /e/)
break IX.3.5
eat VI.5.11
eaves II.7.3
knead V.6.4
meal (= flour) V.6.1
meat V.8.3
speaks V.5.5
steal VIII.7.5
tread IV.6.8/9
wean III.1.4

ME /ɛ:r/ (eME /er/)
bear VI.5.9
mare III.4.5
pears IV.11.8
swear VIII.8.9

ME /e:/
beestings V.5.10
between IX.2.11
cheese V.5.10
creep IX.2.11
feed III.3.1; III.5.1
feet VI.10.1
field I.1.1
geese IV.6.15
green V.10.7
keep IV.6.2
needle V.10.2
niece VIII.1.14
piece VII.2.10
reel V.10.6
see VI.3.2
sheep III.6.1
teeth VI.5.6
three VII.1.3
weeds II.2.1
wheel I.9.5

ME /e:r/
bier VIII.5.9
hear VI.4.2
near IX.2.10
where IX.9.7
year VII.3.4; VII.3.18

ME /o:/
afternoon VII.3.11
boots IX.8.6; VI.14.23
broom V.2.14; V.9.10
cool V.8.11
crook V.3.5
do IX.5.1
fool VII.4.10
foot VI.10.1
goose IV.6.5
hoof III.4.10
(bill)-hook IV.2.6
hoop (= tyre) I.9.10
look III.13.18; VIII.1.23
moon VII.6.3
pool I.3.1; III.3.9
roof V.1.2
root III.9.2; IV.12.1
soot V.4.6

stool III.3.3
tooth VI.5.6

ME /o:r/
board I.8.8; I.10.2/4
door V.1.8
floor V.2.7
ford IV.1.3

ME /ɔ:/ (< OE ā)
bone VI.9.1
both VII.2.11
clothes VI.14.19/20; V.9.7
comb VI.2.4
home VIII.5.2
load II.1.5; II.6.7/8
loaf V.6.9
none VII.1.18
oak IV.10.2
oats II.5.1
spoke I.9.6
toad IV.9.7
toes IV.10.3

ME /ɔ:ld/
cold VI.13.17/18/19
old VIII.1.20/22

ME /ɔ:/ (< eME /o/)
coal IV.4.5
(over)coat VI.4.5/6
foal III.4.1/6
hole IV.1.6; V.3.3; VI.4.3/7
lose IX.3.1
nose VI.4.6

ME /ɔ:r/
boar III.8.7
core VI.11.7
hoarse VI.5.16
more V.1.17; VII.8.13

ME /ai/
chilblains VI.10.6
clay IV.4.2
daisy II.2.10
(a few) days VII.1.19
flail II.8.3
hay II.9.1; IV.6.4
nail II.9.9; VI.7.8
play VIII.6.4
rain VII.6.23
tail III.2.2
whey V.5.8

ME /au/
awns II.5.3
haws IV.11.6
(in) law VIII.1.18
saw VIII.6.15
thaw VII.6.15
straw II.8.2

ME /ɔu/
know VII.5.2
mow II.9.3
snow VII.6.13
throw VIII.7.7

ME /iu/
blue V.10.7
grew IX.3.9
New (Year's Day) VII.4.8
spew VI.13.1
suet V.7.6
suit VI.14.21
Tuesday VII.4.2
tune VI.5.19
useful V.1.16

ME /ɛu/
dew VII.6.7
ewe III.6.6
few VII.1.19; VII.8.21

ME / i/, /ui/
boiling V.8.6
boys VIII.1.3
joiner VIII.5.8
oil V.2.13/14
onion V.7.15/16
poison IV.11.4/5
soil (= earth) VIII.5.8
spoil V.7.10
voice VI.5.17

ME /h/
hair VI.2.1
halfpenny VII.1.15
halter I.3.17
hammer I.7.13
hand VI.7.1
handles I.8.2
hare IV.5.10
hay II.9.1
head VI.1.1
headlands II.3.3
hear VI.4.2
heat II.9.16
hedge IV.2.1
height VI.10.9
herrings IV.9.11
hiccuping IV.8.4
hide VIII.7.6
holiday VIII.6.3
holly IV.10.7
hot V.6.8
hoof III.2.8
horse I.6.5
house V.1.1
how (many) VII.8.11
hub I.9.7
hundred VII.1.15
hurt VI.13.8

ME /hw/
what VII.5.1; VII.8.16/17
wheat II.5.2
wheel I.9.5
whelp III.13.4
where IX.9.7
whey V.5.8
whinny VII.10.3
whip I.5.12
whiskers VI.2.6
white V.10.7
whitlow VI.7.12
Whitsuntide VII.4.8

149

ME /f/
faint VI.13.7
fallow II.1.1
farm I.1.2/3
farmer VIII.4.7
farrow III.8.10
fart (= break wind) VI.13.6
farthing VII.7.2
fat V.7.5
father VIII.1.1
feed III.3.1; III.5.1
feet VI.10.1
fellies I.9.9
fern IV.10.13
fester VI.11.8
fields I.1.1
fifth VII.2.5
fight III.13.6
filly III.4.2
find IX.3.2
finger VI.7.7
fire V.3.1
first VII.2.1
fist VI.7.4
five VII.5.6
foal III.4.1
fog VII.6.9
foot VI.10.1
forehead VI.1.7
forelock III.4.8
ford IV.1.3
forks I.7.9
fortnight VII.3.2
forty VII.1.4
four VII.1.4
fox IV.5.11

funnel V.9.3
furrow II.3.1
furze (= gorse) IV.10.11
pheasants IV.7.8

ME /s/
cinders V.4.3
sack I.7.2
saddle I.5.6
Saturday VII.4.5
saw(dust) I.7.17
scythe II.9.6
second VII.2.3
see VI.3.3
seesaw VIII.7.2
seven VII.1.6
sew V.10.3
sexton VIII.5.4
sight VIII.2.9
silver VII.7.7
six VII.1.5
sixpence VII.7.4
some V.8.4
son VIII.1.4
soot V.4.6
south VII.6.25
sow III.8.6
such VIII.9.7
suck III.7.1
suet V.7.6
suit VI.14.21
suits VI.14.2
sun XI.2.3

ME /θ/
thatch II.7.5/6

thawing VII.6.15
thicken V.7.7
thigh VI.9.3
thimble V.10.9
thin II.4.2
third VII.2.4
thirsty VI.13.10
thirteen VII.1.11
thirty VII.1.13
thistle II.2.2
thousand VII.1.16
thumb VI.7.6
thunder VII.6.21
Thursday VII.4.3

ME /θr/
thread V.10.2
three VII.1.3
threepence VII.7.3
thresh II.8.1
threshold V.1.12
throat VI.1.12
throw VIII.7.7

ME /v/
very IV.11.5; VIII.3.2
vest VI.14.9
vinegar V.7.19
voice VI.5.17

ME /w/
unt (= mole) IV.5.4
woman VIII.1.6
(kindling-) wood V.4.2
wool III.7.5
won't IX.4.5

Alphabetical List of Words Used

about 3.3
afternoon 3.32
apples 2.1
April 3.7
arm 2.3
arse 2.3
ask 2.3
aught 4.6
awns 2.12

bacon 3.7
baking board 3.7
bat 2.1
beans 3.18
bear 3.31
beestings 3.15
beside 3.1
between 3.15
bier 3.31
blue 4.9
boar 3.51
board 3.51
boggy 2.7
boiling 4.16
bone 3.37
boots 3.32
both 3.37
bowl 4.6
boys 4.10
braces 3.7
breast 3.18
break 3.24
broom 3.32
broth 2.11
brought 4.6
bull 2.16
bullock 2.16
burst 2.19
bushes 2.16
butcher 2.16
butter 2.16

cabbage 2.1
carrots 2.1
cart 2.3
cat 2.1
cattle 2.1
chaff 2.3
cheese 3.15
chilblains 4.1
churn 2.19
cinders 5.2
clay 4.1
clothes 3.37
clouds 3.3
coal 3.47
coat 3.47
cocks 2.7
coffin 2.11
cold 4.6
collar 2.7
colt 4.6
comb 3.37
cool 3.32
core 3.51

corn 2.11
coughing 2.11
cousins 2.16
cow 3.3
creep 3.15
crook 3.32
cross 2.11
curds 2.19
curse 2.19
cut 2.16

daisy 4.1
daughter 4.6
days 4.1
deaf 3.18
dead 3.18
dew 4.13
do 3.32
dock 2.7
dog 2.7
door 3.51
down 3.3
dozen 2.16
drowned 3.3
drunk 2.16
duck 2.16
durst 2.19
dust 2.16

east 3.18
Easter 3.18
eat 3.24
eaves 3.24
ewe 4.13

faint 5.2
fallon 5.2
farrow 5.2
farm 2.3, 5.2
farmer 5.2
fart 5.2
farthing 5.2
fat 5.2
father 5.2
feed 3.15, 5.2
feet 3.15, 5.2
fellies 5.2
fern 5.2
fester 5.2
few 4.13
field 3.15, 5.2
fifth 5.2
fight 5.2
filly 5.2
find 5.2
finger 5.2
fire 5.2
first 5.2
fist 5.2
five 3.1, 5.2
flash 4.1
flap 2.1
floor 3.51
foal 3.47, 5.2
fog 2.7, 5.2

fool 3.32
foot 3.32, 5.2
ford 5.2
forehead 5.2
forelock 5.2
ford 3.51
forks 2.11, 5.2
fortnight 5.2
forty 2.11, 5.2
four 5.2
fox 2.7, 5.2
frogs 2.7
frost 2.11
funnel 5.2
furrow 2.19, 5.2
furze 2.19, 5.2

gable 3.7
gate 3.7
geese 3.15
girth 2.19
gold 4.6
gorse 2.11
grass 2.3
grave 3.7
great 3.18
green 3.15
goose 3.32
grew 4.9

hair 5.3
halfpenny 5.3
halter 5.3
hames 3.7
hammer 5.3
handles 5.3
hare 5.3
harvest 2.3
haws 2.12
hay 4.1, 5.3
head 5.3
headlands 5.3
head 3.18
hear 3.31, 5.3
heat 3.18, 5.3
hedge 5.3
height 5.3
herrings 5.3
hiccuping 5.3
hide 5.3
hoarse 3.51
hog 2.7
holiday 5.3
hole 3.47
holly 2.7, 5.3
home 3.37
hoof 3.32, 5.3
hook 3.32
hoop 3.32
horse 2.11, 5.3
hot 5.3
house 3.3, 5.3
how 5.3
hub 5.3
hundred 2.16, 5.3